Deconstructing the Administrative State

DECONSTRUCTING THE ADMINISTRATIVE STATE

The Fight for Liberty

by Emmett McGroarty,
Jane Robbins, and Erin Tuttle

American Principles Project Foundation
Washington, D.C.

LIBERTY HILL PUBLISHING

Liberty Hill Press
2301 Lucien Way #415
Maitland, FL 32751
407.339.4217
www.libertyhillpublishing.com
First Printing

Published for:

American Principles Project Foundation
1130 Connecticut Avenue, N.W., Suite 425, Washington, D.C. 20036
202-503-2010
appfdc.org

by

Sophia Institute Press
Box 5284, Manchester, N.H. 03108
1-800-888-9344
www.SophiaInstitute.com Sophia Institute Press

Title: Deconstructing the administrative state : the fight for liberty / Emmett McGroarty, Jane Robbins, and Erin Tuttle.
Description: Washington, D.C. : American Principles Project Foundation, [2017] | Includes bibliographical references.
Identifiers: LCCN 2017041935 | ISBN 9781622826049 (hardcover : alk.paper)
Subjects: LCSH: Bureaucracy — United States. | United States — Politics and government.
Classification: LCC JK421 .M358 2017 | DDC 320.973 — dc23 LC record available at https://lccn.loc.gov/2017041935

Cover design by Perceptions Design Studio.

Printed in the United States of America.

ISBN-13: 9781545621660

To the American activists who understand that our freedom is fragile and who bravely hold the line against those who would extinguish it

Contents

Foreword

The last decade has seen a number of significant grassroots move-
ments in America: the TEA Party movement, the anti–Common
Core movement, the campaign to elect Donald Trump to "drain
the swamp" in Washington. The common thread of these initiatives is the widespread frustration of American citizens with the
relentless imposition of policies they disagree with and never
voted for.

Where do these policies come from? Who came up with them?
Where can people go to object? Who can be held accountable
if things go wrong?

This book illuminates the dark recesses that spawn the developments so maddening to millions of Americans. It explains
the problem in terms of the growth of the administrative state.
The administrative Leviathan has effected major shifts in policy
without the consent of the people, transferring control over vast
swaths of policy-making from elected officials to anonymous
technocrats and all but eliminating true accountability.

As explained in these pages, these seismic shifts originated in
the progressive movement of the late nineteenth and early twentieth century. This book describes the biological habitat of the
resulting administrative state—the relationships and methods

leveraged to accomplish these antidemocratic goals. But it also traces the philosophical underpinnings that are nothing less than a direct attack on constitutional government. The constitutional structure—the system of checks and balances and of power dispersed between the federal government and the states—is under assault.

The goal: to destroy the very principle of self-government. No more reliance on the will of the people, but rather on the self-reinforcing opinions of a cadre of experts.

This book also delves into an even darker aspect of the progressive assault on the constitutional order. The success of the progressive revolution depends not merely on creating alternative structures and transferring power to them, but on reshaping the American mind so that citizens will be conditioned to accept the new order. For over a century the system of public education has been gradually remade in the progressive image, and the indoctrination proceeds apace.

But it hasn't triumphed yet. The very existence of the nationwide frustration, even anger, and of the increasing grassroots rebellion against the tyranny of the administrative state demonstrates that the American core is still there. The people still treasure American ideals and won't let them go without a fight.

This book provides a blueprint for the battle—what Congress must do, what the judiciary must do, and what the states must do to regain their lost autonomy. It connects the popular impulse to protect the Constitution with the steps that can be taken to achieve that noble goal. When the people understand the problem, they can fix it. We have faith that they will.

—Frank Cannon

Deconstructing the Administrative State

Introduction

"Hello, American sailor. Hello, freedom man."

> —Greeting from a man rescued in the South China Sea
> by the USS *Midway*, as related by President Reagan,
> Farewell Speech, January 11, 1989

Driving to work each day, you pass a construction site for a multiuse development that's going up beside a light-rail station. You've read in the newspaper that the county council had suddenly changed zoning laws to facilitate this development, but it all seemed to happen without much public notice or debate.

The whole light-rail project puzzles you. You live in a suburban area with spacious neighborhoods. Taking the train to work isn't an option for you, both because it doesn't run very near your office and because you frequently need your car during the day for offsite meetings. Most of your friends are in similar situations. But local decision-makers seem to have decided that spending millions on light-rail is good stewardship of taxpayer money, even though the subway system that was built years ago has to be heavily subsidized because nobody rides it. You've noticed that various "Smart Growth" groups have sprung up to promote mass transit and increasingly dense development.

Deconstructing the Administrative State

One reason for the mass-transit push, you gather, is the federal research showing the danger of fossil fuels and their contribution to climate change. You've read about scientists who disagree with that conclusion, but practically every statement you've heard from the federal government supports it. Accounts of these statements appear in newspapers, on television, and all over the Internet, so you have the impression that significant human-caused climate change is a scientific fact.

Your children certainly believe that. They've learned in school about the coming devastation from climate change. They don't seem to be learning much about chemistry or biology, which you find a bit concerning, but the school insists that the new science standards that it's implementing are cutting-edge and will train your kids to think like scientists.

At dinner one night, your third-grader describes his class's visit to a NASA center. You wait to hear about the wonders of the universe, the scientists who study them, and "the giant leap for mankind." Instead, your son shows you the NASA "carbon footprint calculator," which inquires, among other things, how often your family eats "animal based products"; how often you recycle; whether you live in a multifamily house; and how often "you travel in a car each week … (versus a bike or public transportation)." Your son proceeds to estimate the family "carbon footprint."

The dinner conversation turns to current politics. Although you worry about the country's seeming leftward drift, your teenager chimes in that socialism isn't actually so bad, and that more collectivism would protect people from being left behind. If the deplorables are really mean enough to oppose this, he suggests, maybe it's a good idea to have more knowledgeable people making the decisions.

Introduction

After dinner, you try to help your fifth-grader with her math homework. The calculation methods she's required to use seem silly and inefficient, yet the principal assured concerned parents at the PTA meeting that this math instruction will work out in the long run because their children will develop deeper conceptual understanding. But you seem to recall that something very much like this was tried twenty years ago or so, and that people finally gave up on it. Maybe it's different this time.

One of your friends was very involved in fighting this weird math and other curriculum standards in the legislature. She testified about the issue before a committee, but the state department of education officials defended the standards and made vague warnings about losing funding if the state tried to do anything different. Also, to your friend's surprise, a couple of people from the state chamber of commerce and from a large corporation testified that this way of teaching will be good for the economy because it will develop the workforce. They also handed out to the legislature glossy reports highlighting all the federal research showing how effective this pedagogy is. You wonder what chamber-of-commerce officials and business owners know about teaching math or anything else, but their presentations (along with whatever the department-of-education bureaucrat said about funding) seemed to douse any interest the legislators had in investigating the problem.

Speaking of school, there are rumblings from a local activist group that it will start insisting that all restrooms, locker rooms, and sports teams be opened up to students of both sexes. They claim that federal law requires this. You wonder how that could be, since you're pretty sure Congress hasn't passed any such law, but you've read about other schools going in this direction, so maybe you missed something.

Deconstructing the Administrative State

One thing all school officials seem to agree on is that the system needs more money. The tax base in your western state seems unusually narrow, especially compared with states such as Texas, which reaps great benefits from its oil and gas. But for some reason, vast tracks of wilderness land in your state are off-limits to mineral exploration and even agriculture. Everywhere you turn there's a national park or national monument or national something else that means the federal government gets to call the shots about how that land is used.

Getting more and more fed up with Congress on several issues, you work to elect good conservatives. But when they get elected, for some reason they seem to be relegated to the less powerful committees and almost never make it into party leadership—unless they abandon some of the principles that made you want them there in the first place. So you become more and more cynical that anything will ever change. Listening to the words of the Founding Fathers every July 4, you wonder: Is this the way they meant it to be?

These developments that concern so many Americans aren't disconnected trends that just happen to coincide. Rather, they result from a sustained, relentless, more-than-century-long assault on the federalist system that was established by our Constitution in 1789. The attacking force is the political philosophy of progressivism.

The work that follows arose from our study of the American system of governance—the constitutional structure. But the starting point has to be the individual. It's axiomatic that one's view of the individual, of human nature, shapes one's view of government, education, and economics. The founding generation—for all their flaws, for all our flaws—had a deep reverence for the individual and therefore for the American people. They

Introduction

started with the "self-evident" truth that all men are created equal, that sovereignty flows from the people, and that it originates in the infinite Creator — the most powerful existing political description of man's dignity. The Founders' worldview shaped the constitutional structure. It also ignited a continuing struggle to be faithful to those principles, which serve as a moral compass.

The goal of the constitutional structure is to protect the independence of the states — ultimately to protect the rights of individuals — and to ensure that government is citizen-directed. To achieve this, power is diffused not only among the three branches of the federal government but also between the federal government and the states.

But any governing philosophy will provoke a reaction, an attempt to put forth an improved, competing view. In the late 1800s, the political philosophy of progressivism, which differs radically from that of the Founders, took hold among American elitists. This worldview is based on the belief that individual human beings aren't created in the image of anything, that they have no "natural rights" that government can't infringe, and that they can be herded into an efficient economic, political, and social system created and guided by experts empowered to determine the best course of action and impose it on the citizenry for their own good.

As a consequence of their cynical view of human nature, progressives had little respect for a constitutional structure designed to ensure citizen-directed government and to protect individual rights. They did have extreme confidence in the burgeoning fields of social sciences, and they believed that experts could successfully guide society. They further believed that the American people would — with a little assistance — change their mind-sets to accept management by experts more willingly.

7

Deconstructing the Administrative State

Progressive ideology took root in academia and among America's political parties. Throughout the twentieth century and into the current one, progressives relentlessly advanced their competing ideology. They sought, quite blatantly, to reshape the constitutional structure, by formal changes where they could and otherwise by changes in practice.

To implement their ideology of a society managed by experts (the administrative state), several overarching changes were necessary. First, progressives had to quell the notion of eternal truths, because that concept threatens the primacy of the administrative state in two respects: (1) it impairs the efficiency of the expert, whose programs and policies may have to yield to citizens' rights and privileges; and (2) it undermines the progressive idea of government by trial and error. If policy-makers face lines they cannot cross, they can't explore all possible scenarios for creating the most efficient government.

The second requirement for implementing progressive policies was to transfer power to experts in the executive branch (or, if the executive branch is controlled by constitutionalists, to the judiciary). Such power must include large swaths of policy-making authority that under the constitutional structure properly resides with the legislature, where it's closest to the people.

Third, state government had to be subdued, because it was a threat to the efficiency with which experts could implement their reforms and, due to its proximity to the people, a threat to the authority of experts. Progressives had to find a way "to make town, city, county, state, and federal governments ... interdependent and co-operative."[1]

---

[1] Woodrow Wilson, "The Study of Administration," *Political Science Quarterly* (July 1887).

And fourth, there was the problem of the American people themselves, whom the prominent progressive Woodrow Wilson described as "selfish, ignorant, timid, stubborn, or foolish with the selfishness, the ignorances, the stubbornnesses, the timidities, or the follies of several thousand persons."[2] They would have to be trained to respond, animal-like, to the experts.

In this work we examine the power shifts within the constitutional structure, how they were accomplished, and how they are operating today. Some of these are *de jure* shifts made by constitutional amendment and Supreme Court decisions. Others are *de facto* shifts developed to evade constitutional limitations. This work explains how progressives accomplished that, and the operation of the structures they created. Their techniques include the following:

- creating schemes to work around the constitutional structure, such as cooperative-federalism programs, "ghost governments," and independent commissions;
- distributing federal grants, sometimes directly to state subsidiaries rather than to state governments;
- creating public-public and public-private partnerships;
- reshaping the American mind by replacing traditional education with progressive education, including control over pedagogy, standards, curricula, and teacher training;
- generating vast quantities of "research" to justify federal policies;
- expanding the definition of "public health" to justify federal policies;

[2] Ibid.

- aligning the economic interests of powerful private organizations to the imposition of federal policies;
- in some states, simply removing millions of acres of land from state and private control.

We also discuss how the administrative state tries to shape the views, or will, of citizens. We offer solutions to rebalance the constitutional structure and reestablish the proper respect for the American citizen.

The constitutional structure has been severely compromised. Too often decision-making doesn't primarily reflect the will of the people, but instead reflects the views of elitist special interests. The great compound republic—our system of dual sovereign governments—has been neutralized, and every check and balance has failed, except one. Furthermore, the ascendency of the administrative state has enabled special interests to exploit the decision-making process and to block reforms that might lessen their influence.

The last remaining check and balance is the American people. As we note in the penultimate chapter, the special-interest establishment has already conceded its fear of informed, freeborn citizens. What's needed now to restore the Constitution is one more rising by the people.

We don't pretend that such a restoration will be easy. It will require a degree of citizen involvement unprecedented in recent American history. But thanks to the TEA Party movement and other activist groups born of concern over Obama administration overreach, the foundation for such a resurgence is there. We have to build on what these patriots have done to educate and organize. If America as we've known it is to be saved, we have no choice.

Chapter 1

The Constitutional Structure

America's founding rests on an idea, a revolutionary principle that "all Men are created equal, that they are endowed by their Creator[3] with certain unalienable Rights, that among these are Life, Liberty, and the Pursuit of Happiness."[4] This idea sources human dignity in the infinite, beyond human compromise and corruption. Its universal embrace lifts all. It's the strongest political expression of the individual's dignity, an antidote to man's

---

[3] In positing the source of the rights with the Creator, the Founders sourced those rights in the all-powerful, that is, a source beyond the power of any person (king or otherwise), entity, or government to detract from or compromise. That formulation is history's strongest, most immutable statement of individual rights and dignity.

[4] Declaration of Independence (1776), par. 2. See also the Massachusetts Constitution (1780), pt. 1, art. I: "All men are born free and equal, and have certain natural, essential, and unalienable rights." *The Founders' Constitution* (Chicago: University of Chicago Press, 2000), vol. 1, chap. 1, doc. 6, http://press-pubs.uchicago.edu/founders/documents/v1ch1s6.html. See also Virginia Declaration of Rights (1776) § 1: "All men are by nature equally free and independent, and have certain inherent rights." *The Founders' Constitution*, vol. 1, chap. 1, doc. 3, http://press-pubs.uchicago.edu/founders/documents/v1ch1s3.html.

evils throughout the course of world history. With respect to all "earthly" powers, the people are the "original supreme Sovereign." By and large, the American people have accepted that principle, and those words, and made them part of our culture. That principle[5] serves as the animating force of the American Experiment.[6] In furtherance of it, the Framers drafted, and the states ratified, the Constitution. As stated by James Wilson, a signer of the Declaration of Independence and the Constitution and subsequently a Supreme Court justice: "On the same certain and solid foundation [our constitutional] system is erected."[7] Among the Constitution's overarching purposes were "to form a more perfect Union" and secure "the Blessings of Liberty to ourselves and our Posterity."[8]

The "constitutional structure" refers to, among other things, the division and the balance of powers among the branches of government, the division of power between the federal government and the states, the status of the federal government and the states as separate sovereigns, and the people as the ultimate earthly sovereign. Over the years, but especially recently, the Supreme Court has devoted much discussion to the constitutional structure. It has done so for good cause: "The fragmentation of

---

[5] See, *e.g.*, U.S. Constitution, preamble: "in Order to … secure the Blessings of Liberty to ourselves and our Posterity."

[6] For example, its pursuit serves as America's political redemption. It inspired the abolitionist movement and undergirded the Gettysburg Address.

[7] James Wilson, Address to the Pennsylvania Ratifying Convention (December 4, 1787), *The Founders' Constitution*, vol. 1, chap. 2, doc. 14, http://press-pubs.uchicago.edu/founders/documents/v1ch2s14.html.

[8] U.S. Constitution, preamble.

power produced by the structure of our Government is central to liberty, and when we destroy it, we place liberty at peril."[9]

In a unanimous 2011 decision, the Supreme Court noted that federalism (the relationship between the federal government and the states and the interrelationships among the states) serves a greater purpose than merely preserving "the integrity, dignity, and residual sovereignty of the States":[10]

> Federalism is more than an exercise in setting the boundary between different institutions of government for their own integrity. "State sovereignty is not just an end in itself: 'Rather federalism secures to citizens the liberties that derive from the diffusion of sovereign power.'"[11]

Thus, the proper end of federalism is not just the autonomy of the states, but the liberty of the individual.

To protect that liberty and ensure that government is citizen-directed, the Framers developed and the states ratified a "compound republic."[12] "As every schoolchild learns, our Constitution establishes a system of dual sovereignty between the States and the Federal Government."[13] In that system, state government—the government closest to the people and the one with the smaller geographic boundaries—is the general

---

[9] National Federation of Independent Business v. Sebelius, 567 U.S. 519, 707 (2012) (dissenting opinion).

[10] Bond v. United States, 564 U.S. 211, 221 (2011).

[11] Ibid., quoting New York v. United States, 505 U.S. 144, 181 (1992).

[12] James Madison, "Federalist No. 51," in Alexander Hamilton, John Jay, and John Madison, *The Federalist Papers*, ed. Clinton Rossiter (New York: Penguin, 1961).

[13] Gregory v. Ashcroft, 501 U.S. 452, 457 (1991).

government (*i.e.*, the one with the broader powers). As James Madison noted:

> The powers delegated by the proposed Constitution to the federal government are *few and defined*. Those which are to remain in the State governments are numerous and indefinite. The former will be exercised principally on external objects, as war, peace, negotiation, and foreign commerce; with which last the power of taxation will, for the most part, be connected. The powers reserved to the several States will extend to all the objects which, in the ordinary course of affairs, concern the lives, liberties, and properties of the people, and the internal order, improvement, and prosperity of the State.[14]

The "Federal Government 'is acknowledged by all to be one of enumerated powers,' which means that 'every law enacted by Congress must be based on one or more of' those powers."[15] For example, the Constitution specifies that Congress may:

> "coin Money," "establish Post Offices," and "raise and support Armies." The enumeration of powers is also a limitation of powers, because "the enumeration presupposes something not enumerated." The Constitution's express conferral of some powers makes it clear that it

---

[14] James Madison, "Federalist No. 45," emphasis added. See also Alexander Hamilton, "Federalist No. 33": "The purpose of the Necessary and Proper clause 'is expressly to execute [the enumerated] powers.'"

[15] United States v. Comstock, 560 U.S. 126, 133 (2010), quoting McCulloch v. Maryland, 17 U.S. 316, 4 Wheat. 316, 405 (1819) and United States v. Morrison, 529 U.S. 598, 607 (2000). See also *Sebelius*, 567 U.S. at 533–535.

does not grant others. And the Federal Government "can exercise only the powers granted to it."[16]

As Chief Justice Roberts noted in *National Federation of Independent Businesses v. Sebelius,* the ratification of the Bill of Rights "made express what the enumeration of powers necessarily implied: 'The powers not delegated to the United States by the Constitution ... are reserved to the States respectively, or to the people.'"[17]

In contrast, state governments need not identify authority in the Constitution for their actions. "The States thus can and do perform many of the vital functions of modern government—punishing street crime, running public schools, and zoning property for development, to name but a few—even though the Constitution's text does not authorize any government to do so."[18]

This structure ensures that "powers which 'in the ordinary course of affairs, concern the lives, liberties, and properties of the people' were held by governments more local and more accountable than a distant federal bureaucracy."[19] Furthermore, because the police power is controlled by the states individually, the constitutional structure:

> allows local policies "more sensitive to the diverse needs of a heterogeneous society," permits "innovation and experimentation," enables greater citizen "involvement in democratic processes," and makes government "more

---

[16] *Sebelius,* 567 U.S. at 534–535, internal citations omitted.
[17] Ibid., 535 (quoting U.S. Constitution, Amendment 10).
[18] *Sebelius,* 567 U.S. at 535–536.
[19] Ibid., 536, quoting Madison, "Federalist No. 45."

responsive by putting the States in competition for a mobile citizenry."[20]

The Framers intended that the constitutional structure would protect individual rights to the extent that a bill of rights would be unnecessary. "As Alexander Hamilton put it, 'The Constitution is itself, in every rational sense, and to every useful purpose, A BILL OF RIGHTS.'"[21] In furtherance of that, the Constitution erects several barriers to protect individual rights and to ensure that government is citizen-directed. First, as noted above, the state government—the government closest to the people—would have general authority (*i.e.*, most of the power), and the federal government would have the limited powers needed to address truly national interests (*e.g.*, war and relations with foreign powers).

Second, the federal government would be divided into three branches, each with checks and balances to guard against incursions from the other branches.

Third, neither the federal nor the state governments would have a monopoly of power. As Hamilton noted:

> In a single republic, all the power surrendered by the people is submitted to the administration of a single government; and the usurpations are guarded against by a division of the government into distinct and separate departments. In the compound republic of America, the power surrendered by the people is first divided between

---

[20] *Bond*, 564 U.S. at 221, quoting Gregory v. Ashcroft, 501 U.S. 452, 458 (1991).

[21] *Sebelius*, 567 U.S. at 535, quoting Alexander Hamilton, "Federalist No. 84."

two distinct governments, and then the portion allotted to each subdivided among distinct and separate departments. Hence a double security arises to the rights of the people. The different governments will control each other, at the same time that each will be controlled by itself.[22]

"By denying any one government complete jurisdiction over all the concerns of public life, federalism protects the liberty of the individual from arbitrary power."[23]

Fourth, the state governments and the people would have powerful checks to rein in the federal government's tendencies to usurp state decision-making. To that end, Hamilton observed:

It may safely be received as an axiom in our political system that the State governments will, in all possible contingencies, afford complete security against invasions of the public liberty by the national authority.[24]

Likewise, James Madison emphasized the watchdog role of the state legislatures:

The State Legislatures will jealously and closely watch the operations of this Government, and be able to resist with more effect every assumption of power, than any

---

[22] Madison, "Federalist No. 51."

[23] *Bond*, 564 U.S. at 222.

[24] Alexander Hamilton, "Federalist No. 28." See also Alexander Hamilton, "Federalist No. 85": "We may safely rely on the disposition of the state legislatures to erect barriers against the encroachments of the national authority."

other power on earth can do; and the greatest opponents to a Federal Government admit the State Legislatures to be sure guardians of the people's liberty.[25]

But to function as intended, the constitutional structure requires a strong state government. In the words of Thomas Jefferson:

> It is important to strengthen the state governments: and as this cannot be done by any change in the federal constitution (for the preservation of that is all we need contend for) it must be done by the states themselves, erecting such barriers at the constitutional line as cannot be surmounted either by themselves or by the general government. The only barrier in their power is a wise government. A weak one will lose ground in every contest.[26]

Samuel Adams predicted dire consequences of feeble governors and state legislatures:

> Unless great care should be taken to prevent it, the Constitution in the Administration of it would gradually, but swiftly and imperceptibly run into a consolidated government pervading and legislating through all the States, not for federal purposes only, as it professes, but in all cases whatsoever: such a government would soon totally annihilate the Sovereignty of the several States so necessary

---

[25] 1 Annals of Cong. 457, June 8, 1789 (Joseph Gales, ed. 1790).

[26] Thomas Jefferson to Archibald Stuart, December 23, 1791, in *The Papers of Thomas Jefferson*, vol. 22, *6 August 1791–31 December 1791*, ed. Charles T. Cullen (Princeton: Princeton University Press, 1986), 435–437, Founders Online, National Archives, http://founders.archives.gov/documents/Jefferson/01-22-02-0410.

to the Support of the confederated Commonwealth, and sink both in despotism.[27]

This was the mind-set of the Framers. But later political philosophers thought they had a better idea.

---

[27] Samuel Adams to Richard Henry Lee, August 24, 1789, in *The Original Writings of Samuel Adams*, ed. Harry A. Cushing, vol. 4, 1778–1802 (New York: G. P. Putnam's Sons, 1904).

Chapter 2

Progressivism versus the Constitution and the Individual

Above [the citizenry] arises an immense and tutelary power that alone takes charge of assuring their enjoyment and of looking after their fate. . . . It would resemble paternal power if, like it, it had as a goal to prepare men for manhood; but on the contrary it seeks only to fix them irrevocably in childhood. . . . It attends to their security, provides for their needs, facilitates their pleasures, conducts their principal affairs, directs their industry, settles their estates, divides their inheritances; how can it not remove entirely from them the trouble to think and the difficulty of living?

This is how it makes the use of free will less useful and rarer every day; how it encloses the action of the will within a smaller space and little by little steals from each citizen even the use of himself.

— Alexis de Tocqueville, *Democracy in America*, II, IV, 6

Progressivism in America is an ideological rejection of the founding principles, positing instead that greater government control by the "right" people will bring about a better society.

The founding, we have noted, rests on the particular view of the individual as the ultimate sovereign over his earthly affairs.

Deconstructing the Administrative State

Statist policies advanced by progressivism have, as Tocqueville forewarned, wrought "a smaller space" for the individual to live. As the ensuing chapters will demonstrate, the citizen has lost both security in the ownership in his land (the disposition of lands) and substantial control over his built environment (the configuration of cities and towns). Distrusting the citizen's ability to direct his own affairs, progressivism has centralized decision-making, rendering it more distant and less accountable, and as a later chapter will show, has embarked on vast, unmoored data collection on him—wholly unrelated to national security. But the most profound change that progressivism seeks is to steal "from each citizen even the use of himself" by interfering with the education and civic formation of youth and by reshaping the autonomous citizen into a mere creature of the state whose will is enclosed in an ever-shrinking space.

WHAT IS PROGRESSIVISM?

Professors Ronald J. Pestritto and William J. Atto offer a succinct definition of progressivism: "an argument to progress, or to move beyond, the political principles of the American founding."[28]

In contrast to the Framers, early-twentieth-century pro-gressives such as Theodore Roosevelt, Woodrow Wilson, and Herbert Croly denied the existence of permanent principles of human nature and wise government. They "countered that the ends and scope of government were to be defined anew in each historical epoch."[29] They believed that the Constitution and the

[28] Ronald J. Pestritto and William J. Atto, eds., *American Progressivism: A Reader* (Lanham, MD: Lexington Books, 2008), 2.
[29] Ibid., 3.

Declaration of Independence were tailored to the political and social situation as it existed at that time, but that those documents didn't express fundamental and transcendent principles equally applicable to all historical settings.

Progressives seized on the societal changes of the early twentieth century to advance their cause. They argued that industrialization and its attendant social and economic effects rendered the constitutional structure inadequate to the task of solving modern-day problems. Progressive icons Woodrow Wilson and Frank Goodnow "argued that government needed to adjust its very purpose and organization to accommodate modern necessities" and that "history had made obsolete the Founders' dedication to protecting individual rights and their consequent design of a carefully limited form of national government."[30]

Instead, progressives embraced the "science of administration," which Wilson defined as "seeing every day new things which the state ought to do, [and seeing] clearly how it ought to do them."[31] As Pestritto and Atto explain, "[The progressives] coupled this perspective of historical contingency with a deep faith in historical progress, suggesting that, due to historical evolution, government was becoming less of a danger to the governed and more capable of solving the great array of problems besetting the human race."[32]

---

[30] Ronald J. Pestritto, *The Birth of the Administrative State: Where It Came from and What It Means for Limited Government*, no. 16 in the First Principles Series, Heritage Foundation, November 20, 2007, http://www.heritage.org/.

[31] Woodrow Wilson, "The Study of Administration," Pestritto and Atto, *American Progressivism*, 191–210, 193, originally in *Political Science Quarterly* 2 (July 1887): 197–222.

[32] Pestritto and Atto, *American Progressivism*, 3.

Deconstructing the Administrative State

Progressives' enthusiasm for the science of administration was inspired by European bureaucratic organizations and behavioral studies, particularly those from Germany. Insights gleaned from studying these structures could, they thought, guide the administration of government and greatly reduce the need for deliberation among politicians about the prudent course of action. Experts could develop and implement policy and do so with more reliability than the constitutional structure would allow.

Progressives had a particular vision of how modern society should be approached—one that sprang from their view of the nature of man, which, of course, dictated their view of economics, education, and government. They insisted that man did not have God-given dignity, and ordinary citizens and those whom they elect are ill-suited for making specialized policy decisions (transportation, immigration, sanitation, taxation, etc.[33]) in the complex, modern world. As argued by prominent progressive John Dewey, "What has counting heads, decision by majority and the whole apparatus of traditional government to do with such things?"[34] Instead, greater prominence must be accorded to trained technicians, or "experts," applying the process of scientific inquiry to decide matters of public policy and, ultimately, to determine the public's best interest.[35] Both crisis (*e.g.*, the financial crisis of the early twenty-first century) and success (*e.g.*, the "peace dividend" of the 1990s) call for more government management of the individual.

[33] John Dewey and Melvin L. Rogers, *The Public and Its Problems: An Essay in Political Inquiry* (Athens: Swallow Press, 1954), 124–125.
[34] Ibid.
[35] Ibid.

Progressives recognized that the independent American spirit, informed by history and grounded in the founding principles, would resist rule by an administrative state. To support implementation of their philosophy, progressive historians reinterpreted history in order to undermine Americans' dedication to the founding. Charles Beard and J. Allen Smith (foreshadowing Howard Zinn) attacked the popular understanding of the Founders as wise patriots risking everything to launch a new nation; rather, they argued, the Founders designed a system to maintain their own economic and political supremacy.[36] If the people could be brought to believe that the Founders' intentions were misplaced, then so too would be any allegiances to their guiding principles. These historians argued in favor of "an aggressive, popular movement that stressed democratic means to realize political and social reform."[37]

Several principles underlay progressive philosophy:

- Rejection of natural rights as a principle of government: Locke was wrong, progressives argued, and the founding documents based on his error now constituted an obstacle to societal progress.[38] As Woodrow Wilson once advised during a speech, "If you want to understand the real Declaration of Independence, do not repeat the preface."[39]

---

[36] Pestritto and Atto, *American Progressivism*, 8–9.

[37] Ibid., 8.

[38] Ibid., 3–4.

[39] Woodrow Wilson, "An Address to the Jefferson Club of Los Angeles, May 12, 1911," in *The Papers of Woodrow Wilson*, 69 vols., ed. Arthur S. Link (Princeton, N.J.: Princeton University Press, 1966–1993), 23:34, cited in Pestritto and Atto, *American Progressivism*, 30.

- Replacement of natural rights by social expediency: the individual is obligated to act in the best interests of society.[40]
- The theory of "living" and "organic" government, guided by "living" and "organic" documents, for the purpose of addressing unforeseen social ills.[41]
- Increased power for government to address such ills for the good of the whole.[42]
- The separation of administration from politics, committing the former to objective "experts" who would operate for the common good without having to answer to the electorate.

If the idea of pursuing the people's best interest in possible defiance of the people's preferences seems contradictory, it was. As Pestritto and Atto explain, while progressives very much wanted to democratize national political institutions, their inclination in administration was just the opposite — to shield administrative agencies from political influence, so that administrators could be free to make policy on the basis of their expertise.[43] Moreover, progressives, most famously Woodrow Wilson, "believed that administrators, unlike ordinary politicians, could be objective and could focus on the good of the whole people — [but] oddly, their ability to do so rested primarily on being freed from electoral accountability."[44] When progressives speak about "democracy," they intend something outside the constitutional structure.

[40] Pestritto and Atto, *American Progressivism*, 4.
[41] Ibid., 6.
[42] Ibid.
[43] Ibid., 1.
[44] Ibid., 20.

Progressivism versus the Constitution

The denial of natural rights may seem an abstract philosophical idea, but it has critical practical consequences. Acknowledging that certain rights are unalienable impairs the efficiency of the expert, whose programs and policies may have to yield to citizens' rights and privileges. Of even more practical significance, such acknowledgment undermines the science of administration, which requires a trial-and-error process to determine optimal public policy (Dewey referred to this as "experiential" government, or government by experience). Mimicking real scientists, progressives envision government as a never-ending set of experiments, or learning by doing. The citizen, like a guinea pig in a cage, has no choice but to become part of the experiment.

For their part, traditionalists, conservatives, and libertarians decry failed government program after failed government program. But to the progressive the results are excusable, because even failure will point the way to ultimate societal efficiency. Furthermore, each failed attempt provides a handy excuse to retool the bureaucracy with more power, more citizen money, and more information collected on the citizenry. As James W. Ceaser, University of Virginia professor of politics, recently observed:

> Modern progressives have the same confidence in national public administration as did the original progressives, who spoke in broad and bold strokes in favor of "social engineering" and "social control." Given the 20th-century experience with totalitarian governments, few dare to use this language today. Yet modern progressives do not hesitate to urge federal agencies to prod, nudge, and command in ever-increasing spheres of activity.

Deconstructing the Administrative State

National administration remains the progressives' primary instrument for transforming American society.[45]

Because progressivism is incompatible with the founding principles, its advancement has required some changes — *de facto* or *de jure* — to the constitutional structure.

First, there was the matter of the legislatures. The Constitution delegates policy-making duties "to a small number of citizens elected by the rest ..."

> to refine and enlarge the public views by passing them through the medium of a chosen body of citizens, whose wisdom may best discern the true interest of their country and whose patriotism and love of justice will be least likely to sacrifice it to temporary or partial considerations.[46]

The Constitution "vests powers over domestic policy-making in Congress, subject to the President's veto."[47] Congress would study — including consultation of experts — and deliberate on the issues of the day and formulate policy in accordance with the public will.[48]

But this system is incompatible with the progressive preference for policy-making and -implementation by experts. Power

---

[45] James W. Ceaser, "What Next for the Left? The Progressives Go from Bad to Worse," *Weekly Standard*, February 8, 2016.

[46] James Madison, "Federalist No. 10."

[47] Jessica Mantel, "Procedural Safeguards for Agency Guidance: A Source of Legitimacy for the Administrative State," *Administrative Law Review* 61, no. 2 (Spring 2009): 359. See Keith E. Whittington, "The Place of Congress in the Constitutional Order," *Harvard Journal of Law and Public Policy* 40, no. 3 (June 2017).

[48] See Whittington, "The Place of Congress."

would need to be shifted away from the legislature and to the bureaucracy and, once there, insulated from political interference to the extent possible. Referencing "eminent German writers," Wilson argued:

> administration lies outside the proper sphere of *politics*. . . . Although politics sets the tasks for administration, it should not be suffered to manipulate its offices.[49]

"Constitutions . . . properly concern themselves only with those instrumentalities of government which are to control general law." Thus, Wilson argued, legislatures should merely set "broad plans of governmental action." The administrator, or bureaucrat, "is not and ought not be a mere passive instrument." He "should have and does have a will of his own in the choice and means for accomplishing his work."[50]

But what of the danger of concentrating power in unaccountable officials? Wilson wasn't bothered by that. The pride in one's expertise and the incentive to achieve personal success, he argued, would protect against abuse. Power would not corrupt; rather, "the greater [the bureaucrat's] power the less likely is he to abuse it, the more is he nerved and sobered and elevated by it."[51] Wilson asserted, "Bureaucracy can exist only where the whole service of the state is removed from the common political life of the people, its chiefs as well as its rank and file."[52]

Through broadly crafted statutes, strained court decisions, and unchecked executive action, the result of this shift is bureaucracies

---

[49] Woodrow Wilson, "The Study of Administration," cited in Pestritto and Atto, *American Progressivism*, 191–210, 201.

[50] Ibid., 203.

[51] Ibid., 204.

[52] Ibid., 206.

set up like mini-governments unto themselves. Congress has given executive agencies broad, frequently ambiguous, grants of power. The agencies craft regulations that have the force of law and essentially add content to the statute. With varying degrees of due process, the agencies judge whether a private party or state has violated the regulations. The agencies can levy penalties and fines and determine the meaning of the laws and regulations they administer, interpretations to which the courts give great deference.[53]

Beyond shifting legislative power to the administrative state, progressives faced the second problem of America's compound republic. One purpose of that structure was to ensure that government was as close to the people as possible and citizen-directed, something problematic to the centralized administrative state. Thus, progressives sought functionally to undo that division: the science of administration had to find a way "to make town, city, county, state, and federal governments ... interdependent and co-operative, combining independence with mutual helpfulness."[54]

Third, there was the problem of the American people themselves. In the words of Woodrow Wilson:

> The people, who are sovereign have no single ear which one can approach, and are selfish, ignorant, timid, stubborn, or foolish with the selfishness, the ignorances, the

---

[53] For a discussion of the delegation of legislative powers to the agencies, the combination in those agencies of some legislative and judicial powers with executive powers, and the degradation of the political accountability of those agencies, see Pestritto, "The Birth of the Administrative State."

[54] Woodrow Wilson, "The Study of Administration," cited in Pestritto and Atto, *American Progressivism*, 209.

stubbornnesses, the timidities, or the follies of several thousand persons—albeit there are hundreds who are wise.[55]

Wilson argued that America's success in developing and embracing its constitutional system "embarrasses us" and would make it difficult to institute the necessary reforms:

> A truth must become not only plain but also commonplace before it will be seen by the people who go to their work very early in the morning; and not to act upon it must involve great pinching inconveniences before these same people will make up their minds to act upon it.[56]

Wilson lamented that Americans had secured their Constitution and were "wide awake and quite intent upon having [their] own way anyhow." Wilson offered a chilling view as to how the citizen should interact with the expert:

> It is quite pathetic to see a whole book written by a German professor ... saying to his countrymen, "Please try to have an opinion about national affairs"; but a public ... docile and acquiescent in learning what things it has *not* a right to think and speak about imperatively.... It will submit to be instructed before it tries to instruct.[57]

Wilson then contrasted that with what progressives faced in the United States. "In trying to instruct our own public opinion, we are dealing with a pupil apt to think itself quite sufficiently instructed beforehand."[58]

[55] Ibid., 199.
[56] Ibid., 200.
[57] Ibid., 205.
[58] Ibid.

But the progressives held out hope that the American people could evolve. They hoped that, on most issues, the people could be swayed, that progressive education could reshape the American mind to render it receptive to policy prescriptions from the expert. The science of administration would have to find a way to "make public opinion efficient without suffering it to be meddlesome."[59] The progressive intent is to transfer power away from the legislature — where it is closest to the people and where competing views are investigated, debated, and weighed — and to the bureaucracy, where experts would inform, or lecture, citizens as to what society needs and, therefore, what must be.

This would turn the American Experiment on its head: instead of responding to the will of the people, government would instruct the people.

Will progressivism succeed in changing the American mindset? Has it already done so? Writing for *Fortune* in 1952, William H. Whyte Jr. observed:

> This vision of a new elite guiding us to the integrated life has inspired some interesting speculations (*e.g.*, Aldous Huxley's *Brave New World*, George Orwell's *Nineteen Eighty-Four*). The real danger, however, is something else again. It is not that the layman will be pushed around by the social engineers: it is that he will become one himself. Rather than the pawn of experts, he will be the willing apprentice — and embrace groupthink as the road to security.[60]

<hr />

[59] Ibid.

[60] William H. Whyte Jr., "Groupthink," *Fortune* (March 1952), http://fortune.com/. Whyte contends that "three mutually supporting ideas" are advancing this dynamic: "(1) that moral values

Whyte's prophecy of "the real danger" is coming to fruition in three ways. First, the titanic administrative state, coupled with the evisceration of the constitutional structure, makes it much more difficult for passionate citizens to engage successfully — that is, without "spinning their wheels" — in the political process. It changes their incentives and makes it more likely that they will forfeit their role in citizen-directed government to attend to pursuits that they view as more productive.

Second, through its ersatz research and wide-ranging administrative pronouncements, the administrative state has falsely established itself as superior to the citizen in the decision-making process. This encourages citizens to be less discerning and to accept its policies, even those of questionable or false validity. Whyte questioned why, "in a country with the sort of healthy political and economic base that has historically nourished individualism," citizens would accept the decision of the state over their own. His answer was that, in some cases, people have been conditioned to believe that "the system ... attends to these things [public policies] so much better than the individual, and he might just as well relax and enjoy it."[61]

Third, many politicians, including Republicans, seem to have succumbed to the progressive vision to the detriment of their faith in the citizen. Whether consciously or not, they have accepted the progressive assumption that the American Experiment and its founding principles and values aren't applicable

---

and ethics are relative; (2) that what is important is the kind of behavior and attitudes that make for the harmonious functioning of the group; (3) that the best way to achieve this is through the application of scientific techniques."

[61] Ibid.

to modern society. They fear that invoking those principles in defense of prudent legislation and policies will be rejected by the people as antiquated. They fear that the people don't care about these principles and, thus, the good fight cannot be fought. In place of defending the founding principles, they have adopted the progressive ideas of collaboration and compromise even if compromise means, as it always does in the political realm, that traditional principles and values must give way.

In the penultimate chapter, we discuss the crossroads that members of Congress face when they get to Washington and why the perverted system in Washington actually "weeds out" men and women of strong character. That system—and that mind-set—must change.

PROGRESSIVISM VERSUS INDIVIDUAL FREEDOM

During the early twentieth century, one of the most prominent proponents of progressive theory was John Dewey (1859–1952), a professor of philosophy and education at Columbia University Teachers College. Widely recognized as the "father of modern education," Dewey was also a leading progressive theorist. He believed the grand American Experiment had failed, and if democracy in American society were to survive, it must be reconstructed. Like his fellow progressives, he denied any philosophy "in which the particular ideas of individuality and freedom were asserted to be absolute and eternal truths; good for all times and all places."[62] To Dewey, the value of individuality and freedom should be judged by whether the application of those ideas brought

[62] John Dewey, "The Future of Liberalism," *Journal of Philosophy* 32 (April 1935): 225, reprinted in *John Dewey: The Later Works*,

about positive social outcomes. Whatever advanced society's best interest—whether greater individual liberty and less government control, or less individual liberty and more government control—would be deemed right. Nothing was absolute. Events, values, and ideas had to be examined through the lens of historical relativity—everything was relative to that time and place.

According to Dewey, the emphasis on individuality and liberty arose in reaction to the British political environment. The demand for "freedom of the taxpayer from governmental arbitrary action" drove the desire for individual liberty and a distrust of government.[63] The understanding of government as a threat to individual rights provided a "valiant service" to society during this period, because it succeeded in "sweeping away ... an innumerable number of abuses and restrictions."[64]

But Dewey found the liberal notion, particularly as expressed by the Framers, that government action and individual freedoms are antithetical to each other to be ephemeral and outdated. He argued that government had become "popular" and "the servant of the people," and he lamented the Framers' failure to envision a day when government would be "an instrument for securing and extending the liberties of individuals."[65] With the changes of the Industrial Revolution, that day had come. Dewey believed that liberty could no longer be secured without state intervention in social matters. The state could not survive without securing

---

1925-1953, ed. Jo Ann Boydston (Carbondale, IL: Southern Illinois University, 2008), 11:290.

[63] Ibid., 289.

[64] Ibid., 290.

[65] Ibid., 291; John Dewey, "Liberalism and Social Action," in *John Dewey: The Later Works*, 11:8.

the terms of liberty as much through the "positive construction of favorable institutions, legal, political and economic as ... in removing abuses and overt oppressions."[66] In "The Progressive Movement and the Transformation of American Politics," Professor Thomas G. West describes this fundamental difference between the Framers' and the progressives' views of the role of government as one of "protecting individuals" from the encroachment on their liberties versus that of "creating individuals" through government programs.[67]

Dewey argued that firmly holding on to economic, political, and religious traditions thwarted social progress because it prevented new "collective ideas" from taking hold. As an example, he proffered that the American economic tradition was preventing American society from solving the economic problems of the Depression:

> We are taught to believe that all start equal in the economic race without any external handicaps being imposed on any persons and that reward and victory go to those of superior personal energy, ability, industry, and thrift, while, barring the exceptional cases of physical disease and accident, those who fall behind do so because of individual defects. We are taught that in this equal struggle between individuals all the great virtues of initiative, self-respect, self-help, standing on one's own feet, moral independence, and the rest are acquired.

[66] John Dewey, "The Future of Liberalism," in *John Dewey: The Later Works*, 11:291.

[67] Thomas G. West and William A. Schambra, *The Progressive Movement and the Transformation of American Politics*, no. 12 in the First Principles Series, Heritage Foundation, July 18, 2007, http://s3.amazonaws.com/thf_media/2007/pdf/fp12.pdf.

Now these things may have been true once. They are not true now. Industry is mainly collective and corporate today, and economic opportunities are dependent upon collective conditions.[68]

As we will see, modern-day progressives are building on their predecessors' work, and implementing their philosophy and agenda, through ingenious schemes that require little or no public defense — because the public has no idea what is happening.

CORRUPTING THE CONSTITUTIONAL STRUCTURE BY CONSTITUTIONAL AMENDMENTS AND JUDICIAL DECISIONS

Three realities have influenced the effectiveness of the constitutional structure: (1) constitutional amendment, (2) judicial decisions, and (3) the day-to-day practices of the federal and state governments. This work addresses primarily the last item on that list, but a brief overview of the first two provides the context for discussion of the last.

Formal Structural Changes That Weakened States' Power

The Framers intended that the U.S. House of Representatives would reflect the concerns of the people, and they thus provided for that body to be elected directly by the people.[69] But because the state governments would possess broader, general authority, the Framers made sure those bodies have a means to repel federal encroachment and thereby protect the state decision-making

---

[68] John Dewey, "The Economic Situation: A Challenge to Education," in *John Dewey: The Later Works*, 6:128–129.

[69] U.S. Constitution, Art. I, § 2.

done at the behest of state citizenry. To accomplish this, they empowered the state legislatures to elect U.S. senators.[70]

This harkens to a key function of the constitutional structure. The people authorize government to exercise a portion of their power. As we've noted, the Framers crafted a structure that divides the power between governments and among branches. But common sense requires that the various governments and branches have the means to protect the power—which has been delegated to them by the people—from incursions by other branches and other governments. Several developments, though, have weakened the ability of state governments to protect their power.

In the late 1800s, progressives persuaded some states to begin loosening their legislatures' control over the selection of U.S. senators. This began with chipping away the legislatures' selection of nominees and culminated in 1913 with the ratification of the Seventeenth Amendment: direct election of senators by a state's citizens. Though seemingly an enhancement of the power of the people, direct election turned out to be a reckless innovation.

A senator who was chosen by the state legislature, as the Constitution originally provided, had a personal interest in protecting the autonomy and constitutional authority of that legislature as the governing body of the state. But removing that power from the state legislature allowed election of senators who would be less responsive to, and protective of, that body:

---

[70] See James Madison, "Federalist No. 62": "... giving to the State governments such an agency in the formation of the federal government as must secure the authority of the former, and may form a convenient link between the two systems."

The framers understood that the mode of electing (and especially reelecting) Senators by state legislatures made it in the self-interest of Senators to preserve the original federal design and to protect the interests of the states as states (*see* Article I, Section 3, Clause 1). This understanding was perfectly encapsulated in a July 1789 letter to John Adams, in which Roger Sherman emphasized that "[t]he Senators, being eligible by the legislatures of the several states, and dependent on them for reelection, will be vigilant in supporting their rights against infringement by the legislative or executive of the United States."[71]

State citizens entrusted their governments with vast powers and responsibilities. Moreover, as the Court in *Bond v. U.S.* noted, state sovereignty is integral to the protection of the rights of the individual from federal incursion. In stripping the legislatures of the appointment of senators, the Seventeenth Amendment deprived states and state citizens of their ability to guard against federal overreach as well as to guard against special-interest lobbying in Washington.[72] Nor can the people provide an effective check through their U.S. senators and House members because, as noted below, the federal government often hides behind state actors and thus shrouds its true influence over state policy.

[71] "Popular Election of Senators," in *The Heritage Guide to the Constitution*, eds. David F. Forte and Matthew Spalding (Washington, D.C.: Heritage Foundation, 2014), http://www.heritage.org/constitution/#!/amendments/17/essays/178/popular-election-of-senators.

[72] See Todd J. Zywicki, "Senators and Special Interests: A Public Choice Analysis of the Seventeenth Amendment," *Oregon Law Review* 73 (1994): 1007.

Judicial Decisions That Expanded Federal Power

The Supreme Court has paved several avenues for the enlargement of federal power, several of which are discussed below. These decisions left the states vulnerable to federal incursion, especially on the heels of the Seventeenth Amendment. As we'll see, Congress and the executive branch set about to exploit these avenues aggressively.

One such avenue is an expansive interpretation of the Commerce Clause. The Constitution accords Congress the power "To regulate Commerce ... among the several States."[73] The purpose of that clause is to ensure the free flow of commerce among the states.[74] Over the years, the Court has interpreted the Commerce Clause power expansively: "as interstate commerce has become ubiquitous, activities once considered purely local have come to have effects on the national economy, and have accordingly come within the scope of Congress' commerce power."[75]

Congress may not, however, "simply 'commandee[r] the legislative processes of the States by directly compelling them to

---

[73] U.S. Constitution, Art. I, § 8.

[74] See, *e.g.*, James Madison, "Federalist No. 42": "The defect of power in the existing Confederacy to regulate the commerce between its several members [has] been clearly pointed out by experience."

[75] *New York*, 505 U.S. at 144, 158, citing Katzenbach v. McClung, 379 U.S. 294 (1964) and Wickard v. Filburn, 317 U. S. 111 (1942). See also *Sebelius*, 567 U.S. at 536–537: "The power over activities that substantially affect interstate commerce can be expansive. That power has been held to authorize federal regulation of such seemingly local matters as a farmer's decision to grow wheat for himself and his livestock, and a loan shark's extortionate collections from a neighborhood butcher shop," internal citations omitted.

enact and enforce a federal regulatory program.' "[76] The Court will "strike down federal legislation that commandeers a State's legislative or administrative apparatus for federal purposes."[77] It will hold a federal statute or regulatory scheme unconstitutional if states don't have a choice in participating—that is, if they don't "freely agree to have their powers employed and their employees enlisted in the federal scheme."[78] For example, the Court has struck down federal legislation compelling law-enforcement officers to perform federally mandated background checks on handgun purchasers.[79] And it has invalidated provisions of a statute that would compel a state either to take title to nuclear waste or to enact particular state waste regulations.[80]

Another judicially created avenue for federal domination is the Court's interpretation of the Spending Clause, found in the Constitution at Section 8 of Article I. That clause authorizes Congress to tax and spend: Congress may "lay and collect Taxes, Duties, Imposts and Excises, to pay the Debts and provide for the common Defence and general Welfare of the United States."[81] Section 8 then enumerates "legislative fields"—specific subject matter—in which Congress may legislate.[82]

In its 1936 decision *U.S. v. Butler*, the Supreme Court held that Congress may tax and spend for the "general welfare" and that this confers a power on Congress separate and distinct from

---

[76] *New York*, 505 U.S. at 161, quoting Hodel v. Virginia Surface Mining, 452 U.S. 264, 288 (1981).

[77] *Sebelius*, 567 U.S. at 577.

[78] Ibid., at 648 (Scalia, Kennedy, Thomas, and Alito, JJ, dissenting).

[79] See Printz v. United States, 521 U. S. 898, 924 (1997).

[80] *New York*, 505 U.S. at 174–176.

[81] U.S. Constitution, Art. I, § 8.

[82] U.S. v. Butler, 297 U.S. 1, 65 (1936).

those later enumerated "legislative fields."[83] As the Chief Justice discussed in *National Federation of Independent Business v. Sebelius*, there are two ways in which the Spending Clause, as interpreted by the Court, enables Congress to affect activities it otherwise could not: (1) Congress may "enact a tax on an activity that it cannot authorize, forbid, or otherwise control"[84] and (2) "Congress may offer funds to the States, and may condition those offers on compliance with specified conditions."[85] The federal government frequently, and quite effectively, uses that power to "induce the States to adopt policies that [it otherwise] could not impose."[86]

The Court has established four criteria to evaluate the constitutionality of such federal grants—in other words, whether the federal government has exceeded its authority. The conditions placed on federal grants to states must (1) "be in pursuit of the 'general welfare,'" (2) be unambiguous so as to enable "the States to exercise their choice [to accept the federal conditions] knowingly, cognizant of the consequences of their participation," (3) be germane "to the federal interest in particular national projects or programs," and (4) not otherwise run afoul of the Constitution.[87] In Supreme Court jurisprudence, most discussion has centered on the second condition: the states' free choice to accept or reject the federal terms.

---

[83] Ibid., 65–66.

[84] *Sebelius*, 567 U.S. at 537, citing *License Tax Cases*, 72 U.S. 462 (1867).

[85] Ibid., citing College Savings Bank v. Florida Prepaid Postsecondary Education Expense Board, 527 U. S. 666, 686 (1999).

[86] See ibid., citing South Dakota v. Dole, 483 U.S. 203, 205–206 (1987), conditioning federal highway funds on states' raising their drinking age to twenty-one.

[87] *Dole*, 483 U.S. at 207–210.

With respect to both Commerce Clause and Spending Clause matters, it's critical that states have a free choice whether to participate in federal programs or regulatory schemes.[88] For example, as the Court has repeatedly held, Spending Clause legislation is "much in the nature of a contract."[89] Following that line of thought, the Court reasons:

> The legitimacy of Congress's exercise of the spending power "thus rests on whether the State voluntarily and knowingly accepts the terms of the 'contract.'" ... Respecting this limitation is critical to ensuring that Spending Clause legislation does not undermine the status of the States as independent sovereigns in our federal system.[90]

As held by the Supreme Court, the rule is that Congress may use its spending power to create incentives for states to implement federal policies, but "when 'pressure turns into compulsion,' the legislation runs contrary to our system of federalism."[91]

---

[88] *New York*, 505 U.S. at 167-69, citing *Hodel*, 452 U. S. 264, 288 (1981). As the Court in *New York* notes: "This arrangement, which has been termed 'a program of co-operative federalism,' is replicated in numerous federal statutory schemes." 505 U.S. at 167–168, internal citations omitted.

[89] See, *e.g.*, Barnes v. Gorman, 536 U.S. 181, 186 (2002), quoting Pennhurst State School and Hospital v. Halderman, 451 U.S. 1, 17 (1981).

[90] *Sebelius*, 567 U.S. at 577, quoting *Pennhurst*.

[91] Ibid., 577–578, quoting Steward Machine Company v. Davis, 301 U. S. 548, 590 (1937). By today's standards, the legislation in *Steward* was rather simple. It involved a federal tax on employers that was abated if the businesses paid into a state unemployment plan that met certain federally specified conditions. An employer sued, alleging that the tax was impermissibly

In *Sebelius*, the Chief Justice further argued that allowing the federal government to force states to implement a federal program would threaten the political accountability that is key to the constitutional structure. Quoting precedent, he reasoned that "where the Federal Government directs the States to regulate, it may be state officials who will bear the brunt of public disapproval, while the federal officials who devised the regulatory program may remain insulated from the electoral ramifications of their decision."[92]

After noting the principles in those cases, however, the Chief Justice opined that such danger doesn't exist "when a State has a legitimate choice whether to accept the federal conditions in exchange for federal funds. In such a situation, state officials can fairly be held politically accountable for choosing to accept or refuse the federal offer."[93] He observed that typically the Court will "look to the states" to defend their sovereignty by simply not accepting the "federal blandishments when they do not want to embrace the federal policies as their own."[94] The Chief Justice famously admonished, "The States are separate and independent sovereigns. Sometimes they have to act like it."[95] As we'll see,

---

"driv[ing] the state legislatures under the whip of economic pressure into the enactment of unemployment compensation laws at the bidding of the central government." The Court acknowledged the danger that the federal government might employ its taxing power to exert a "power akin to undue influence" upon the states.

[92] Ibid., 578, quoting *New York*, 505 U.S. at 169.

[93] Ibid.

[94] Ibid., 579, citing Massachusetts v. Mellon, 262 U. S. 447, 482 (1923).

[95] Ibid.

though, the federal government takes an abusive and divisive approach in its relations with the states, such that states' simply rejecting federal schemes and programs may be easier said than done.

The Court in *Sebelius* discussed whether the states could freely decide whether to participate in the Medicaid-expansion program under the Patient Protection and Affordable Care Act (Obamacare).[96] Under the statutory scheme, if a state didn't significantly expand its Medicaid program to meet federal requirements, it would lose all its Medicaid funding. The Court struck down this provision, reasoning that, due in large part to the size of the threatened loss in funding, states were left with no real option but to agree to Medicaid expansion.

Thus, the Act was held unconstitutional with respect to that aspect of Medicaid funding.[97]

Judicial Empowerment of the Administrative State — *Chevron*

The administrative state has metastasized, growing ever larger and unmoored from the system of checks and balances. Administrative agencies — that is, the experts — "as a practical matter ... exercise legislative power, ... executive power ... and judicial

---

[96] See ibid., 574–585, opinion of Chief Justice Roberts, at Section IV, joined by Justice Breyer and Justice Kagan; opinion of Justice Ginsburg, at Section V, joined by Justice Sotomayor; and opinion of Justices Scalia, Kennedy, Thomas, and Alito, at 671–689.

[97] See ibid. (opinion of Chief Justice Roberts at Part IV, joined by Justice Breyer and Justice Kagan); and opinion of Justices Scalia, Kennedy, Thomas, and Alito, at 671–689 (Sect. IV A-E).

power."[98] With broad delegations of power to the experts and with the overall size of the bureaucracy growing, the office of the president is also stretched in terms of providing any effective check. The progressive dream of rule by experts is more reality than not.

In the progressive view, the point of an administrative state is to enable efficient and effective policy-making by experts. It does this in several ways: combining the three governmental functions (legislative, executive, and judicial) into one; delegating legislative power to entities unaccountable to the people; and establishing a quasi-judicial process that "prioritizes efficiency and social justice rather than the rights of individual citizens."[99] All these techniques defy the principles of separation of powers, due process, and equal protection of the laws that form the foundation of the Constitution.

Congress has theoretically established a framework for overseeing the administrative state. Enacted in 1946, the Administrative Procedure Act (APA)[100] sets out the governing framework for federal executive-branch and independent agencies. The APA requires courts that review agency action to decide "all relevant questions of law, including the interpretation of constitutional or statutory provision."[101] Despite this mandate for broad

[98] City of Arlington v. Federal Communications Commission, 569 U.S. __, 133 S. Ct. 1863, 1877 (May 20, 2013) (Roberts, CJ, Kennedy and Alito, JJ, dissenting).

[99] See Joseph Postell, "From Administrative State to Constitutional Government," Heritage Foundation, December 14, 2012, http://www.heritage.org/political-process/report/administrative-state-constitutional-government#_ftn38.

[100] 5 U.S.C § 500ff.

[101] See John F. Duffy, "Administrative Common Law and the Original Meaning of Judicial Review under the APA," Federalist

judicial review, the Supreme Court has imposed its own limits on the scrutiny it will apply to agency action, giving agencies wide latitude to enforce their own policy preferences. It has genuflected to rule by experts.

In *Chevron, USA, Inc. v. Natural Resources Defense Council, Inc.* (1984),[102] the Court addressed a challenge to the Environmental Protection Agency's interpretation of the phrase "stationary sources" in the Clean Air Act. The Court upheld the EPA's interpretation, finding that the agency permissibly filled in a "gap" left by Congress in the definition of the statutory term. Justice Stevens approvingly quoted Supreme Court precedent that "the power of an administrative agency to administer a congressionally created ... program necessarily requires the formulation of policy and the making of rules to fill any gap left, implicitly or explicitly, by Congress."[103]

Under what has become known as this "*Chevron* deference," a court reviewing an agency's statutory interpretation must first decide whether "Congress has directly spoken to the precise question at issue."[104] If Congress is determined to have spoken either ambiguously or not at all, the court should uphold the agency's interpretation, as long as it is a "reasonable" or "permissible" reading of the statute. The *Chevron* Court summed up: a challenge

---

Society Administrative Law Practice Group Newsletter 3, no. 2 (Summer 1999), http://www.fed-soc.org/.

[102] 467 U.S. 837 (1984).

[103] Ibid., 843, quoting Morton v. Ruiz, 415 U.S. 199, 231 (1974).

[104] Elizabeth Slattery, "Who Will Regulate the Regulators? Administrative Agencies, the Separation of Powers, and Chevron Deference," Heritage Foundation, May 7, 2015, http://www.heritage.org/courts/report/who-will-regulate-the-regulators-administrative-agencies-the-separation-powers-and#_ftn17.

"must fail" if it "really centers on the wisdom of the agency's policy, rather than whether it is a reasonable choice within a gap left open by Congress."[105] The Court thus gives deference to bureaucrats' statutory and regulatory interpretations in such instances.

Chevron deference has since been expanded to the question of "an agency's interpretation of the scope of its authority (not simply its interpretation of the law)."[106] That is, a court should defer to the agency's opinion even on the question of whether the statute at issue is ambiguous.[107] In a more recent case, the Court justified its *Chevron* deference in terms right out of the progressive handbook: "In our increasingly complex society, replete with ever-changing and more technical problems, Congress simply cannot do its job absent an ability to delegate power under broad general directives."[108]

Several justices (including Alito, Breyer, Scalia, and Thomas) have expressed concern about the "aggrandizement of the power of administrative agencies," especially under the *Chevron* doctrine.[109] Similarly, the most recent arrival to the Court, Justice Gorsuch, has previously argued the incompatibility of *Chevron* deference with the separation of powers and due process established by the Framers:

> [When an agency is allowed almost unfettered power to interpret law,] that's a problem for the judiciary. And it

[105] *Chevron*, 467 U.S. at 866.

[106] Slattery, "Who Will Regulate?"

[107] *Arlington*, 133 S. Ct. 1863 (2013).

[108] Mistretta v. U.S., 488 U.S. 361, 372 (1989). Interestingly, as discussed in the chapter on property, the Court has also used this reasoning in the evisceration of private-property rights.

[109] Slattery, "Who Will Regulate?"

is a problem for the people whose liberties may now be impaired not by an independent decision-maker seeking to declare the law's meaning as fairly as possible ... but by an avowedly politicized administrative agent seeking to pursue whatever policy whim may rule the day.[110]

Gorsuch summed up *Chevron* as adding "prodigious new powers to an already titanic administrative state."[111]

Perhaps the addition of Gorsuch to the Court will result in changes to *Chevron* deference. In addition, the House of Representatives has, for two Congresses in a row, passed legislation (on an almost party-line vote) that would overturn *Chevron* by prohibiting courts from conducting a deferential review of agency action.[112] (A constitutional challenge might be expected on the grounds that this law would improperly interfere with judicial functions, but at least one constitutional scholar has opined that this "is really a question of statutory interpretation, which Congress should be able to control.")[113] So *Chevron*'s days may be numbered. For now, though, federal agencies operate under the assumption that, if challenged by citizens harmed by their actions, the Supreme Court has directed the judiciary to bend over backward to side with the federal agencies.

---

[110] Gutierrez-Brizuela v. Lynch, 834 F.3d 1142, 1153 (10th Cir. 2016) (Gorsuch, concurring).

[111] Ibid., 1155.

[112] Vikram David Amar, "*Chevron* Deference and the Proposed 'Separation of Powers Restoration Act of 2016': A Sign of the Times," Justia Verdict, July 26, 2016 (referring to legislation in the 2015-16 Congress), https://verdict.justia.com/.

[113] See ibid.

The Court's Half-Hearted Defense
of the Constitutional Structure

As we've seen, the Court has repeatedly used strong rhetoric to affirm the importance of the constitutional structure in defense of state sovereignty. Of more importance, that rhetoric has affirmed the purposes of the compound republic: to protect individual liberty and to ensure that government is citizen-directed. The Court has even added the gloss that the compound republic sets states in competition for a mobile citizenry — something that bears itself out in, for example, the westward expansion of the frontier days; the African-American migrations to the Northeast, the Midwest, and the West; and the recent migrations into Texas.

But when the Court moves from rhetoric to its actual holdings, it too often abandons the recognition of states as complex entities and embraces a simplistic description. Certainly, as the Chief Justice opined in *Sebelius*, the states have to act like "separate and independent" sovereigns. But it's the Court that fails to consider them as such. It treats a state as a simple plaintiff — much like an individual — objecting to a single, static transaction. Such an analysis may have been sound when the Court decided *Steward Machine Company v. Davis* in 1937, but not now.

Over the ensuing eighty years, as discussed in this work, the federal government has unleashed wave after wave of grants and regulatory schemes on the states, many of them interlocking. It has lured generations of governors with short-term revenue programs to decorate their short-term tenures but which left their states with long-term financial commitments. It has built up state bureaucracies to administer ongoing federal grants. It has bent the loyalties of those bureaucracies toward the federal government and away from their own legislature and people. It has skipped over state governments and given grants directly to local government. It has created boards and commissions to shape policy in the states. It has released billions of dollars' worth of biased research to buttress its favored policies. In short, it has created a complex web of incentives and relationship structures designed to enhance its power at the expense of the states' power.

This is the context in which the Court resorts to a century-old analysis, developed long before the federal evisceration of state government, to chastise states for not acting like separate and independent sovereigns. Unless and until it updates its analysis, its decisions will simply not reflect political reality. The Court expects the states to act like sovereign governments in the face of federal overreach, yet it seems oblivious that the federal Leviathan has crippled the functioning of state government and impaired the ability of the states to make independent, reasonable decisions. To borrow from the Court's reasoning in *Bond*, that would be one thing if the only issue were state sovereignty for its own sake. But it's not. At issue are the rights of the people, as free citizens, to control their government. Given the deteriorating landscape of federalism, the Court must be more vigilant in protecting the constitutional structure.

AN OVERVIEW OF DEFECTS IN THE PRESERVATION OF STATE SOVEREIGNTY

Despite the Seventeenth Amendment and Court decisions that have undermined federalism, the constitutional structure remains a stumbling block for progressive governance. Progressive "experts" cannot dictate policy if state legislatures are guarding against federal intrusion and enacting legislation in response to citizens' desires. To work around that problem, progressives have developed mechanisms to subdue state sovereignty. Those mechanisms include the following:

- conditional-funding programs (grants, cooperative agreements)
- cooperative-federalism schemes
- direct funding to state subsidiaries
- propagation of "ghost governments" and independent commissions
- massive federally funded "research" to justify federal policies
- public-public partnerships
- public-private partnerships

As we'll see, these mechanisms marginalize both Congress and state government, especially state legislators. They undermine the constitutional structure to bring about government by experts. These mechanisms will be discussed in detail in subsequent chapters, but here is an overview:

Conditional-funding programs. Conditional-funding programs corrupt the intended relationship between the federal government and the state and between a state's executive and legislative branches. In response to the lure of the federal dollar, the state executive — including elected, appointed, and career officials — turns attention away from the state legislature and the people and toward federal agencies. It readies itself for the federal money, rationalizing the adoption of policies preferred by federal agencies. It lobbies the legislature to make changes to state law to qualify for the conditional dollar. In certain instances, the state executive will receive funding from the federal government for executive-agency jobs, a reality that at the very least gives the appearance of a divided loyalty.

These funding schemes involve parties of vastly disparate power. The federal government supplies money and, through the grant or cooperative agreement, secures promises from the supplicant state. It tends to use ambiguities in the agreement and in relevant federal statutes, regulations, and guidance documents as leverage over the states. It will even misinterpret the clear or settled meanings of such documents to gain further leverage.

Even beyond federally incubated divided loyalties, the states are hard-pressed to mount an effective response to such techniques. They have fewer legal resources than the federal government. They invariably have federal- and state-imposed performance deadlines that weaken their negotiating power with the federal government. Deadlines must be met, and that may mean bowing to federal interpretations, no matter how unreasonable.

Cooperative-federalism schemes. Cooperative-federalism schemes — programs in which the federal government and state government work together for joint goals — present multiple difficulties. These schemes tend to pair federal goals with state regulatory schemes designed to meet the federal goals. Even more so than with conditional-funding schemes, the states find themselves having to deal with ambiguous or misinterpreted federal legal pronouncements and without the time or resources to rebut them.

Direct funding to state subsidiaries. The federal government also freely jumps over state government to deal directly with political subsidiaries of the state. This cuts the state legislature out of the picture and is sometimes done purposely to undermine action or inaction by state government.

Propagation of "ghost governments." Another technique for undermining state government is the federal government's creation of "ghost," or parallel, government-like structures. These entities operate largely independent of the state legislatures. They have federally specified policy portfolios and are structured for political dominance over legislatures and local government.

Deconstructing the Administrative State

One example of ghost governments is the metropolitan planning organization (MPO), a creature of the Federal-Aid Highway Act.[114] The federal government has made each MPO responsible for transportation planning for its designated area, and it defines an MPO's geographical area with little regard for political boundaries. Federal law prescribes the objectives of transportation policy and dictates the general makeup of the MPO boards.[115] In this way the federal government usurps the autonomy of state and local governments over transportation planning within their jurisdictions.

Federally funded research to justify federal policies. National goals established by federal agencies are often influenced by policy reports issued by federal commissions or organizations such as the National Science Foundation and the National Research Council.[116] In some cases, the reports are merely ruses to create a body of literature to justify the federal agency's agenda.

---

[114] Currently, all MPOs are governed by federal legislation called Moving Ahead for Progress in the 21st Century (MAP-21), as updated by the December 2015 passage of the Fixing America's Surface Transportation Act (FAST Act).

[115] 23 CFR § 450.310(d)(1). The FAST Act requires that the representation of MPOs with a population over 200,000 people "shall consist of (i) Local elected officials, (ii) Officials of public agencies that administer or operate major modes of transportation in the metropolitan area, including representation by providers of public transportation; and (iii) Appropriate State officials."

[116] The National Research Council is the principal operating arm of the National Academy of Sciences and the National Academy of Engineering. The Research Council is a private, nonprofit institution that provides science and technology advice under a congressional charter.

The research organizations or commissions inevitably reach the same conclusion: the current structures aren't working, the problems are systemic, and the federal government must step in to avoid a collapse. Examples, as discussed in detail later in this work, include issuance of reports demanding greater federal involvement in both education and "public health," broadly defined. In the face of such "research," how can states say no?

Public-public partnerships. This brings us to public-public partnerships — collusion among multiple agencies to usurp state decision-making and drive a federal agenda. A good example is the initiative of the Departments of Housing and Urban Development (HUD) and Transportation (DOT) and the EPA to counter the purported negative effects of urban sprawl. These agencies formed the Interagency Partnership for Sustainability, leveraging grants and technical assistance from multiple departments to push state and local agencies to include Smart Growth principles[117] in transportation planning, zoning ordinances, and land-use patterns.[118]

[117] In general, Smart Growth initiatives adhere to the following principles: Mix Land Uses; Take Advantage of Compact Building Design; Create a Range of Housing Opportunities and Choices; Create Walkable Neighborhoods; Foster Distinctive, Attractive Communities with a Strong Sense of Place; Preserve Open Space, Farmland, Natural Beauty, and Critical Environmental Areas; Strengthen and Direct Development Towards Existing Communities; Provide a Variety of Transportation Choices; Make Development Decisions Predictable, Fair and Cost Effective; Encourage Community and Stakeholder Collaboration in Development Decisions. See "Smart Growth Principles," Smart Growth Online website, http://smartgrowth.org/smart-growth-principles/.

[118] "About Us," Partnership for Sustainable Communities (PSC) website, https://www.sustainablecommunities.gov/mission/about-us.

Public-private partnerships. Public-private partnerships provide yet another tool for the breakdown of the constitutional structure. The Interagency Partnership for Sustainability, mentioned above, extended a variety of grants[119] to private businesses (such as real estate developers[120]) and nonprofits (such as universities, civic groups, and community groups) to implement its reforms. By spreading the federal largesse among the local community, federal agencies create a constituency for its agenda and the perception of popular support.

Public-private partnerships also present an opportunity for federal agencies to do an end run around federal laws. Such relationships must be examined to determine whether federal agencies are paying others to do what it is prohibited from doing under federal law. As discussed in later chapters, the U.S. Department of Education provided funding to private (as well as public) entities to develop national standards, curriculum, and student assessments—all of which it is prohibited from doing under federal law.

STATE OFFICIALS SUM UP THE PROBLEM

In testifying before the Senate Judiciary Committee in 1995, Nebraska Governor Ben Nelson remarked, "When I was elected governor in 1990 and prepared my first budget, I honestly

---

[119] "Federal Grant Opportunities," Reconnecting America website, http://reconnectingamerica.org/resource-center/federal-grant-opportunities/.

[120] U.S. Department of Urban Housing and Development, Docket No. FR-5600-N-19, Notice of Funding Availability (NOFA) for HUD's Fiscal Year 2012 Choice Neighborhoods Initiative: Implementation Grants 16-17 (2012).

wondered if I was actually elected governor or just branch manager of the state of Nebraska for the federal government."[121] To help understand the breakdown of the constitutional structure, consider statements by former and current state officeholders on education policy-making—an area that is, with certain narrow exceptions (*e.g.*, civil rights, the education of the children of servicemen and women stationed overseas, and federal enclaves, such as the District of Columbia), the exclusive domain of state decision-making. As former Louisiana Governor Bobby Jindal stated, "Federal mandates, money, and threats bend [state] officials' necks stiffly towards Washington."[122] Amy Edmonds, a former Wyoming state legislator, elaborates on that sentiment:

> We continue to give lip service to the fairytale that states have control over the development and delivery of education in public schools. This is simply not true. The federal government has effectively created a system of "incentives" using the power of the federal purse to hammer states into submission. Wyoming, like most states, does not develop education policy that makes sense for our rural Western public schools, we develop policy based on what the federal government wants us to do. But we slap the word Wyoming in front of the legislation and say it's state based. It's utter lunacy.

[121] Roger Pilon, "Federalism, Then and Now," *inFocus Quarterly* (Winter 2015): 3, available at Jewish Policy Center, https://www.jewishpolicycenter.org/.

[122] Bobby Jindal, *K–12 Education Reform: A Roadmap* (Alexandria, Va.: America-Next, 2015), 21, http://www.americanext.org/.

Ingenious though they are, these mechanisms depend for their success on citizens and state and local officials who either will not recognize what is happening to the federalist structure or will accept the transformation as either necessary or inevitable. Successful implementation requires that not only the government but also the individual must change. That happens through education, which we shall explore in our next chapter.

Chapter 3

Reshaping the American Mind

We've got to do a better job of getting across that America is freedom—freedom of speech, freedom of religion, freedom of enterprise. And freedom is special and rare. It's fragile; it needs protection.

—President Ronald Reagan, Farewell Speech, January 11, 1989

"Stamping In" the Correct Attitude

Federalism ties into education policy in a profound, often over-looked way. In its purposes of protecting both states' rights and the liberty of the individual, federalism rests on the idea that the individual will direct government. Thus, while the citizen is the ultimate party protected, he also serves as the final check on government behavior.

But in practice, only a well-educated individual is capable of holding the primary position in the constitutional structure. This doesn't mean that a citizen must have a college education, and, in fact, many citizens without college educations more ably fulfill their civic duties than do those with degrees. What it does mean, though, is that only a citizen who recognizes truth, who understands the basis for his rights, who appreciates the struggle for civil society to protect those rights, and who can empathize and communicate with others can truly fulfill his constitutional role.

Many conservatives and traditionalists don't consciously recognize the individual as the keystone of the constitutional structure. Progressives don't make that mistake. They have relentlessly set about to reprogram the rugged individual who launched the American Experiment into a servant of the state — one who won't resist as the constitutional structure that guards his dignity is torn down.

The recent intolerance of diverse political thought, Western values, and American exceptionalism on college campuses isn't the beginning of a new political movement — it's the realization of progressive efforts that began about a hundred years ago. The grand experiment of early-twentieth-century progressives such as John Dewey and his cadre of educators, to rewire the mind of the American citizen through politicizing instruction in the school system, has finally borne fruit. The purpose of this chapter is to show how the education system has been designed to serve that progressive goal — to condition students to reject the principles of a constitutional republic in favor of rule by an administrative state. Familiarity with that effort is essential to understanding the erosion of the constitutional structure.

Traditional Education

The purpose of a traditional, or classic liberal, education is to develop the intellect of the individual so that he can reach his potential, fully participate in civic life, and exercise his rights. It enables the student to pursue the truth, to chart his course in life, and to become a person of virtue and of substance in his family, his community, and his country. It equips him to exercise his liberties fully and to appreciate the beauty in life. Traditional education focuses on the conveyance of knowledge, of academic content, not on current events, multiculturalism, or the low trajectory of workforce skills.

Through the study of mathematics, language, literature, science, history, and the arts, the traditional model transmits the knowledge and skills necessary for students to think critically about the events, issues, and concerns they will have to grapple with in life. It fosters an appreciation for the beauty in life and encourages children to think creatively.[123] It presents the body of knowledge in a sequential, orderly fashion through direct instruction, primarily teacher lectures and books. Under that model, a student is individually responsible for his work and is tested and graded on his mastery of content.

In *Left Back: A Century of Failed Reforms*, education historian Diane Ravitch points out that American public schools differed from their counterparts in Europe, where class structures limited a traditional education to the elite. Americans viewed the traditional public school education as enabling any child, regardless of class or position, to achieve the American dream. In doing so, the public schools were faithful to, and helped fulfill, America's promise of equal opportunity for all.[124]

In that respect, a traditional public education for all students was one of America's great cultural achievements. It's a dynamic that mirrors the development and propagation of the Declaration of Independence's statement regarding the rights and equality of man.

Providing a traditional education to all is a civic virtue. It is unitive — the highest form of assimilation. Traditional education

---

[123] Diane Ravitch, *Left Back: A Century of Failed School Reforms* (New York: Simon and Schuster, 2000), 15.
[124] Ibid., 19–21.

embraces the study of Western civilization, which includes the classical cultures of Greece and Rome, the Judeo-Christian influence, and the Enlightenment of the modern era.[125] Western civilization gave rise to an understanding of liberty, natural rights, limited government, and free-market economics. From it flowed the Declaration of Independence, the constitutional structure, the Bill of Rights, and the American Experiment.[126] That study exalts the dignity of the individual — and thus the individual student — and leads to the rational embrace of all other individuals as equally vested with dignity. Moreover, the never-ending struggle to be faithful to that founding, while shedding light on

[125] James Kurth, "Western Civilization, Our Tradition," *Intercollegiate Review* (Fall 2003/Spring 2004), 5–13, 5.

[126] For discussion on this point see, *e.g.*, Kurth, "Western Civilization," 6:

> The first of the Western traditions was classical culture. In the realm of politics, for example, Greece contributed the idea of a republic, while Rome contributed that of an empire. Similarly, Greece contributed the idea of liberty, and Rome, that of law. When combined, these ideas gave rise to the important Western concept of *liberty under law*.
>
> ... Christian theology established the sanctity of the individual believer and called for obedience to an authority (Christ) higher than any secular ruler (Caesar), ideas that further refined and supported the concept of liberty under law. Christian institutions, particularly the papacy of the Roman Catholic Church in its ongoing struggle with the Holy Roman Emperor and local monarchs, bequeathed to the West the idea of a separation, and therefore a limitation, of powers.
>
> The third source of Western civilization was the modern Enlightenment, which provided the ideas of liberal democracy, the free market, and the belief in reason and science as the privileged means for making sense of the world.

our imperfection, proves that the founding principle is not mere rhetoric. The authentic study of Western civilization — warts and all — compels faith in the American Experiment.

Excluding or perverting the study of Western civilization leaves citizens ill-equipped to defend against threats to peace and prosperity, whether domestic or foreign. To that end, Michael J. Demiashkevich (1891–1938), a Russian-born professor of education, argued that it is "undemocratic" to deny citizens access to the knowledge of the past: "Independent thinking on the part of citizens is one of the mightiest weapons of self-defense which a democracy can employ against ... demagogues, dictators, and tyrants." As he went on to explain, "Our thinking can properly be called independent when it is not divorced from facts knowable by experience nor from logic, but is independent of deceptive arrangement of facts and of an incorrect interpretation of facts."[127]

Professor of Education William Bagley (1874–1946) wrote during the early twentieth century that the transmission of Western values would provide for an intelligent electorate who would not fall prey to "the want, fear, fraud, superstition, and error which may felter the ignorant as cruelly as the chains of the slave-driver."[128] By expanding their thinking beyond the limits of their current time and place, students gain access to the "highest standards of accurate and fertile thinking, through direct or indirect contacts with the best minds of humanity, and

---

[127] Michael Demiashkevich, "Independent Thinking and Mental Discipline," *Peabody Journal of Education* 12, no. 3 (1934): 135.

[128] William C. Bagley, "An Essentialist's Platform for the Advancement of American Education," *Educational Administration and Supervision* (1938): 241–256, 251.

in that way to put them on solid ground for the critical judgment of their own thinking and that of others."[129]

At the turn of the twentieth century, American education reflected the traditional model. In 1892, the Committee of Ten —a commission created by the National Education Association (NEA)—affirmed the importance of teaching an academic curriculum to all students. The two chairmen of the committee, U.S. Education Commissioner William Torrey Harris and Harvard University President Charles W. Eliot, recommended that all students follow a traditional academic curriculum.[130] Educational equality meant offering the same high-level academic content to all Americans, despite their social circumstances or someone else's opinions about their likely future occupations.

One of the academic tragedies of our times is that, driven by the federal government and progressive interest groups, states have rejected the traditional view of education in favor of a lower-trajectory workforce education model. Ironically, this reversal is often advanced under the guise of "meeting the needs of a modern economy," when it's nothing more than the reinstatement of nineteenth-century European class structures Americans have always rejected. Consequently, many people now view traditional education as something reserved for a small segment of the population, often as a privilege reserved for the children of the rich. That view conflicts with the history of academic achievement arising from traditional education, and it feeds into the progressive goal of a society managed by "experts."

[129] Michael Demiashkevich, *An Introduction to the Philosophy of Education* (New York: American Book Company, 1935), 357.
[130] Ravitch, *Left Back*, 42.

Progressive Education

Supporters of progressive education have employed semantics to link their methods and techniques to "progress" in the field of education. The public has thus been led to believe that progressive teaching methods, such as "learning by doing," are more effective than the "outdated" traditional methods they replaced. Moreover, anyone who questions this claim is quickly dismissed as "opposed to progress and thus a hopeless reactionary."[131] But if progressive education connotes progress, then it raises the question: What is it progressing toward?

While traditional education seeks to transmit Western civilization, progressive education has an openly contrary aim. As explained in the introduction, the goals of the progressive movement are to move away from the principles of the American founding, in rejection of the concepts of natural rights and limited government. Progressive education provides the means to this end: the creation of a new social order underlying politics. In other words, the aim of early progressive educators wasn't to educate students to thrive under the political system as established by the Framers; their aim was to modify that system, in effect to create a *new* order through the schools that would serve the administrative state.[132]

The Father of the Progressive Political Order

In the early twentieth century, progressive educators viewed traditional education with scorn. They believed that a more modern education system was needed to meet the changing demands

---

[131] Augustin G. Rudd, *Bending the Twig: The Revolution in Education and Its Effect on Our Children* (Chicago: Heritage Foundation, 1957), 18.

[132] Ibid.

that technology and industry placed on society. They viewed a traditional education as too "bookish" and "rigid." Subjects such as literature, Latin, and even algebra represented the "dead" past of "aristocratic" Europe. Traditional education, they argued, undermined democracy because it advanced the priorities and well-being of those in power and discounted others by teaching Western traditions and values. Progressives rejected the permanence of Western ideas, particularly the nature of individual rights and their primacy over the state.

During the early twentieth century, these ideas found their way into academia through the work of, among others, Columbia University Teachers College professor John Dewey. Widely recognized as the "father of modern education," Dewey fervently embraced the general progressive political philosophy and sought—quite successfully—to revamp public education to achieve its implementation.

The complete philosophy of John Dewey, published in several books and hundreds of essays, constitutes a rambling, sometimes contradictory, body of literature. Even Dewey admitted that his philosophies were "unstable, chameleon-like, yielding one after another to many diverse and often incompatible influences."[133] Perhaps his belief that nothing is absolute and the truth is continually reestablished through man's evolving experiences lent itself to such confusion. But some of Dewey's views remained consistent throughout his lifetime:

1. God does not exist. All that exists is "domesticated" within nature; there is no supernatural force, no consciousness of mind

---

[133] John Dewey, *From Absolutism to Experimentalism*, in *John Dewey: The Later Works*, 5:155.

outside man's experience on Earth.[134] Thus, the only Creator is mankind itself, and he will achieve salvation through a continuous process of experimentation to perfect the social institutions and functions that govern it:

> [Faith is] the power of [mankind's] intelligence to imagine a future [on Earth] which is the projection of the desirable in the present, and to invent the instrumentalities [social policies and human experiences] of its realization, [which] is our salvation.[135]

2. Man does not possess inherent rights outside of government. Instead, government should "be an instrument for securing and extending the liberties of individuals."[136]

3. Nothing is absolute; truth is relative to the social and economic conditions of the time. If society is to be reconstructed into a collective social order, any notions of absolutes must be "eliminated," including natural rights and natural laws.[137]

4. Capitalism is unacceptable. Production and consumption should be controlled by a powerful central state. According to Dewey, "The principle of private labor for private gain ... has taken on a malign form when linked up with the tremendous

---

[134] Geoffrey O'Connell, *Naturalism in American Education* (New York: Benziger Brothers, 1938), 114.

[135] John Dewey, "The Need for a Recovery of Philosophy," in *Creative Intelligence: Essays in the Pragmatic Attitude*, ed. John Dewey, (New York: Holt, 1917), 69.

[136] John Dewey, "Liberalism and Social Action," in *John Dewey: The Later Works*, 11:8.

[137] Dewey, "The Future of Liberalism," 290–291.

expansion and centralization of power effected by a technological society."[138] Moreover, "society, in order to solve its own problems and remedy its own ills, needs to employ science and technology for social instead of merely private ends."[139]

5. People must be "educated to the recognition of the importance of finding experts and of entrusting administration to them." The constitutional structure ("political beliefs and machinery from a period when science and technology were so immature as not to permit a definite technique for handling social situations and meeting specific social needs") would have to give way to "experts guided by specialized inquiry":

> The questions of most concern at present may be said to be matters like sanitation, public health, healthful and adequate housing, transportation, planning of cities, regulation and distribution of immigrants, selection and management of personnel, right methods of instruction and preparation of competent teachers, scientific adjustment of taxation, efficient management of funds, and so on. These are technical matters, as much so as the construction of an efficient engine for purposes of traction or locomotion. Like it they are to be settled by inquiry into facts; and as the inquiry can be carried on only by those especially equipped, so the results of inquiry can be carried on only by those especially equipped, so the results of the inquiry can be utilized only by trained technicians. What has counting heads, decision by majority and the

[138] John Dewey, "The Social-Economic Situation and Education," in *John Dewey: The Later Works*, 8:65–66.
[139] Ibid., at 69.

whole apparatus of traditional government to do with such things? Given such considerations, and the public and its organization for political ends is not only a ghost, but a ghost which walks and talks, and obscures, confuses and misleads governmental action in a disastrous way.[140]

By the mid-twentieth century, Dewey's philosophy about "right methods of instruction" determined by progressive "experts" had achieved prominence in public education. In a 1940 *Wall Street Journal* column, journalist Thomas F. Woodlock summarized the progressive philosophy held by professors of education at Columbia,[141] which, of course, mirrored that of Dewey.

---

[140] Dewey and Rogers, *The Public and Its Problems*, 124–125.

[141] Thomas Woodlock summarized the philosophy of educators at Teachers College as follows: "(1) We live in a universe without final ends, forms or assignable limits, either internally or externally, of which continuous evolutionary change is all that can be predicted. (2) Man is as much a product of this process as are all other visible things, and is strictly continuous with nature. There is nothing transcendent to the visible universe and man's home is within it. His thinking is a pure product of experience and cannot transcend it. There is no such thing as metaphysics, which is merely a collection of empty dreams and idle fancies. Man has no soul, mind or reason as metaphysicians understand these words. Ideas are merely plans of operations to be performed, not statements of what is or has been. They are merely hypotheses. Experience evolves new standards and values. All human affairs whether personal or associative are merely projections, continuations, complications of the nature which exists in the physical and pre-human world. (3) God as a Being does not exist; He is merely that unification of ideal Values that is essentially imaginative in origin when the imagination supervenes in conduct. There is no such thing as religion in any sense of relation to God. Faith in the sense in which the Western civilization understood it

Woodlock cited the progressives' rejection of God, religion, and, in fact, any fixed standards or values, as well as their utilitarianism, in cautioning that students "educated" in this philosophy would inevitably reject the values underlying the Declaration and the Constitution. But his warning fell flat with progressives, who dismissed the founding principles as relics from a different time and strove to recreate society around a different set of values.[142]

Progressive Educational Methods: From Theory into Practice

Today, the public largely understands the progressive march against federalism through the schools in terms of federal control over policies, procedures, or funding formulas used in school systems. But removing these regulations will do little to remove progressive education content and methods from the classroom. A century after the progressive movement in America began, these methods are ingrained in the education system and will continue to instill collective or "progressive" assumptions and beliefs in the mentalities of students until they are recognized for what they are and reversed.

These education methods demonstrate the elitist, condescending nature of progressive thought. Underlying them is the

---

is impossible for the 'cultivated mind' of the Western world today. (4) There is no enduring moral law of fixed principles. Morals are purely social. The question of 'ought' is merely one of better or worse in social affairs. The only moral end is an abundant life shared by all, achieved by growth itself. There are no absolute moral standards; the moral and the social quality of conduct are identical. There is nothing absolutely and unchangingly good."

[142] Thomas F. Woodlock, "Thinking It Over," *Wall Street Journal*, December 27, 1940, 4.

supposition that, if theories of evolution show a link between man and lower animals in the physical sense, then a similar connection exists with the mind. If man's mind is nothing more than an advanced animal mind, it can be trained using the same behavioral techniques.

Edward Thorndike, a professor at Teachers College whose career spanned forty years, instructed generations of educators on many of the classroom techniques he developed to "train" students. Thorndike refined the stimulus-response techniques developed by Wilhelm Wundt of Germany (1832–1920)[143] and that linked psychology with the field of education. The marriage of education to psychology led to the development of the progressive theory of "learning by conditioning." Lawrence Cremin, former president of Teachers College (1974–1984), summarized Thorndike's theory in his book *The Transformation of the School*:

> What was the nature of the experiments? Basically, they involved an animal in a problem box, a situation in which a specific behavior, like pressing down a lever, was rewarded with escape from the box and a bit of food. The animal was placed in the box, and after a period of random activity, it pressed the lever and received the reward.

Thorndike called the process by which the animals tended to repeat rewarded behaviors ever more efficiently and economically "learning," and out of his experiment came a new

[143] William Wundt was a German philosopher, physician, physiologist, philosopher, and professor, known today as one of the founding figures of modern psychology. His pioneering work in experimental psychology inspired many of the educators discussed in this paper to employ the science of psychology in educational practices.

theory of learning and a new "law" founded on that theory. The theory maintained that learning involves the wedding of a specific response to a specific stimulus through a physiological bond in the neural system, so that the stimulus (S) regularly calls forth the response (R). In Thorndike's words, the *bond* between S and R is "stamped in" by being continually rewarded. And from this follows what Thorndike called the "law of effect"—namely, that a satisfactory outcome of any response tends to "stamp in" its connection with a given situation, and conversely, that an unsatisfactory outcome tends to stamp out the bond or connection.[144]

These methods, however, are effective only in teaching students to exhibit certain behaviors, not to teach them academic content. Obviously, it would be futile to try to teach complex subjects such as algebra or geometry using the stimulus-response technique. It can't be done; one must *learn* the material.

But progressives were less concerned about academic content than about adapting the psychological-conditioning aspects of the stimulus-and-response theory to teaching methods. Dewey and others believed such methods could "stamp in" the correct attitudes, habits, and beliefs that students should possess in a future, collectivist society. These pedagogical methods, such as the "child-centered" curriculum (the child, not the teacher, selects activities) or "experiential" learning (learning by doing), are the instruments to "train" students to this new mind-set.

In *Impressions of Soviet Russia*, Dewey recounted a conversation he had with a Soviet educator who explained that the outside

---

[144] Lawrence A. Cremin, *The Transformation of the School: Progressivism in American Education, 1876–1957* (New York: Alfred A. Knopf, 1961), 111.

influences of the family, the church, and parochial interests often reversed the good work done by the schools in instilling the preferred dispositions and mental habits. Dewey sympathized with him, as any "thorough-going" collectivist would, and agreed that the traditional family can be "hostile to a truly communal life."[145] His praise of the Soviet techniques used to "undermine" the "importance and uniqueness of family life" in a child's education is disturbing:

> It is obvious to any observer that in every western country the increase of importance of public schools has been at least coincident with a relaxation of older family ties. What is going on in Russia appears to be a planned acceleration of this process. For example, the earliest section of the school system, dealing with children from three to seven, aims, in the cities, to keep children under its charge six, eight and ten hours per day, and in ultimate ideal (although far from present fact) this procedure is to be universal and compulsory. When it is carried out, the effect on family life is too evident to need to be dwelt upon.[146]

In 2015, President Barack Obama's secretary of education, Arne Duncan, advocated for such a system, stating that schools shouldn't be just a place for learning but rather "community centers ... open 12, 13, 14 hours a day with a wide variety of afterschool programming." He continued that because youth violence is a "public health crisis in the United States," the idea of "public

---

[145] John Dewey, *Impressions of Soviet Russia*, in *John Dewey: The Later Works*, 3:227–230.
[146] Ibid., 230–231.

boarding schools" was being considered. He concluded there are "just certain kids we [the government] should have 24/7."[147]

Soviet educators used on their students a psychological technique known as social behaviorism, a technique Dewey considered to have great pedagogical value. Briefly stated, bureaucrats charged teachers with uncovering any conditions in the home that might undermine the preferred collectivist mind-set; the teachers then had to modify the student's educational plan to offset the effect. For example, if the conditions of a student's family life were found to be religious, the teacher would stamp out the individualistic tendencies inherent in religious worship by pairing the student with a devout atheist during school activities. In this way, the group would condition the student to reject his family belief system. Dewey applauded this mental manipulation of students and declared that Soviet schools were more democratically organized than our professedly democratic schools in America.[148]

Of course, by "democratic" Dewey was referring to the progressive definition, which had to do with the economic opportunities provided through a managed economy. Dewey thought there was much for the United States to learn from the Soviet model of education if, as he wished, American society were to be transformed into a new social order.

How Progressive Education Conditions Students to Accept Rule by Experts

In *Education and Experience*, Dewey defined education as "a social process," whose quality is measured by "the degree in which

---

[147] "Youth Violence Prevention Summit, Federal Officials," May 12, 2015, video, 47:18, C-SPAN, https://www.c-span.org/.

[148] Dewey, *Impressions of Soviet Russia*, 228–229, 240–241.

individuals form a community group."[149] All learning must be accomplished through experience. It must be "active" through engagement in projects and other activities, not "passive" through reading books or listening to teachers' lectures. He advocated a pedagogy (a method by which content should be taught) in which teachers "arrange conditions that are conducive to community activity and to organization which exercises control over individual impulses by the mere fact that all are engaged in communal projects."[150] Dewey theorized that by continually subjecting students to group work, observing the rules of everyday living in communal life would become habit and man would eventually become less competitive over resources.

Dewey's theories are central to modern education's call for group work, collaboration, group consensus, and problem-based learning. Those techniques gained ground and are now common in the classroom and the instruction in the schools of education, even though early-twentieth-century progressive educators admitted in the National Education Association's *Cardinal Principles* (discussed later) that they are designed not to educate, but rather as a "device" for "collective thinking":

> Among the means for developing attitudes and habits important in a democracy [new social order] are the assignment of projects and problems to groups of pupils for cooperative solution and the socialized recitation whereby the class as a whole develops a sense of collective

---

[149] John Dewey, *Experience and Education* (New York: Simon and Schuster, 1938), 58.
[150] Ibid.

responsibility. Both of these devices give training in collective thinking.[151]

In the article "Groupthink," mentioned in chapter 2, William Whyte observes how constant group activities had made the youth of the 1950s more inclined than previous generations to establish collectively their personal beliefs and values:

> While youngsters are not inclined to philosophize, their attitude toward life adds up to a fairly discernible set of values. It could be described as a "practical" relativism. The old absolute moral values are disappearing. There is still black and white, to be sure, but it is no longer determined by fixed precepts; it is determined rather by what the group thinks is black and white—and if someone does things the way his group does, well, who is to censure him for his loyalty?[152]

In sum, the goal of Dewey and his disciples was to replace the philosophies of Western civilization—those found in traditional education—with progressive philosophy. They would de-emphasize content and classical academic subjects in favor of activities that centered on the individual's daily interactions with the community and that conditioned his mind to accept collectivism. To that end, Dewey dismissed the "absorbing of facts and truths," which is central in a traditional education, as "so exclusively individual an affair that it tends very naturally to

---

[151] Commission on the Reorganization of Secondary Education, National Education Association, *Cardinal Principles of Secondary Education* (Washington, D.C.: National Education Association, 1918), 14.
[152] Whyte, "Groupthink."

pass into selfishness."[153] If education were to lead the next generation to socialism, it would have to be much less intellectual and much more social.

"Daring the Schools [to] Build a New Social Order"

For the first half of the twentieth century, progressive education steadily gained ground. The leading progressive educators at the turn of the century believed that, in the new industrialized era, democracy could be preserved only through the collective sharing of the nation's resources, and that this would bring economic security for every individual; without that, freedom would be impossible. These progressives took it upon themselves to use schools to redefine democracy and freedom.

Some historians view progressive education reformers as falling into different camps, most notably "pedagogical" and "administrative" progressives. Pedagogical progressives are associated with the educational methods of John Dewey (such as "learning through experience," and "inquiry-based learning") and believed in the child-centered approach, where the curriculum was differentiated based on the student's interests. Administrative progressives (sometimes referred to as "social-efficiency" progressives) also believed that children should receive a differentiated education, but for different reasons. They advocated sorting students according to their ability and class into various educational tracks which were, in turn, designed to meet the projected needs of the workforce and society.[154] There is debate as to the extent to which

[153] *John Dewey: The School and Society and The Child and the Curriculum* (Chicago: University of Chicago, 1990), 15.

[154] David F. Labaree, "Progressivism, Schools and Schools of Education: An American Romance," *Paedagogica Historica* 41, nos. 1, 2 (February 2005): 277.

each camp achieved its reforms, but parents familiar with their children's schoolwork are sure to notice the influence of both.

While there are other distinguishing features among the various progressive school-reform efforts of this time, they all shared certain characteristics: (1) a discrediting of the notion that all children should have a traditional (liberal) education; (2) the belief that the authority of parents, teachers, and school leaders was secondary to that of experts in the new schools of education; and (3) the experts' claim that a democratic education was only possible through a differentiated curriculum.[155] Under this idea of a democratic education, only a small segment of students would continue to get an academic education and the rest would be sorted into programs for training according to their future position in the workforce or the home.[156]

Schools of education and pedagogical departments of American universities were the cradle of progressive educational theory. These early school reformers set about to undermine the assumptions of a traditional education, particularly the importance of teaching academic subjects, and to encourage schools to replace traditional subjects with practical studies.[157] Schools of education provided a platform to spread these new curricular objectives by inculcating them in teachers in training.

George S. Counts was a leader in advancing this ideology. Following appointments at several prominent schools of education, such as the University of Washington, Yale, and the University of Chicago, he served as professor of education at Teachers College from 1927 through 1941.

[155] Ravitch, *Left Back*, 88.
[156] Ibid, 89.
[157] Ibid.

Reshaping the American Mind

In his 1932 address to the Progressive Educational Association, entitled *Dare the School Build a New Social Order?*, Counts declared, "The times are literally crying for a new vision of American destiny." He challenged the teaching profession to "eagerly grasp the opportunity which the fates had placed in their hands," and use their positions to become social reformers for progressive causes.[158] He argued that American traditions must evolve in order to survive the greed of capitalism and that the new American mind-set must "assume an essentially collectivistic pattern" in which all the country's resources "must be dedicated to promotion of the welfare of the great masses of the people."[159]

> Freedom without a secure economic foundation is only a word: in our society it may be freedom to beg, steal, or starve. The right to vote, if it cannot be made to insure the right to work, is but an empty bauble. Indeed, it may be less than a bauble: it may serve to drug and dull the senses of the masses.... If all of us could be assured of material security and abundance, we would be released from economic worries and our energies liberated to grapple with the central problems of cultural advance.[160]

Among these outdated traditions, Counts included "the democracy of the past." He insisted that "democracy should not be identified with political forms and functions—with the federal constitution, the popular election of officials, or the practice of

[158] George S. Counts, *Dare the School Build a New Social Order?* (New York: John Day, 1932), 54.
[159] Ibid., 43–46.
[160] Ibid., 50.

79

universal suffrage." In its place, he advocated for a new democracy, suitable for an industrialized era, that "has little to do with our political institutions: it is a sentiment with respect to the moral equality of men."[161]

Although at first blush this idea might seem compassionate and perhaps even reasonable, it rejects out of hand the sovereignty and political power of the individual. "We, the experts," it holds, "will determine what must be done. We must not be encumbered by notions of 'rights' and the constitutional structure, and you the people will benefit because we will make decisions for you." Those sentiments included a call to divert the mission of schools away from teaching academic content—an extremist vision that citizens would have rejected were the question put to them.

In the view of Counts and his cohorts, schools should serve as a tool for solving the problems of society caused by unrestrained capitalism and unregulated industrialization. A traditional education stood in the way of this goal, because it was "serving the cause of perpetuating ideas and institutions suited to an age that is gone."[162] Instead, teachers should organize the curriculum around social problems in order to reshape public opinion in support of progressive solutions. Counts continued to rise in prominence and would serve as president of the American Federation of Teachers from 1939 to 1942.

Ellwood P. Cubberley, an early-twentieth-century progressive, also advanced the transformation of schools into progressive change agents. Cubberley received his Ph.D. from Teachers College and at various points during his career served as president

---

[161] Ibid., 40–41.
[162] Ibid., 5.

of Vincennes University, superintendent of schools in San Diego, and from 1917 through 1933 dean of the Stanford University School of Education. He was a pioneer in developing school administration as a specialized profession, an effort that was firmly grounded in the belief in the expert. While giving a nod to democracy, he "argued that power ought to rest firmly in the hands of a knowledgeable elite."[163] Cubberley, for example, advocated for the election of school-board members citywide rather than by ward in order to "eliminate the 'inevitable representation' from the poorer wards."[164] Betraying his lack of faith in the citizenry to make educational decisions for themselves, Cubberley declared, "'Each year, the child is coming to belong more and more to the state and less and less to the parent,'" a statement that reflects his support for the school to sort students into various vocations according to the needs of the state.[165] The political institutions through which the people controlled government needed to be weakened, all the better to give the expert free rein to influence and direct the citizenry.

The Influence of Communism on Progressive Educators

American educators weren't the only ones to embrace progressive education. Dictator Joseph Stalin, impressed with the opportunity to bend the attitudes of students toward collectivism, adopted this philosophy as a blueprint for Soviet schools. Eager to observe the implementation of progressive education on a large scale,

---

[163] Robert Welker, *The Teacher as Expert: A Theoretical and Historical Examination* (Albany: State University of New York Press, 1992), 22.
[164] Ibid., 20.
[165] Ibid., 23.

many of the Teachers College faculty visited the Soviet Union in the early years of Stalin's dictatorship. Although (or perhaps because) Stalin limited their visits to a few schools of his choosing, these professors returned with glowing accounts of the schools' success. Their pilgrimages left them not only heartened by the collectivist transformation of Russian society, but certain that a similar revolution in America was right around the corner.[166] As one professor of education observed, "Many of them returned challenging everything American, breathing fire and defiance to property, the profit system, and the Constitution, and beating the tom-tom for a new social order."[167]

In *Impressions of Soviet Russia*, Dewey wrote of the wonder he experienced during his 1928 visit. Despite the well-known gross abuses and political oppression suffered by the Soviet people at the hands of Stalin, Dewey wrote that the revolution had been a blessing for them:

> I can hardly do better than record the impression, as overwhelming as it was unexpected, that the outstanding fact in Russia is a revolution, involving the release of human powers on such an unprecedented scale that it is of incalculable significance not only for that country, but for the world.[168]

For Dewey, the realization of a collectivist society was like watching a dream come true. To see his educational methods, his

---

[166] Augustus G. Rudd, "Education for the New Social Order" (address delivered before the National Society of New England Women, New York, February 26, 1948), in *Vital Speeches of the Day* 14, no. 23 (September 15, 1948): 1–2.

[167] Ibid.

[168] Dewey, *Impressions of Soviet Russia*, 207.

life's work, being fully employed in the transformation of Russian society had to resemble Dr. Frankenstein's watching his monster come to life. Dewey's writing on the subject was almost maniacal as he noted the "omnipresence" of propaganda in Soviet schools and praised the genius of Soviet educators in what can be described only as the brainwashing of their students:

> In Russia the propaganda is in behalf of a burning public faith. One may believe that the leaders are wholly mistaken in the object of their faith, but their sincerity is beyond question. To them the end for which propaganda is employed is not a private or even a class gain, but is the universal good of universal humanity. In consequence, propaganda is education and education is propaganda.[169]

Dewey argued that it would take more than establishing collectivist economic and political *institutions* for communism to succeed; the *mind-set* of the Russian people would also have to become less individualistic and more cooperative. He praised the "direct and concentrated effort" of the schools to stamp out the "individualistic psychology" still "ingrained" in most pupils and to "create habits so that persons will act cooperatively and collectively." He wrote with a sense of pride that the Soviet schools had become the "ideological arm of the Revolution."[170] The experiences of the Soviet Union reinforced the progressive belief that the American mind-set would have to be transformed to further the development of a cooperative, collectivist society.

[169] Ibid., 222.
[170] Ibid., 221–224.

How Progressives Took Control of the American Education System

As we have seen, John Dewey—the man credited as the most influential person in the history of American education—was for all practical purposes an atheist and a fervent socialist. It might seem unremarkable that atheism and socialism would be tolerated today, but how did that come about in the early twentieth century, when the general American population was strongly opposed to those ideas? During the 1932 election, only 2.3 percent of voters selected a socialist candidate (there were two: Norman Thomas and Verne Reynolds).[171] Gallup polling shows that even until 1958, 82 percent of Americans claimed they would never vote for an atheist—even if he were otherwise the perfect candidate.[172] So how did a group of progressive educators advancing anti-American ideas engineer such radical changes in American schools?

The following examination of how Dewey and his Columbia colleagues quietly undermined the American form of government is not, unfortunately, merely a history lesson. The same structures and networks are still in play. Recognition of these dynamics, how they work, and their intended purpose is the first step in restoring the authority of states and localities over education, and ultimately in restoring a fully functioning constitutional structure.

To grasp the influence of this small group of early progressive theorists on today's education system, one must recognize that,

---

[171] See "United States Presidential Election, 1932," *Wikipedia*, last updated August 14, 2017, https://en.wikipedia.org/.

[172] See "The Presidency," Gallup, http://www.gallup.com/poll/4729/presidency.aspx.

at the time of their ascendency to prominence, there was no national policy on education. Yet, without invitation or even a perceived need for it, progressive educators took it upon themselves to create a narrative to instruct the localities as to the best practices and methods for student learning. Without another education powerhouse to advance a competing view, progressives were free to establish a national narrative, one that continues today, based on progressive assumptions and methods of education. By establishing schools of education (Teachers College was the first, established in 1898) and utililizing national professional associations (the National Educational Association [NEA], established in 1857, and the American Federation of Teachers [AFT], established in 1916), progressives were able to embed their ideas into educational practice and block competing views.

In *Managers of Virtue*, Professor David Tyack explains how this small clique of radical theorists from Teachers College worked to place their followers, many of them former students, into positions from which they could propagate progressive theories:

> [The network was] an informal association of individuals who occupied influential positions (usually in university education departments or schools, as policy analysts or researchers in foundations, and as key superintendents), who shared common purposes (to solve social and economic problems by educational means through "scientific" diagnosis and prescription), who had common interests in furthering their own careers, and who had come to know one another mostly through face-to-face interactions and through their similar writing and research. They controlled important resources: money, the creation of

reputations, the placement of students and friends, the training of subordinates and future leaders, and influence over professional associations and public legislative and administrative bodies.[173]

Because progressive educators initially established schools of education within the university system (Dewey at Columbia, Counts at Columbia and the University of Chicago, Cubberley at Stanford), they continued to enjoy unchallenged control over these schools' design and development. The significance of this is hard to overestimate, and it explains how they were so successful in establishing progressive education as the unwavering paradigm of educational thought in America.

David Labaree, a professor of education at Stanford, attests to the fact that progressive education remains the status quo in schools of education:

> Within the community of professional educators — by which I mean classroom teachers and the education professors who train them — pedagogical progressivism provides the words we use to talk about teaching and learning in schools. And within education schools, progressivism is the ruling ideology. It is hard to find anyone in an American education school who does not talk the talk and espouse the principles of the progressive creed.[174]

---

[173] David Tyack and Elisabeth Hansot, *Managers of Virtue: Public School Leadership in America, 1820–1980* (New York: Basic Books, 1982), 130.

[174] Labaree, "Progressivism, Schools and Schools of Education," 277.

Despite the failures of progressive education, its stranglehold over schools of education and the educational establishment as a whole prevents the embrace of traditional methods. This is the reason educational progress never seems to materialize; the "scholars" continually return to the structure of progressive educational theory and tinker around the edges instead of teaching proven, more effective practices.

Progressivism, the NEA, and
Early Intrusion by the Federal Bureaucracy

As the country moved into the twentieth century, progressives were gaining influence in education policy-making. In contrast, the influence of traditionalists—such as those who had drafted the Committee of Ten report in 1892—began to wane. Not surprisingly, the NEA formed a new committee—one stacked with progressives—to draft guidance on the organization and development of secondary education. In 1918, the Bureau of Education at the U.S. Department of the Interior published the NEA's recommendations in a bulletin titled *Cardinal Principles of Secondary Education: A Report of the Commission on the Reorganization of Secondary Education, Appointed by the National Education Association.*

The committee designed a blueprint that would destroy the foundation of the constitutional structure: schools would no longer prepare students for active citizenship under the existing American order but would instead prepare them for a new order of a collectivist, expert-managed society. In so doing, the committee advanced a key goal of progressivism: of changing—actually undermining—the American political system.

As we shall see, despite initial opposition from citizens and teachers, *Cardinal Principles* became a staple in the instruction of future teachers at schools of education. Because these schools were created and staffed by progressives, few faculty members within this small group disagreed with the premises and claims of *Cardinal Principles*. Eventually, many of the report's recommendations became standard practice in schools. This has negatively influenced education in two important ways.

First, *Cardinal Principles* rejected the Committee of Ten's affirmation that the aim of education was to develop the intellect of individuals to the fullest. Instead, the schools were to "distribute men and women to those tasks in life where their abilities will count most and their defects least,"[175] similar to the Marxist saying: "From each according to his ability, to each according to his need." Each student's educational path would be "differentiated" based on the school's opinion of his academic ability and likely future employment. The new aim of education was to teach students the practical skills they would use in their everyday living and future jobs. Instead of developing intellect, schools were to help students discover interests and abilities that, in the judgment of the school, would best serve society.

Changes to the education system were unavoidable, the report argued, because increased immigration, urbanization, and a complex economy had changed the "character" of the school population. There was now a large number of pupils with "varying capabilities, aptitudes, social heredity, and destinies in life" who were considered incapable of learning the same academic subjects as earlier generations of Americans. They instead needed

---

[175] Bureau of Education, Department of the Interior, *Report of the Committee of the National Council of Education on Economy of Time in Education* (Washington, D.C.: Government Printing Office, 1913), 34.

an alternative education that would help them find their place in society.[176] The radical nature of this idea is frequently overlooked. It rejected providing a liberal education to help every student fulfill his potential. Instead, it sought to replace that with the paternalistic idea that schools would guide students to their place in society.

Embracing this philosophy, Woodrow Wilson—who before his political career was a professor of political science and president of Princeton University—advocated for an education system differentiated between liberal education for the elites and workforce training for the masses. According to Wilson, "We want one class of persons to have a liberal education, and we want another class of persons, a very much larger class ... to forgo the privileges of a liberal education and fit themselves to perform specific difficult manual tasks."[177]

Wilson's views were becoming a reality. The rising professors of education contended that it was democratic (*i.e.*, all students would have an opportunity, just not the same opportunity) to parse out an academic education to an elite group while relegating the rest to the lower trajectory of workforce training.

In contrast, William Bagley and Charles Judd argued that a school that "gives to one class of children one set of ideas and ideals and to another class an entirely different set of ideas and ideals will make for social distinctions that are dangerous in a democracy."[178] While progressives were creating different edu-

---

[176] Bureau of Education, *Cardinal Principles*, 8.

[177] Woodrow Wilson, "The Meaning of a Liberal Education" (address to the New York City High School Teachers Association, New York, January 9, 1909).

[178] W. C. Bagley and Charles H. Judd, "Enlarging the American Elementary School," *School Review* 26, no. 5 (1918): 313–323. See Ravitch, *Left Back*, 93.

cational paths based on bureaucratic projections of the child's future, students were enrolling in academic courses in record numbers.[179] Parents frequently resisted the experts' views;[180] they wanted their children to have what Woodrow Wilson had described as "the privileges of a liberal education." Like the parents of the elite, they wanted their children to know civilization's great thinkers, writers, scientists, and heroes, not be engaged in mere job-training that leaves one to the mercy of others. They were Americans, like the colonists before them, and they rejected an arbitrary authority's denying their right to shape their own lives.

Nonetheless, the progressives forged ahead. They believed sorting the masses of students according to an expert's view of their ability and station in life was not only socially efficient but the kinder course of action. Earl Russell of Teachers College scoffed that schools must not "rouse the ambitions and aspirations in the oncoming generations" if their future place in society cannot fulfill them. Russell also wrote (more ominously) that the progressive model would act as a means of social control, at least for "the masses" who, if educated in the same manner as future leaders, would cause social instability.[181]

The second negative influence of *Cardinal Principles* was its embrace of the new "science" of education, or pedagogical methods, espoused by the new schools of education. These theories held that pedagogy, or how students are taught, is more important than content, or what they are taught. David Klein writes that the struggle between content and pedagogy was, and continues

---

[179] Ravitch, *Left Back*, 81.

[180] Ibid., 163.

[181] James E. Russell, "The Trend in American Education," *Educational Review* 32 (June 1906): 39.

to be, at the heart of the battles between progressive and traditional education:

> At first glance, such a dichotomy seems unthinkable. There should no more be conflict between content and pedagogy than between one's right foot and left foot. They should work in tandem toward the same end, and avoid tripping each other. Content is the answer to the question of what to teach, while pedagogy answers the question of how to teach.
>
> The trouble comes with the first step. Do we lead with the right foot or the left? If content decisions come first, then the choices of pedagogy may be limited. A choice of concentrated content precludes too much student centered, discovery learning, because that particular pedagogy requires more time than stiff content requirements would allow. In the same way, the choice of a pedagogy can naturally limit the amount of content that can be presented to students. Therein lies the source of the conflict.[182]

A traditional education crowds out the pedagogical techniques for creating a collectivist mentality. Complex subjects, such as algebra and geometry, have to be substantially dumbed down for use with progressive methods, such as group discussions or hands-on activities. Thus, *Cardinal Principles* discouraged a curriculum built on academic subjects, or knowledge, and advised a curriculum centered on the "activities" of an individual's life, or "skills." Health, command of fundamental processes (math

---

[182] David Klein, "A Brief History of American K–12 Mathematics Education in the 20th Century," in *Mathematical Cognition*, ed. James Royer, (2003): 177–178.

and English), worthy home-membership, vocation, citizenship/ civic education (including "training in collective thinking" and group projects), worthy use of leisure, and ethical character (as defined by progressives) were included in students' education on par with traditional academic subjects.[183] This curriculum rested on the utilitarian idea that children should be taught only what they will need to know as determined, of course, by experts' forecast as to their future place in society.[184] In furtherance of that idea, *Cardinal Principles* followed the progressive formulation of democracy as a collectivist enterprise:

> The purpose of democracy is so to organize society that each member may develop his personality primarily through activities designed for the well-being of his fellow members and of society as a whole.[185]

The federal government's publishing of *Cardinal Principles* is an early example of its intrusion into state policy-making. As the century marched on, the broader federal bureaucracy—often unmoored from its authority—would hone its skill at shaping public opinion and state policy through commissions and reports.

Progressives Take Over the Content of Science Instruction

The restructuring of education away from a sequential study of facts to a curriculum organized around societal issues was, and still

---

[183] Commission on the Reorganization of Secondary Education, National Education Association, *Cardinal Principles of Secondary Education* (Washington, D.C.: National Education Association, 1918) 14. Ravitch, *Left Back*, 124.

[184] Ravitch, *Left Back*, 124.

[185] *Cardinal Principles*, 9. See Ravitch, *Left Back*, 124.

is, advanced under the guise that the latter better "engages" students. The theory behind *Cardinal Principles* held that if students were interested in what they were learning, they would become better learners. But one consequence of this theory is that American students receive inadequate instruction in the fundamentals.

More than sixty years after *Cardinal Principles* was released, Robert Kromhout and Ron Good observed that content experts continue to express grave concerns with centering science curricula on social issues. They quote their colleague Dr. Paul Ragland, chairman of the Geology Department at Florida State University, on this point:

> It seems to me that the most compelling arguments against societal issues being the organizing force for K–12 science textbooks are (1) despite lip-service and loud proclamations to the contrary, the basics simply do not get taught under such a system, and (2) a body of scientific knowledge must be taught in an orderly and systematic manner, building upon previously learned information as one proceeds, and societal issues normally do not provide that logical, orderly framework....
>
> It is certainly true that the average junior high school student, for example, can be more easily motivated toward science if societal issues are emphasized. To make them the organizing force, however, would be disastrous.[186]

That depends, of course, on one's definition of "disastrous." To progressives, restructuring the curriculum around social problems

---

[186] R. Kromhout and R. Good, "Beware of Societal Issues as Organizers for Science Education Reform," *School Science and Mathematics* 83, no. 8 (1983): 649–650.

encourages students to accept the new "democratic" way of solving them. The smokescreen of "engaging" students allows this agenda to advance.

But despite the disapproval of real scientists such as Dr. Ragland, school curriculum continues to be structured around the same topics to inculcate progressive social attitudes. In fact, the situation has become worse. Today, social issues and "activities" serve as the backbone of the Next Generation Science Standards (NGSS), written in 2011 under the direction of Achieve, Inc. (the same organization that wrote the controversial Common Core national standards for English language arts and mathematics). The process that resulted in the NGSS will be described in chapter 6. The discussion here focuses on the progressive bias of the standards.

The Thomas B. Fordham Institute, though an outspoken fan of the Common Core standards, couldn't bring itself to endorse the NGSS. The Fordham Institute gave the NGSS a grade of C and rated the standards "inferior" to those of twenty-two states. Among other things, a lack of basic science content and failure to prepare students for college or careers in STEM fields were cited as major deficiencies.

In an extensive critique, the Fordham Institute noted the NGSS's "animus toward content coupled with a near-fixation on practices."[187] In physical science, it observed that "it would be impossible to derive a high school physics or chemistry course from the content included in the NGSS."[188] If not scientific facts

---

[187] Paul R. Gross with Douglas Buttrey, Ursula Goodenough, Noretta Koertge, Lawrence Lerner, Martha Schwartz, and Richard Schwartz, *Final Evaluation of the Next Generation Science Standards* (Washington, D.C.: Thomas B. Fordham Institute, 2013), 19.
[188] Ibid., 10, 31.

and knowledge—content—what is it that fills the hundreds of pages of science standards for K–12 education?

According to the Fordham Institute's report, the NGSS writers "suffer from the belief—widespread among educators—that practices are more important than content,"[189] and they engage in "a systematic pruning of substantive content so as to make way for a vast expansion of science 'practices.'"[190] The Fordham Institute reviewers characterized the "practices" as "skills," "applications," "activities," "inquiry learning," and "hands-on learning"—essentially the same methods developed by Dewey and his colleagues and encouraged in *Cardinal Principles*. The reviewers explained that the practices, which are often called "processes" in standards documents, are largely divorced from content and focused on the behaviors of scientific inquiry: how scientists think (reason scientifically), communicate (speak, write, and argue about scientific issues), and act (gather data, make presentations).[191] Although accepting the limited use of these practices in science education, the Fordham Institute argued that they should never be a substitute for content. The NGSS fail to achieve this balance by making a "practice" or "process" integral to *every* standard, which requires students to "take the form of some action, activity, or behavior."[192]

These practices are often "sold" to parents and educators as necessary to develop "critical thinking skills." Yet the report quoted University of Virginia psychologist Daniel Willingham, who points out what should be obvious to any educator: "Critical

[189] Ibid.
[190] Ibid., 19.
[191] Ibid.
[192] Ibid., 21.

thinking is not a set of procedures that can be practiced and perfected while divorced from background knowledge. Thus, it makes sense to consider whether students have the necessary background knowledge to carry out a critical thinking task you might assign."[193] On this point, the report concludes that a good set of standards is not designed primarily to encourage mastery of "practices" or to encourage "inquiry-based learning"; rather, "the purpose is to build knowledge *first* so that students will have the storehouse of information and understanding that they need to engage in the scientific reasoning and higher level thinking that we want for all students."[194]

Not surprisingly, the content that the NGSS does include emphasizes political issues, such as global warming, environmentalism, and sustainable communities. Large swaths of the standards address two major topics: Human Impacts on Earth Systems and Global Climate Change. These topics are present at almost every grade level from K through 12, ensuring that a large part of a student's science education will be devoted to them.

The purpose of the Human Impacts on Earth Systems standards is to answer the overarching question, "How do humans change the planet?"[195] In grade after grade, the NGSS require instruction on how humans negatively affect the earth and on how to mitigate this damage through individual behavior and regulatory action. For example, the NGSS provide targeted goals for what students should know at the end of specific grade bands:

[193] Ibid., 18.
[194] Ibid., 12.
[195] "ESSC3C: Human Impacts on Earth Systems," Next Generation Science Standards, https://ngss.sdcoe.net/.

- *By the end of grade 5.* Human activities in agriculture, industry, and everyday life have had major effects on the land, vegetation, streams, ocean, air, and even outer space. But individuals and communities are doing things to help protect Earth's resources and environments. For example, they are treating sewage, reducing the amounts of materials they use, and regulating sources of pollution such as emissions from factories and power plants or the runoff from agricultural activities.

- *By the end of grade 8.* Changes to Earth's environments can have different impacts (negative and positive) for different living things. Typically, as human populations and per-capita consumption of natural resources increase, so do the negative impacts on Earth unless the activities and technologies involved are engineered otherwise.

- *By the end of grade 12.* The sustainability of human societies and the biodiversity that supports them requires responsible management [regulation] of natural resources. Scientists and engineers can make major contributions —for example, by developing technologies that produce less pollution and waste and that preclude ecosystem degradation. When the source of an environmental problem is understood and international agreement can be reached, human activities can be regulated to mitigate global impacts (*e.g.*, acid rain and the ozone hole near Antarctica).[196]

The purpose of the Global Climate Change standards is to answer the question, "How do people model and predict the

---

[196] Ibid.

effects of human activities on Earth's climate?"[197] Students discuss existing global-climate-change models and simulations and discuss global climate change as "shown to be driven by both natural phenomena and by human activities" and how it "will have large consequences for all of Earth's surface systems."[198]

Like the Human Impact standards, the NGSS Global Climate Change standards provide goals for students' learning at the end of certain grade bands:

- *By the end of grade 5.* If Earth's global mean temperature continues to rise, the lives of humans and other organisms will be affected in many different ways.
- *By the end of grade 8.* Human activities, such as the release of greenhouse gases from burning fossil fuels, are major factors in the current rise in Earth's mean surface temperature (global warming). Reducing human vulnerability to whatever climate changes do occur depend [*sic*] on the understanding of climate science, engineering capabilities, and other kinds of knowledge, such as understanding of human behavior and on applying that knowledge wisely in decisions and activities.
- *By the end of grade 12.* Global climate models are often used to understand the process of climate change because these changes are complex and can occur slowly over Earth's history. Though the magnitudes of humans' impacts are greater than they have ever been, so too are humans' abilities to model, predict, and manage current and future impacts. Through computer simulations and other studies, important discoveries are still being

[197] Ibid.
[198] Ibid.

made about how the ocean, the atmosphere, and the biosphere interact and are modified in response to human activities, as well as to changes in human activities. Thus science and engineering will be essential both to understanding the possible impacts of global climate change and to informing decisions about how to slow its rate and consequences—for humanity as well as for the rest of the planet.[199]

The NGSS do not simply require students to learn about global climate change and answer questions about it; instead, students are expected to affirm it as fact and marshal evidence to support their affirmation. For example, a middle-school standard reads that students should "clarify evidence of the factors that have caused the rise in global temperatures over the past century." Students may include evidence of both "human activities (such as fossil-fuel combustion, cement production, and agricultural activity) and natural processes (such as changes in incoming solar radiation or volcanic activity)."[200] However, NGSS guidance documents specify that the "emphasis is on the major role that human activities play in causing the rise in global temperatures," not on natural phenomena.[201]

At the date of publication, eighteen states had adopted the NGSS since the standards were completed in 2011. The remaining states face a relentless campaign from the education establishment to adopt the standards. For example, the National

---

[199] Ibid.
[200] "MS-ESS3-5: Earth and Human Activity," Next Generation Science Standards, http://www.nextgenscience.org/pe/ms-ess3-5-earth-and-human-activity.
[201] Ibid.

Association of School Boards of Education (NASBE) has pushed adoption of the NGSS by state school boards, which generally exercise authority over state academic standards. Efforts to reject the NGSS face a barrage of "expert" reports from the NASBE to refute any concerns raised. And standards are written to allow bureaucratic control over teaching content and are invariably aligned with standardized tests. That mechanism enables bureaucrats to evaluate teachers and schools based on how students perform on the test — ensuring that teachers do in fact teach as required by the standards.

Progressives Take Over the Content of "Social Studies" Instruction

After the publication of *Cardinal Principles*, progressives began a curriculum-revision movement that continues today. Particular attention was directed to what used to be called "history." Because the study of Western civilization culminates in, and affirms, citizen-directed government and undermines the primacy of experts, it had to be marginalized. The study of history in the early elementary grades was one of the first victims. "History" was changed to "social studies," better to present on the variety of topics necessary to shape the child's morals.

In 1934, the American Historical Association's Commission on Social Studies recommended a social-studies curriculum that was very much in keeping with *Cardinal Principles*. As we shall see, it was also in line with the curriculum used by Soviet educators called the Complex System, which Dewey had observed during his visit to the USSR a few years prior. Both curricula begin with activities centered on the student's immediate environment. Those experiences are then extended into the broader society to link the individual to the collective society.

The American Historical Association's description on the social-sciences curriculum includes the following:

> Instruction in the social sciences should begin in the earli-est years of schooling, not with the life and institutions of some people remote in time, space, and cultural develop-ment, but with the life and institutions of the surrounding community—the simple social relationships of the family and the neighborhood and the modes of providing food, clothing, shelter, medical care, education, recreation, cultural opportunities and security of person.[202]

Instead of learning history through stories of great events and heroes (*i.e.*, material that actually interests children), students would be fed "social studies," weaving in strands of sociological and economic thought, to groom them for participation in a collectivist society.[203] Before progressives revised the history cur-riculum, stories about Indian life, pioneers, explorers, American heroes, and events in American history were staples in grades 1 through 3. Much of that content was replaced with the study of the student and his relationship with society. An example is *Expanding Horizons*, a popular replacement curriculum written by Professor David Hanna (who earned his doctorate at Teach-ers College). Operating from the theory that children should begin their studies with what they know best—themselves and their families—and then gradually expand their scope to

[202] Diane Ravitch, "Tot Sociology: Or What Happened to History in the Grade Schools," *American Scholar* 56, no. 3 (Summer 1982): 348, quoting American Historical Association: Com-mission on the Social Studies (1934).
[203] Ibid., 345–346.

broader society, this curriculum focuses on mundane topics such as "how the mail gets delivered" and "the role of public health inspectors."[204]

It's worth examining the similarities between the new social-studies curriculum and the Complex System about which Dewey wrote so admiringly in *Impressions of Soviet Russia*. Following this pedagogical model, Dewey explained that students perform activities centered on things they can observe in their environment—for example, the neighborhood—and then extend that experience, or learning activity, into the broader social system:

> Each [Soviet] province has its own experimental school, that supplements the work of the central or federal experimental stations, by studying local resources, materials and problems with a view to adapting school work to them. The primary principle of method officially laid down is that, in every topic, work by pupils is to begin with observation of their own environment, natural and social.[205]

The activities selected by the teacher had to align with the long-term economic and social plan established by the Soviet regime.[206] In practice, the teacher would study the local environment, both natural and social, and select activities for the students that utilized the local resources in order to serve the greater Soviet aims.

This type of education method profoundly influences the way students understand society and their place in it. Early on, in

[204] Ibid., 346.
[205] Dewey, *Impressions of Soviet Russia*, 236–237.
[206] Ibid., 238.

both the Complex System and American social-studies courses, the student is taught that the importance of one's individual circumstances—his family, neighborhood, and church—can be understood only in connection with national and international industrial life. The purpose of one's life is to support society as a collective enterprise. It is to subordinate one's dreams and ideals to what society determines is best.

Moreover, the instruction of the child is not undertaken for his personal benefit. Rather, as Dewey argued, every educational procedure is "conscious[ly] controlled" to produce a "comprehensive social purpose," or socially useful work.[207] By focusing study on how the individual and his community should interact, the schools could redefine that relationship and establish a new social order. The inclusion of contemporary problems or current events makes students aware of social and economic injustices, and encourages them to accept the progressive policies needed to bring about change. Progressives hoped that students would "become aware of society's many flaws and develop a desire to ameliorate those ills, thus making it difficult, if not impossible, for the curriculum to instill a spirit of nationalism or respect for American culture."[208]

Dewey commended the Soviets' Complex System for its strict requirement that every educational activity be directly connected to the creation of a new social order, not the private, personal benefit of the student. He found it to be "that educational system in which our professed progressive democratic

[207] Ibid., 230.
[208] Kathleen Porter-Magee, Lucien Ellington, and James Leming. "Where Did Social Studies Go Wrong?" (Washington, D.C.: Thomas B. Fordham Foundation, 2003), 126.

ideas are most completely embodied, and from which accordingly we might ... learn much more than from the system of any other country."[209] In his estimation, some progressive educational methods — even the Project Method, which was similar to the Complex System — fell short of the Soviet system because student classroom activities didn't always serve a social purpose.

The first four years of the American elementary social-studies curriculum are still organized around the study of the social relationships within the home, the school, the neighborhood, and the local community, often shown in textbooks as concentric circles to emphasize the interdependence between the individual and the community.[210] But the generations of teachers who have assumed that this approach — known as expanding environments or expanding horizons — has been validated by research would search in vain for supporting data.[211] In fact, there is no evidence to support it, and its use in schools results from a political decision to create a "socially efficient" school system that molds children to accept certain progressive values, not the least of which is to accept their place in the new order of collectivism.[212]

Overcoming Parental Rejection of Progressive Education Methods

As this discussion shows, Dewey was enthusiastic about the Soviets' use of the education system to create citizens to serve the

---

[209] Dewey, *Impressions of Soviet Russia*, 241.
[210] Ravitch, "Tot Sociology," 347.
[211] Ravitch, *Left Back*, 258; Ravitch, "Tot Sociology," 345ff.
[212] Ravitch, *Left Back*, 51–53; "Tot Sociology," 345ff.

State's workforce needs—the children were no longer students but rather human capital. In America, the related effort took the form of "social efficiency" education, designed not only to transfer power from the individual to government but also to meet the needs of the economy, a mindset prevalent among today's education reformers. But this form of progressive education, as Professor David Labaree observes, was a tough sell to parents and to good teachers:

> Social efficiency education, when examined closely from the perspective of American traditions of democratic equality and individual opportunity, was not an attractive sight.... As an educational process, it was mechanistic, alienating, and dull, with a dumbed-down curriculum and a disengaging pedagogy. This was a coldly utilitarian and socially reproductive vision of schooling, and the offer it made to students—learn a skill and take your place in the workforce—was hard to get excited about and easy to refuse.[213]

Not surprisingly, parents in the early twentieth century rejected progressive efforts to reform American schools in the socially efficient methods embraced by the Soviets. Such a curriculum seemed designed to douse a child's interest in history. When the riveting story of Paul Revere's ride is replaced with "how postal routes are designed," children will naturally disengage from the subject. Perhaps that's the point. This drab fare was appealing to neither students nor parents; local communities and parents still preferred children to learn reading, writing,

---

[213] Labaree, "Progressivism, Schools and Schools of Education," 255–288.

geography, languages, mathematics, literature, grammar, the sciences, history, and so forth.[214]

This rejection didn't phase progressive educators, who believed the delay in implementing their reforms—caused by concerns from parents, local communities, and classroom teachers—was simply a "cultural time lag," until they swayed public opinion or replaced existing teachers and administrators with those trained in their methods.[215] After all, they were the experts, not parents.

Labaree writes that, because educators at that time lacked the authority to override the decisions of parents and local school boards, progressive educators eventually sought to gain the "consent" of teachers and parents by sugarcoating the methods:

> Into this efficient and heartless environment, the romantic educational vision of the pedagogical progressives introduced welcome elements, such as natural learning, student-centered teaching, an interest-based curriculum, and possibilities for personal fulfillment and social improvement. Therefore, having education schools imbue student teachers with commitment to this kind of engaging and optimistic form of teaching and learning helped make the whole prospect of social efficiency education seem a little more palatable.[216]

Today's progressive teaching methods are the same as those espoused by early progressives. The difference is that modern progressives no longer unabashedly admit that one purpose of

---

[214] Ravitch, *Left Back,* 163.

[215] Ibid.

[216] Labaree, "Progressivism, Schools and Schools of Education," 287.

these methods is the social indoctrination of students into a collective economic system, and most teachers are probably unaware of these intentions. But that purpose is clear in a modern description of progressive pedagogy offered by Labaree. He writes that, in the lingo of American education today:

> Progressivism means pedagogical progressivism. It means basing instruction on the needs, interests and developmental stage of the child; it means teaching students the skills they need in order to learn any subject, instead of focusing on transmitting a particular subject; it means promoting discovery and self-directed learning by the student through active engagement; it means having students work on projects that express student purposes and that integrate the disciplines around socially relevant themes; and it means promoting values of community, cooperation, tolerance, justice and democratic equality. In the shorthand of educational jargon, this adds up to "child-centered instruction," "discovery learning" and "learning how to learn." And in the current language of American education schools there is a single label that captures this entire approach to education: constructivism.[217]

While Labaree believes that the social efficiency—or administrative—progressives have greatly influenced education, he questions the classroom influence of pedagogical progressives. Regardless, the progressive march seems relentless under current school conditions: veteran, traditional teachers retire and are replaced by young education-school graduates marinated in the progressive pedagogies; curricula aligned to the low-trajectory

[217] Ibid., 277.

Common Core standards are taught; and progressive content in subject areas such as social studies and science is unquestioningly accepted by teachers. Moreover, the increasingly centralized curricula and assessments, and the required accountability to the "experts" in the education bureaucracies, are designed to stamp out any noncompliance by a rogue teacher. If classroom practice hasn't fully caught up with the progressive theories of the education schools, that day cannot be long in coming.

PROGRESSIVE EDUCATION — THE TRIUMPH OF IDEOLOGY OVER TRUE EDUCATION

Do these methods of "learning" outperform traditional education in increasing academic content knowledge? Not according to the evidence, a fact not generally taught in education schools. Such methods "require background knowledge but they do nothing to teach it."[218] They cause students to waste time thinking about the wrong things rather than committing essential knowledge to long-term memory, which is critical to real learning.[219] In reality, the replacement of books with activities limits the range of learning to subjects that are tangible or observable, and denies students access to the great minds of the past.

But progressives aren't particularly concerned with improving academic knowledge; they have a different goal in mind. To

---

[218] Daisy Christodolou, *Seven Myths about Education* (New York: Routledge, 2014), 98.

[219] Paul A. Kirschner, John Sweller, and Richard E. Clark, "Why Minimal Guidance during Instruction Does Not Work: An Analysis of the Failure of Constructivist, Discovery, Problem-Based, Experiential, and Inquiry-Based Teaching," *Educational Psychologist* 41, no. 2 (June 2010): 75–86.

progressives, the social and emotional development of the student is at least as important as acquiring academic knowledge. Learning activities are performed in groups, without grades. While this process is cloaked in terms of promoting "collaboration" among students, which can appeal to parents, it's actually a method to enforce collectivism and eradicate individualism. (Imposition of social-emotional learning, or SEL, carries with it enormous other risks to children's psychological health and privacy[220] and to parental authority, but those risks are beyond the scope of this work.)

After years of lackluster student achievement, an objective observer would wonder why progressive educational methods are still advanced through federally driven efforts, such as the Common Core and the NGSS. But when it's recognized that the philosophy of Dewey and like-minded progressive educators was to promote a centrally controlled society, the answer becomes obvious: these methods condition Americans to accept the bureaucratic authority of government.

In *The Abolition of Man*, C. S. Lewis wrote of the "new" educational methods advanced in a progressive education textbook that he called *The Green Book*.[221] Lewis took objection to a lesson in which the authors decry assigning labels of value to objects. In this case, calling a waterfall "sublime" was deemed wrong because "it appears to be saying something very important about

---

[220] Jane Robbins and Karen Effrem, "Schools Ditch Academics for Emotional Manipulation," *Federalist*, October 19, 2016, http://thefederalist.com/.

[221] Lewis used the title *The Green Book* to avoid publicly admonishing its authors. The actual title was *The Control of Language: A Critical Approach to Reading and Writing*, published in 1939 as a textbook for secondary students in British schools.

something, and actually it is only saying something about our own feelings." Lewis conceded that the student will most likely draw no conscious inference from what he's taught. But the damage is done:

> The very power [of the lesson] depends on the fact that they are dealing with a boy: a boy who *thinks* he is "doing" his "English prep" and has no notion that ethics, theology, and politics are all at stake. *It is not a theory they put into his mind, but an assumption, which ten years hence, its origin forgotten and its presence unconscious, will condition him to take one side in a controversy which he has never recognized as a controversy at all.*[222]

Lewis suspected that the authors themselves "hardly know what they are doing to the boy, and he cannot know what is being done to him." This is the power of indirect methods of mental conditioning. One doesn't have to teach a student to reject capitalism, or that rule by experts is better than representative government, or that the American Experiment has failed, or that the American culture of self-defense is bad, and so forth: the student will eventually come to these conclusions on his own. He will do so because progressives have embedded an assumption in the child's mind that the collective is more than the individual; they have embedded the values that support progressive policies. Later, when someone asks the child's position, he will tend to rely on the embedded assumption — the assumption he was conditioned to believe in English class or math class. Lewis understood this. Communists, socialists, and progressives

---

[222] C.S. Lewis, *The Abolition of Man*, chap. 1, emphasis added.

understand this. Conservatives, libertarians, and traditionalists tend not to understand this and thus remain continually baffled by the changes in each generation. A national Reason-Rupe survey conducted in 2014 suggested that these indirect methods of bending the mind of Americans to accept a new collectivist order are working. The survey found that 58 percent of college-aged Americans reported a positive view of socialism while only 28 percent of senior citizens did.[223]

Progressives' desire to essentially change the constitutional structure so that government policy and society are shaped by experts rather than by citizens can be fulfilled only if progressive educational methods go unchallenged and their academic failures remain hidden. Progressives thus need a continuing body of policy reports and studies, of various types, to provide a colorable basis for those policies. Here, the federal government has eagerly stepped in to help. Various federal agencies, such as the U.S. Department of Education and the National Science Foundation, have funded schools of education, state departments of education, and research organizations to produce "evidence" in support of progressive educational methods. With this "research," wholly ineffective and indeed harmful methods of education are perpetuated by schools of education and policy-making governmental bodies. It is to this structure of corrupted research that we now turn.

---

[223] Emily Ekins, "Poll: Americans Like Free Markets More Than Capitalism and Socialism More Than a Government-Managed Economy," Reason.com, February 12, 2015, http://reason.com/poll.

Chapter 4

Federally Funded Research —
Shaping the Will of the People

The prospect of domination of the nation's scholars by Federal employment, project allocations, and the power of money is ever present — and is gravely to be regarded. Yet, in holding scientific research and discovery in respect, as we should, we must also be alert to the equal and opposite danger that public policy could itself become the captive of a scientific-technological elite.

— President Dwight D. Eisenhower,
Farewell Address, January 17, 1961

The Framers intended that legislatures would ensure that public policy reflects the people's will, with the expectation that the law originates with the people's representatives — from the bottom up — and is not imposed by the State from on high. This expectation threatens the primacy of the administrative state to control public policy. To circumvent it, government agencies use federally funded "research" conducted by "experts" to legitimize the preferred policies of the administrative state and discredit competing policies and programs. In other words, because the constitutional structure doesn't permit unelected bureaucrats to dictate the outputs of the legislative process (*i.e.*, the law), the bureaucrats do the next best thing by controlling the inputs.

As stated earlier, progressives have long argued that rule by experts is superior to representative government. Unlike elected representatives, experts are supposedly freed from political influences and thus would make neutral, objective decisions based on science. But neutrality and objectivity are usually ideals rather than reality in the realm of public policy. As Frederick M. Hess, an education scholar at the American Enterprise Institute, points out, both "expertise and research are contested terrain in a democratic nation."[224] There is no guarantee that research will be unbiased or that those who conduct it will have the necessary level of expertise. Political considerations frequently determine what gets researched and what the results should look like, especially when supported with federal funding. Inevitably, politicians, special-interest groups, and bureaucrats use the research to influence public support for their preferred policies.

As this chapter will explain, federally funded research is often conducted as a political ruse to provide federal agencies with a body of literature to advance the adoption of progressive legislation and policies. The research essentially becomes the means by which public opinion, elected officials, and the overall decision-making process of governance are influenced to support progressive policies that increase federal control over individuals and state and local government. (It's important to keep in mind that, while the examples provided in this chapter are limited to research

[224] Frederick M. Hess, ed., *When Research Matters: How Scholarship Influences Education Policy* (Cambridge, MA: Harvard Education Press, 2008), 3.

conducted or authorized by federal agencies, state legislatures are not immune from the corrupting influence. As chapter 7 will illustrate, the same bogus research used to misinform transportation and housing policies in Congress has trickled down to the states.)

FEDERAL GOVERNMENT EXPENDITURES ON RESEARCH AND DEVELOPMENT

Despite complaints from progressive groups that national research efforts are underfunded, substantial amounts are allocated for research to various federal agencies (see table 1). Because the federal government has no single source of funding for Research and Development (R&D), the federal R&D budget is calculated by aggregating the components of each agency's R&D budget. The research budgets are developed internally by the agencies, submitted to the Office of Management and Budget (OMB) for review and approval, and added to the president's budget submission to Congress.

The table below compares FY2017 R&D funding ($148 billion) to Trump's proposed 2018 budget ($117 billion). While Trump's 2018 budget made cuts to R&D funding for most major federal research agencies, it appears Republican members of Congress are unwilling to make them. Although the Senate had yet to pass a 2018 budget at the time of publication, the House budget (which passed 219-206) included a 4.9% ($7.7 billion) increase over current spending for federal research funding.[225]

[225] "FY 2018 R&D Appropriations Dashboard," American Association for the Advancement of Science, October 3, 2017, accessed October 9, 2017, https://www.aaas.org/page/fy-2018-rd-appropriations-dashboard.

Deconstructing the Administrative State

Department/ Agency	FY2017 CR Annualized	FY2018 Proposed	Change 2017–2018
Defense*	71,196	53,396	-25%
Health and Human Services	32,322	26,144	-19%
Energy	15,007	13,408	-11%
NASA	13,329	10,327	-23%
NSF	6,106	5,371	-12%
Agriculture	2,614	1,991	-24%
Commerce	1,811	1,567	-13%
Veterans Affairs	1,346	1,357	1%
Interior	989	818	-17%
Transportation	914	923	1%
Homeland Security	707	564	-20%
Patient-Centered Outcomes	463	533	15%

*   Unlike previous years, totals for development spending in FY 2018 do not include the DOD Budget Activity 07 (Operational System Development) due to changes in the definition of Development. These funds are requested in the overall FY 2018 budget request.

Department/ Agency	FY2017 CR Annualized	FY2018 Proposed	Change 2017–2018
Smithsonian	255	304	19%
EPA	510	277	-46%
Education	257	246	-21%
Other	617	471	-24%
Total	148,443	117,697	-21%

Table 1. Federal R&D Funding by Agency, FY2017-FY2018 (mandatory and discretionary budget authority, dollar amounts in millions)[226]

Federal agencies often have a large degree of discretion over how research funding is spent, including the types of research projects that will be funded. As we shall see, this flexibility allows federal agencies to conduct research not in the name of science but to advance a political agenda.

It's worth dispelling the misconception that all research conducted by federal agencies focuses on sophisticated, ground-breaking science on matters of national importance. The National Science Foundation (NSF), for example, was established "to promote the progress of science; to advance the national health, prosperity, and welfare; to secure the national defense; and for other purposes." Yet, many NSF grants are of questionable

---

[226] United States Office of Management and Budget, Analytical Perspectives: Budget of the United States Government, Fiscal Year 2018. Washington, D.C.: U.S. G.P.O., 2018, table 18-2.

scientific value, as pointed out by Senator Jeff Flake in a 2016 report:[227]

Do drunk birds slur when they sing?	$5,000,000
What has more hairs — a squirrel or a bumble bee?	$753,000
Where does it hurt the most to be stung by a bee? [On the nose.]	$1,000,000
How many shakes does it take for a wet dog to dry off?	$390,000
Are Republicans or Democrats more disgusted by eating worms?	$855,000

Because federal agencies fall under the executive branch, there is little that members of Congress can do to stop such frivolous grants. However, Congress can control research funding by (1) determining the level and allocation of funding for the overall agency budgets and (2) imposing substantive requirements as to the direction of the research as well as "process" requirements on the disbursement of funds (see chapter 13). Outside these measures and normal oversight authority, Congress has little control over the selection of research projects.

HISTORY OF THE FEDERAL ROLE IN SCIENTIFIC RESEARCH

Before World War II, the federal government had little involvement in scientific R&D. In that era, the small amounts of federal

[227] Senator Jeff Flake, *Twenty Questions: Government Studies That Will Leave You Scratching Your Head*, website of Senator Jeff Flake, https://www.flake.senate.gov/public/.

R&D funding supported mission-oriented research in agriculture, national defense, and natural resources. Government employees conducted that research in small government laboratories and experimental stations.[228]

During World War II, President Franklin Roosevelt issued an executive order creating the Office of Scientific Research and Development (OSRD) to, among other responsibilities, "serve as the center for the mobilization of the scientific personnel and resources of the Nation in order to assure maximum utilization of such personnel and resources in developing and applying the results of scientific research to defense purposes."[229] The OSRD awarded $450 million in federal contracts to industry and university scientists for defense-related research.[230]

Roosevelt commissioned OSRD director Vannevar Bush to head a committee charged with determining whether the lessons from that effort could "be profitably employed in times of peace." Bush was to report on the feasibility of creating a national research structure based on the OSRD model, which would sponsor leading university scientists and nonprofit research institutions to advance a broad agenda that would "improve the national health, create new jobs and enterprises, and raise the standard of living."[231] The

[228] Institute of Medicine, National Academy of Sciences, National Academy of Engineering, and National Research Council, *Allocating Federal Funds for Science and Technology* (Washington, D.C.: National Academies Press, 1995), 41–50. https://doi.org/10.17226/5040.

[229] Exec. Order No. 8807, 6 Fed. Reg. 3207 (June 28, 1941).

[230] Office of Scientific Research and Development (OSRD) Collection, Library of Congress, https://www.loc.gov/rr/scitech/trs/trsosrd.html.

[231] Daniel J. Kevles, "The National Science Foundation and the Debate over Postwar Research Policy, 1942–1945: A Political

resulting report, *Science: The Endless Frontier,* was released in 1945 and recommended the creation of the NSF.

Analyzing this report, Daniel J. Kevles explains that during World War II's early years those of a "liberal political persuasion" were concerned "about the extent to which defense research was dominated by big business in alliance with the leading universities."[232] In their opinion, most of the private market's technologically related research had been "determined to a disturbingly large degree by how big business responded to market forces rather than by an assessment of national needs."[233] Progressives encouraged the use of federal funding to address public-policy concerns and advance the social programs of the New Deal.

Some members of Congress, business leaders, and many university scientists — whom the funding was intended to support — objected to the call for a national science agency. They feared that federal support of scientific research would open the door to political control of the academic world.[234] The president of the National Academy of Sciences at the time, Frank Jewett, also cautioned against such an agency, warning that "federal aid to academic research in any form [is] a threat to the freedom of science."[235]

Committee members also disagreed over how the new agency would be structured. One faction wanted the agency to be managed by a director appointed by and responsible to the president. The other wanted a presidentially appointed part-time board of private citizens, mainly scientists, to choose a director who would

---

Interpretation of Science — the Endless Frontier," *Isis* 68, no. 1 (March 1977): 17.

[232] Ibid., 5.

[233] Ibid., 7.

[234] Ibid., 18.

[235] Ibid., 11.

answer not to the president but to the board.[236] The disagreement centered on the degree of programmatic autonomy the new agency would have. Would it be responsible to the president, and thus its research ultimately controlled by political considerations? Or would it support research determined by the agency's director?[237]

While the president's leadership could be tainted by political considerations and special-interest groups on any subject, it's also subject to the checks and balances of the constitutional structure. In contrast, an independent board is largely impervious to checks and balances and susceptible to domination by biased bureaucrats as well as special interests.

When President Truman finally signed legislation creating the NSF in 1950, the agency's administrative structure was the result of a compromise. The law authorized the president to appoint the NSF's director but also required him to share policy-making with a part-time board of private citizens. The arrangement was best described by one of Bush's key staffers as "a new social invention—of government sanction and support but professional guidance and administration."[238] In other words, the taxpayer would fund the agency, but "experts" would control it.

Despite the good intentions of those who created the NSF, the expectation of insulating a federally funded agency from politics was naive. As the case studies in this section will show, the early opponents of the NSF have been proven right: federal research grants have opened the door to political control of the academic world, and "official" scientific theory has now become a reality.

[236] Ibid., 24.
[237] Ibid.
[238] Ibid., 22, internal citations omitted.

BIAS RESULTING FROM GRANTS TO UNIVERSITIES

Federal funding enables federal bureaucrats, for all intents and purposes, to partner with like-minded researchers to skew the information that the public receives and, ultimately, to shape public policy. Since the early twentieth century, a "cozy" relationship has existed between social-science research and expansive progressive policies, with the former serving to validate the latter.[239] As Hess notes, instead of objectively identifying *optimal* policies, social-science research has been conducted to support *specific* policies involving "regulation, new public spending, and the growth of government responsibilities in the process."[240]

Certainly, no party is innocent of injecting bias into research projects. But in the social sciences, an overwhelming majority of researchers lean left—particularly within academia. The lack of ideological balance among university faculty has created what *New York Times* columnist John Tierney calls a "monoculture," with professors identifying as Democrat over Republican by a ratio of 8 to 1 (in sociology the ratio is 44 to 1).[241] The monoculture of leftist ideology among professors not only ensures a healthy dose of indoctrination for students but also creates the overwhelming likelihood of biased research generated by their departments in favor of a leftist agenda.

Uniformity of thought, however, is not the only factor driving "consensus" among university researchers on controversial issues. Federal research grants provide half the funding of university research departments ($37 billion out of $68 billion

---

[239] Hess, *When Research Matters*, 3.
[240] Ibid.
[241] John Tierney, "The Real War on Science," *City Journal* (2016), https://www.city-journal.org/html/real-war-science-14782.html.

total),[242] which places pressure on researchers to align their research with federal parameters. Dr. Judith Curry, former chair of the School of Earth and Atmospheric Sciences at Georgia Institute of Technology, testified to this effect before a Senate subcommittee: "Consensus about dangerous anthropogenic [human-caused] climate change is portrayed as nearly total among scientists with prominence in the field of climate science," despite "substantial and fundamental uncertainties."[243]

Curry's testimony revealed that the Obama administration forced consensus by embedding "an implicit assumption of the dominance of human caused global warming" in the calls for climate-research proposals issued by federal funding agencies.[244] Curry explained that professors in the sciences, eager for research funding, jettisoned their standards of scientific inquiry to be eligible for these grants, and in the process became "another lobbyist group" for the climate agenda:

> "Success" to individual researchers, particularly at the large state universities, pretty much equates to research dollars — big lab spaces, high salaries, institutional prestige,

---

[242] Constant dollar conversions based on the OMB's GDP deflators from the Fiscal Year 2017 budget. See, *e.g.*, National Center for Science and Engineering Statistics, National Science Foundation, "Higher Education Research and Development: Fiscal Year 2015" (2016), updated March 2, 2017, https://ncsesdata.nsf.gov/herd/2015/.

[243] Hearing on "Data or Dogma? Promoting Open Inquiry in the Debate over the Magnitude of Human Impact on Climate Change" before the Subcommittee on Space, Science, and Competitiveness of Senate Committee on Commerce, Science, and Transportation, 114th Cong. 2 (December 8, 2015) (statement of Judith A. Curry, Ph.D.).

[244] Ibid.

and career advancement. At the Program Manager level within a funding agency, "success" is reflected in growing the size of their program.... Divisional administrators are competing for budget dollars against the other Divisions; tying their research to a national policy priority helps in this competition. At the agency level, "success" is reflected in growing, or at least preserving, the agency's budget.

Aligning yourself, your program, your agency with the current political imperatives is a key to "success." It is very difficult to obtain Federal research funding for dissenting science.[245]

When professors and departments within public universities become dependent on federal grant funding, university administrators become less concerned with the priorities of their state legislature, thus diminishing the state's authority over its university system. Moreover, this research is often used in testimony before the state legislature to argue in favor of policies that the people, and even many legislators, may oppose.

WHY FEDERALLY FUNDED RESEARCH IS BIASED

At the Cato Center for the Study of Science, researchers David E. Wojick and Patrick J. Michaels write that within all levels of the federal funding structure, a certain amount of "funding-induced bias" can occur.[246] They define such a bias as "any scientific activity where the prospect of funding influences the

---

[245] Ibid.

[246] Within each department or agency, multiple divisions receive a portion of the allocation for division-level programs. The divisions, in turn, fund the program's individual projects. The funding hierarchy is Congress, department, division, program, project.

result in a way that benefits the funder."[247] In the case of federal activity, such a bias occurs when a federal agency (the funder) funds research (the scientific activity) to generate support for the mission, policy, or paradigm of the agency (the benefit).[248]

Federally funded research is often tied to bolstering the agency's mission and existing policies. In such cases, Wojick and Michaels question whether the government is buying objective science or merely support.[249] They identify three sources of federal funding–induced bias: (1) protecting a policy, (2) growing the mission with a new thrust, and (3) preserving the existing scientific paradigm.[250]

1. *Protecting a policy.* Funding is often directed to research that is related to an existing policy. Here the bias issues are likely to be related to whether the research that gets funded is objective as far as the merits of the existing policy are concerned. In particular, there is the danger that the research will assume the policy, rather than evaluating it.[251]

2. *Growing the mission with a new thrust.* Sometimes research is funded to develop a new mission thrust, such as identifying a new problem that falls under the agency's mission. Here the danger is that the research will assume the new thrust is justified, rather than evaluating it.[252]

---

[247] David E. Wojick and Patrick J. Michaels, *Is the Government Buying Science or Support? A Framework Analysis of Federal Funding-Induced Biases* (working paper no. 29, Cato Institute, Washington, D.C., 2015), 1.

[248] Ibid.

[249] Ibid.

[250] Ibid., 8.

[251] Ibid.

[252] Ibid.

3. *Preserving the existing scientific paradigm.* Agency policies, programs and practices are often based on past [conclusions], which operated under a specific paradigm. When this paradigm begins to be questioned within the scientific community, there is the danger that the agency will simply continue to fund research under the existing paradigm. In effect the agency is taking a side in a scientific controversy, rather than working to resolve that controversy.[253]

Consider the case of climate change and the $21 billion spent by the Obama administration to combat global warming.[254] Although the current progressive paradigm in climate-change theory holds that global warming is significant and that human activity is the main driver, many members of the scientific community, such as Dr. Curry from Georgia Tech, disagree. Nevertheless, research funded by federal agencies (at least until possible revision by the Trump administration) continues to adhere to that paradigm. For example, a quick examination of the Department of Energy's research budget shows unequal funding (funding-induced bias) against forms of energy that are carbon-based (burning fossil fuels). Funding to the division of Energy Efficiency and Renewable Energy (non-carbon-based) was $1.7 billion, whereas the division of Fossil Energy (carbon-based) received only $436 million.[255] Moreover, climate research

---

[253] Ibid., 12.

[254] Obama White House, *Federal Climate Change Expenditures Report to Congress* (Washington, D.C.: White House, 2013), table 7.

[255] National Center for Science and Engineering Statistics, National Science Foundation, Survey of Federal Funds for Research and Development Fiscal Years 2015–2017, table 3 (2017), https://www.nsf.gov/.

is coordinated by the U.S. Global Change Research Partnership (USGCRP), an interagency partnership established by presidential initiative in 1989 and mandated by Congress in the Global Change Research Act of 1990 to "assist the Nation and the world to understand, assess, predict, and respond to human-induced and natural processes of global change."[256] But the research funded by the USGCRP doesn't try to "understand" or "assess" whether global warming exists and, if so, what's causing it. Rather, the research assumes the paradigm that the earth is warming and that the phenomenon is primarily driven by humans. The USGCRP website states this position in plain terms:

> Evidence from the top of the atmosphere to the depths
> of the oceans, collected by scientists and engineers from
> around the world, tells an unambiguous story: the planet is
> warming, and over the last half century, this warming has
> been driven primarily by human activity—predominantly
> the burning of fossil fuels.[257]

HOW FUNDING-INDUCED BIAS IN FEDERAL RESEARCH CAN PRODUCE A FALSE PARADIGM

A funding-induced bias can be amplified when a single funding-induced bias is followed by another, such that the first bias is increased.[258] When one biased activity leads to multiple instances

---

[256] "About USGCRP," GlobalChange.Gov, http://www.global-change.gov/about.

[257] See "Understand Climate Change," GlobalChange.Gov, http://www.globalchange.gov/climate-change/.

[258] Wojick and Michaels, *Is the Government Buying Science or Support?*, 4.

of funding-induced bias, this is referred to as a "cascading amplification." Wojick and Michaels provide a possible sequence of a cascading amplification:

1. An agency receives biased funding for research from Congress.
2. The agency issues multiple biased Requests for Proposals (RFPs).
3. The agency selects multiple biased projects for each RFP.
4. Many projects produce multiple biased articles, press releases, and so forth.
5. Many of these articles and releases generate multiple biased news stories.
6. The resulting amplified bias is communicated to the public on a large scale.[259]

The widespread belief among the public that global warming is significant and primarily human-caused is one such example. Congress funds USGCRP agency partners to advance the paradigm of human-caused global warming. The USGCRP issues RFPs based on that embedded assumption and funds projects to produce biased climate-change models and forecasts. The findings of these projects are published in scientific journals, university press releases, and K–12 science textbooks. And media outlets repeat the biased reports to the public at large.

It's obvious how the cascading amplification of biased federal research can shape public opinion in favor of the agency's mission and bureaucratically preferred policies, and establish the appearance that its findings are universally recognized as

[259] Ibid., 4–5.

true. If an agency can spawn an extensive body of literature and media reports rooted in biased federal research, it will likely dominate the public narrative and bend public opinion in its favor. It will ultimately establish a false paradigm. Once established, a paradigm is a powerful determinant of how scientific inquiry is conducted: it determines what is to be observed, the questions to be asked, and what the answers are expected to look like, and these questions and answers are the focus of research funding.[260]

The Relationship Between Research and the Legislative Process

One problem with federally funded research is its potential negative effect on the legislative process. Along with the Congressional Research Service, federal agencies provide the necessary information for Congress to draft legislation and evaluate existing policies. But federal researchers cannot be assumed to operate without professional or political motivations. When these motivations taint research requested by Congress, the ability to enact sound legislation is undermined. As the Supreme Court noted in *Eastland v. United States Servicemen's Fund*, "The power to investigate is inherent in the power to make laws because '[a] legislative body cannot legislate wisely or effectively in the absence of information respecting the conditions which the legislation is intended to affect or change.'"[261] When a federal agency advances the priorities of the executive or special-

---

[260] Ibid., 6.
[261] See Eastland v. U.S. Servicemen's Fund, 421 U.S. 491, 504 (1975).

interest groups by misrepresenting or withholding information requested by Congress, it undermines the legislative process.[262] This problem is illustrated by the recent treatment of a government scientist who made the mistake of telling Congress the truth as she saw it.

In September 2016, at a joint hearing of the Senate Subcommittee on Oversight and the Senate Subcommittee on Energy of the Committee on Science, Space, and Technology, it was revealed that senior Department of Energy (DOE) employees and management from the Office of Science (a component of the DOE) deliberately withheld information from Congress to quell support for legislation opposed by the Obama administration. These officials also fired a DOE scientist for providing complete answers to committee staff.[263]

The allegations stemmed from the Senate Committee's October 2014 request to the DOE for a briefing on legislation to create a long-term research agenda for the DOE's Low Dose Radiation Research Program (LDRRP). The requested briefing was to include "an overview of the LDRRP, its accomplishments, and expectations moving forward."[264] Senior DOE employees, however, had undisclosed plans to close the LDRRP and redirect funds to President Obama's Climate Change Plan; therefore, they instructed the program manager, Dr. Noelle Metting, to suppress any findings supportive of the LDRRP.

---

[262] Staff of the Committee on Science, Space, and Technology, 114th Congress, *U.S. Department of Energy Misconduct Related to the Low Dose Radiation Research Program* (hereafter Radiation Report), December 20, 2016, 4.
[263] Ibid., 4.
[264] Ibid., 6.

Metting chose instead to present the accurate information, as directed by Congress. After the briefing, the DOE fired her for allegedly having lobbied Congress. In response, Metting insisted that she acted properly by answering the committee members' questions honestly:

> I suggest it is unacceptable that scientists are put under pressure to espouse views that are not their own, and that federal scientists are persecuted for presenting accurate information and professional opinion to those charged with providing funds for the research, Congress.[265]

Unmoved, the DOE issued Dr. Metting a notice of proposed removal from federal service:

> You were cautioned to avoid interjecting contradictory opinions regarding this project. When you gave the presentation, you did not follow instructions or the prepared briefing.... *Your failure to adhere to [the DOE's] talking points while speaking in your professional capacity ... as a DOE official was confusing and undermined the purpose of your presentation.* ... By defying my instructions, you directly undermined [the DOE] management priorities.[266]

As the committee staff report concluded, DOE officials "did not realize or did not care that Congress has a Constitutional right to access uncensored information from the Executive as an inherent aspect of the legislative process."[267] By attempting to withhold such information, the DOE was effectively lobbying

[265] Ibid., 8.
[266] Ibid., 21, emphasis added.
[267] Ibid.

against the legislation in violation of federal law prohibiting any federal agency from influencing in any manner a member of Congress "to favor, adopt, or oppose … any legislation."[268] Furthermore, the report concluded, the DOE's termination of Dr. Metting for speaking honestly with Congress contravenes Article I, which supports Congress's right to such information.[269]

Despite the findings of the committee, the executive branch has taken no action to correct the situation within the DOE; none of the employees involved in the incident were disciplined, and at this writing all are still in service. After several months of unemployment, Dr. Metting reached a settlement with the DOE to return to federal service in a different capacity. She was never allowed to regain access to her research on the LDRRP, which the DOE eventually discontinued.

When federal employees corrupt the legislative process by withholding research, Congress has limited recourse outside of exposing the offense in a hearing, as in Dr. Metting's case, because executive officials aren't accountable to Congress. They essentially say, "Thank you for bringing that to our attention, members of Congress. We will do nothing about it." While Congress can hold offenders in contempt of Congress, it rarely does

[268] 18 USC 1913 reads in pertinent part: "No part of the money appropriated by any enactment of Congress shall, in the absence of express authorization by Congress, be used directly or indirectly to pay for any personal service, advertisement, telegram, telephone, letter, printed or written matter, or other device, intended or designed to influence in any manner a Member of Congress, a jurisdiction, or an official of any government, to favor, adopt, or oppose, by vote or otherwise, any legislation, law, ratification, policy, or appropriation."

[269] Radiation Report, 21.

so. The bureaucracy weathers the temporary public-relations storm and then returns to business as usual.

How Bias in Federal Research Funding Undermines Federalism

Spending billions of tax dollars to produce false, biased research is obviously a misuse of taxpayer money. But how does biased research undermine federalism and advance the administrative state? Unfortunately, such research is used to influence federal and state policy-makers and bend public opinion toward federal domination over state and individual sovereignty interests.

The USGCRP, for example, states that its mission is not simply to conduct research on global climate change to advance science, but to use that science to inform decisions, conduct sustained assessments, and communicate with and educate a range of audiences.[270] The research data is intended not only to inform but to advance the adoption of global-warming "mitigation" strategies. These strategies include measures intended to reduce the amount and speed of future climate change by limiting emissions that trap heat in the atmosphere.[271]

The USGCRP's website states that efforts are "accelerating" at all levels of government to force climate-change "mitigation" strategies on society:

---

[270] U.S. Global Change Research Program and Subcommittee on Global Change Research, 114th Congress, *Our Changing Planet: The U.S. Global Change Research Program for Fiscal Year 2016* (2015), 6.

[271] See "Climate Change," GlobalChange.Gov, http://www.globalchange.gov/climate-change/glossary.

Deconstructing the Administrative State

Preparing for both climate variability and climate change can reduce impacts while also facilitating a more rapid and efficient response to changes as they happen. Such efforts are accelerating at the Federal, regional, state, tribal, and local levels, and in the corporate and non-governmental sectors. Actions to reduce emissions, increase carbon uptake, adapt to changing climate, and increase resilience to impacts can improve public health, economic development, ecosystem protection, and quality of life.[272]

When research places humans at the center of global warming, the considerable leap of blaming human actions for the negative effects of climate change is made possible, which in turn justifies new policies and regulations to control such human actions. If implemented, these strategies have consequences for how the citizen functions in society.

Without funding or staff to conduct competing research, individuals, organizations, state legislators, and local officials are at a significant disadvantage in opposing such programs and policies. The position of the administrative state becomes mainstream, and all others are labeled "fringe." Through the federal-funding mechanism, the federal administrative state can fund what amounts to a dominant public-relations narrative, even when that narrative lacks a sound factual basis. And through grants and regulatory mechanisms, it can sway state bureaucracies to be more loyal to it than to the state's citizens and legislature.

[272] See "Response Options," GlobalChange.Gov, http://www.globalchange.gov/climate-change/response-options.

Chapter 5

Expanding Federal Power by Redefining "Public Health"

I know not what answer to give you, but this, that Power always
sincerely, conscientiously, de tres bon foi, believes itself right.
Power always thinks it has a great soul, and vast views, beyond
the comprehension of the weak; and that it is doing God service,
when it is violating all His laws.

—John Adams, letter to Thomas Jefferson, February 2, 1816

Federal agencies, congressional committees, and the executive branch frequently seek advice from federal research organizations, such as the NSF, the National Research Council (NRC), and the National Academies of Sciences, Engineering, and Medicine.[273] They use the research to establish national priorities

[273] The National Research Council is the principal operating arm of the National Academy of Sciences, Engineering, and Medicine. The National Research Council is a private, nonprofit institution that provides science and technology advice under a congressional charter.

Seven major programs of the National Academies of Sciences, Engineering, and Medicine conduct studies, facilitate workshops, and undertake other activities: Behavioral and

and goals, address complex problems, and inform public-policy decisions related to science, technology, and medicine. In these contexts, the federal research apparatus performs a valuable function.

But the research can also be used more problematically. Federal agencies often fund these research organizations, with their specially created commissions, boards, and committees, to conduct research for the purpose of expanding the role of the federal government. The commissioned reports habitually reach the same conclusion: the current system is failing, systemic changes are needed, and the federal government must take on a larger role. The research products often amount to little more than "push papers" intended to spark a policy shift across federal and state governments, advancing the progressive goal of increasing government regulation of the individual. The research serves to inform, or misinform, the decision-making process of elected officials and steers public opinion in favor of policies that increase federal control over individuals and state and local government.

A good example of this dynamic is the 1988 commissioning of the Institute of Medicine to expand the role of government in healthcare by redefining the concept of public health. This chapter explains how, over time, the consequences of that action shifted the responsibility of healthcare from a private to a public function.

Social Sciences and Education; Earth and Life Studies; Engineering and Physical Sciences; Health and Medicine; Policy and Global Affairs; Transportation Research Board; and the Gulf Research Program.

CASE STUDY: THE PUBLIC-HEALTH SYSTEM

In 1988 the U.S. Public Health Service (through its Centers for Disease Control and the Health Resources and Services Administration) commissioned the Institute of Medicine (IOM),[274] currently known as the National Academy of Medicine, to conduct a study of the nation's public-health system. In response, the IOM convened a committee "to address a growing perception among the Institute of Medicine membership and others concerned with the health of the public that this nation has lost sight of its public health goals and has allowed the system of public health activities to fall into disarray."[275] This wording, included in the preface of the resulting report, *The Future of Public Health*, suggests that the purpose of the study was not to analyze the public-health system objectively and make neutral, scientifically based recommendations; rather, it was to confirm an existing perception of the public-health system held by IOM members and, in turn, by the agencies sponsoring the report.

The report identified the state of "disarray" — a state assumed by the committee — to be caused by the failure of policy-makers and the public to recognize new health concerns related to social,

---

[274] The National Academy of Medicine (formerly the Institute of Medicine) is a private, nonprofit institution that provides health policy advice under a congressional charter granted to the National Academy of Sciences. The National Academy of Science acted under its 1863 congressional charter responsibility as "an adviser to the federal government," as well as its own initiative to "identify issues of medical care, research, and education," to charter the Institute of Medicine in 1970.

[275] Committee for the Study of the Future of Public Health, Institute of Medicine, *The Future of Public Health* (Washington, D.C.: National Academy of Sciences, 1988), 1.

economic, environmental, and biological factors.[276] The existing "public health apparatus originally conceived and constructed to meet a different set of concerns" (epidemic diseases) inadequately addressed these factors.[277] If the government were to provide for an effective public-health system, the definition of "public health" had to be expanded to cover a wider array of concerns, and federal, state, and local government would need to take on a bigger role.[278]

Until this point, the public-health system functioned to control epidemic disease, such as diphtheria, typhoid fever, waterborne illnesses, and other communicable diseases that affected the population at large.[279] To expand the authority of government in general, and the federal government in particular, *The Future of Public Health* argued that epidemic diseases were not the only "threat" to the public health in need of government action. Other health concerns, stemming from behavioral, environmental, biological, and socioeconomic factors also posed a threat that warranted government involvement.[280] The mission of the public-health system could no longer be limited to controlling epidemic diseases, but rather must expand to include "what we, as a society, do collectively to assure the conditions in which people can be healthy."[281] The committee concluded that while private individuals and organizations play a role in the mission of public health, governmental public agencies had

---

[276] Ibid., v.
[277] Ibid.
[278] Ibid.
[279] Ibid., 40.
[280] Ibid.
[281] Ibid., 7

a "unique" role "to see to it that vital elements are in place and that the mission is adequately addressed."[282]

The IOM committee argued that public health is not measured solely by the absence of illness, something that may be largely determined by individuals' genetic makeup, and the prevention and treatment of diseases. Health also included a measure of overall "well-being," which includes "mental and social dimensions" as well.[283] The committee suggested that this correlation "implies the need [for the public-health system] to address factors that fall outside the normal understanding of 'health,' including decent housing, public education, adequate income, freedom from war, and so on."[284] In order to "assure the conditions in which people can be healthy," the public-health system, and in turn the federal government, should be expanded to include the socioeconomic conditions affecting individuals' health. The committee concluded that the failure of the existing public-health system to address these factors was "cause for national concern" and that the health of the public was "threatened" as a result.[285]

By contending that public health, as defined by these new determinants, was threatened, the committee (and the federal agencies that funded its report) attempted to provide an incontrovertible mandate for the federal government to influence, if not control, new areas of policy. The committee acknowledged that its recommendations conflicted with the "mainstream" perspective, which held that "society is made up of individual persons with inalienable rights" and that the purpose of government

[282] Ibid.
[283] Ibid., 40.
[284] Ibid.
[285] Ibid., 2, 19.

was "to protect those rights and ensure the basic conditions necessary for their exercise—civil order, a free market, and equal individual opportunity."[286] To counter this position, it cited "another longstanding tradition in American political philosophy" that viewed government as "a facilitator of the social bond [of shared values] and the policy process as a means of defining positive goals and taking concerted action."

> In general, the philosophy of limited government implied by a concern for individual rights has prevailed. But the theme of positive values and community effort has persisted, and deliberate government steps to combat acknowledged social ills have become increasingly acceptable to most Americans, remaining so even during the renewed stress on individualism in recent years.[287]

The role of the public-health system, according to the committee, was to "achieve a balance between the two great concerns in the American public philosophy: individual liberty and free enterprise on the one hand, just and equitable action for the good of the community on the other."[288]

The committee took this view one step further. It offered that inconsistencies among states in providing "the basics" of public health begged for federal intervention:

> [The basics] of government's responsibility for the people's health encompasses the following elements: assuring a substantive core of activities, assuring adequacy of means and methods, establishing objectives, and providing

[286] Ibid., 42–43.
[287] Ibid.
[288] Ibid., 46.

guarantees. In the ideal health system, the substance of basic services will entail adequate personal health care for all members of the community, the education of individuals about healthy life-styles and the education of the community-at-large, the control of communicable disease, and the control of environmental hazards — biological, chemical, social, and physical. Explicit priorities will be set in each community and at each level of government so that clear objectives guide organized community efforts. *And governments will hold themselves accountable to the people by undertaking to guarantee certain services to all as a matter of justice.*[289]

The committee clarified that government's "obligation to assure conditions in which people can be healthy extend[s] to *requiring* certain of these conditions."[290] The appropriate role of government was to "assure" that these obligations were met.

CASCADING AMPLIFICATION OF THE INSTITUTE OF MEDICINE REPORT

As discussed in chapter 4, biased research can have an "amplification" effect, whereby a single funding-induced bias can trigger another and then another, such that the first bias is amplified.[291] This phenomenon certainly occurred in the realm of public health.

---

[289] Ibid., 54, emphasis added.
[290] Ibid.
[291] Wojick and Michaels, *Is the Government Buying Science or Support?*, 4.

Deconstructing the Administrative State

The Future of Public Health was a classic example of a funding-induced bias, because the research was not objective but rather was conducted to advance the agencies' missions and expand their regulatory authority. The cascading amplification of the initial bias is well documented through the vast body of literature based on, and programs funded under, its findings. In fact, the 1988 report is considered to have been a "landmark" report that laid the foundation for the public-health system to move into a different era; it marks what public-health officials consider the transition from public-health system "1.0 to 2.0."[292]

In a 2016 report, U.S. Department of Health and Human Services (HHS) officials Karen B. DeSalvo and Patrick W. O'Carroll note the significance of the IOM report in transforming the public-health system:

> We conceive of Public Health 2.0 as beginning with this IOM report and continuing to the present day. The IOM Committee characterized the mission of public health as fulfilling society's interest in assuring conditions in which people can be healthy, and defined the core functions of governmental public health agencies as assessment, policy development, and assurance. This seminal report was enormously influential in shaping and reenergizing public health (*e.g.*, by spurring national deliberations leading to the clear articulation of the essential services of public health).[293]

[292] Karen B. DeSalvo, Patrick W. O'Carroll, Denise Koo, John M. Auerbach, and Judith A. Monroe, "Public Health 3.0: Time for an Upgrade," *American Journal of Public Health* 106, no. 4 (April 2016): 621–622.

[293] Ibid.

Subsequent IOM reports and studies, including *The Future of Public Health in the 21st Century* (2003), significantly amplified the bias of the 1988 IOM report. Sponsored by the same federal health agencies[294] as the 1988 report, the 2003 report emerged from the Committee on Assuring the Health of the Public in the 21st Century, a group convened by the IOM to create a framework for assuring population health.

The IOM intended the recommendations of the 2003 report to be "more inclusive than those of the 1988 report" and to "be effectively communicated to and acted upon by diverse communities."[295] In the second report, the committee built upon the 1988 report's definition of public health, adding that it refers to "the health of a population as measured by health status indicators and as influenced by social, economic and physical environments, personal health practices, individual capacity and coping skills, human biology, early childhood development and health services."[296] Under this view, all aspects of society,

---

[294] The IOM report (2003) was jointly sponsored by six Department of Health and Human Services agencies: the Centers for Disease Control and Prevention; the National Institutes of Health; the Health Resources and Services Administration; the Substance Abuse and Mental Health Service Administration; the Department of Health and Human Services Office of the Secretary, Assistant Secretary for Planning and Evaluation; and the HHS Office of Disease Prevention and Health Promotion.

[295] Committee on Assuring the Health of the Public in the 21st Century, Institute of Medicine, *The Future of the Public's Health in the 21st Century: Report Brief* (Washington, D.C.: National Academies Press, 2002), 1.

[296] Ibid., note 1.

including the built environment,[297] social conditions,[298] and economic opportunity, are *determinants* of health and thus within the scope of "the public health.[299] In other words, every aspect of human existence lay within the scope of public health and therefore would be fair game for government meddling.

Citing the growing, seemingly valid, body of research, the 2003 report focused on five conditions (previously identified in yet another IOM report called *Health and Behavior* — note how these biased reports all build on each other) which were found to both "surpass and powerfully interact with 'downstream' elements such as individual behaviors, biological traits, and access to health care services":[300] (1) socioeconomic position, (2) race and ethnicity, (3) social networks and social support, (4) work conditions, and (5) ecological-level influences (economic inequality and social capital).[301] The 2003 report suggested that this more expansive perspective of health required the public-health system to take into account the potential effects of "social connectedness, economic inequality, social norms, and public policies on health-related behaviors and on health

---

[297] The built environment includes transportation, water and sanitation, housing, and other dimensions of urban planning.

[298] Social conditions include, among others, economic inequality, urbanization, mobility, and cultural values, attitudes, and policies related to discrimination and intolerance on the basis of race, gender, and other differences.

[299] Committee on Assuring the Health of the Public in the 21st Century, *The Future of the Public's Health in the 21st Century*, 2.

[300] Committee for the Study of the Future of Public Health, Institute of Medicine, *The Future of Public Health in the 21st Century* (Washington, D.C.: National Academy of Sciences, 2003): 71.

[301] Ibid., 57.

status."[302] While personal health-care services address disease prevention on an individual basis, the government should engage in population-based interventions, including policies that support education, adequate housing, a living wage, and clean air or that attempt to deal with some of the pervasive social and economic inequities that appear to be associated with profound disparities in health status, access, and outcomes.[303] The committee found that, because assuring the conditions that support population health is an important social and political undertaking, "the government and its partners must be committed to a broad array of activities in order to change the conditions for health."[304]

The IOM view of "public health" is so broad as to be arbitrary. It provides no practical limit on what government can lay claim to in the name of public health.

In their report, HHS officials DeSalvo and O'Carroll acknowledge the influence of earlier IOM reports in propelling these social and economic determinants to the forefront of public policy, and they call for action to shift the public-health system into the next era. That "next era" would lead to the creation of communities that "by their nature, promote the public's health and wellness." This expansive control would be necessary to "develop and embrace dramatically enhanced, community-wide approaches to assuring the conditions in which all people can be healthy."[305] No longer would these bureaucrats simply be the "directors of the

---

[302] Committee on Assuring the Health of the Public in the 21st Century, *The Future of the Public's Health in the 21st Century*, 2.
[303] Ibid., 2–3.
[304] Ibid.
[305] DeSalvo et al., "Public Health 3.0," 622.

public health agencies," but rather "chief health strategists" for the entire community, capable of "mobilizing community action to affect health determinants beyond the direct reach of their agencies."[306]

Further evidence of the cascading amplification of the 1988 report can be seen in its use by other agencies to justify new federal regulations and programs. Specifically, the Partnership for Sustainable Communities, as will be discussed later, has required the development of sustainable communities as criteria for Department of Transportation, Housing and Urban Development, and Environmental Protection Agency grants. Under the guise of promoting public health, these grants require the inclusion of "livability" principles in state and local government land-use and transportation plans and zoning ordinances. These federal agencies have linked certain urban-planning elements (public transportation, transit-oriented developments, and so forth) with a wide spectrum of public and individual health issues, such as asthma, cancer, obesity, mental health, substance abuse, crime exposure, cardiovascular disease, and social and health inequity.[307] An underlying theory of this research is that suburban sprawl has led to an increased dependence on automobiles and less use of public transit, bicycling, and walking, all of which contribute to increased pollution and less physical activity by individuals.[308] Despite the absence of medical research directly relating the adoption of "livability" principles

---

[306] Ibid.

[307] National Association of County and City Health Officials, *Statement of Policy: Healthy Community Design*, September 9, 2003, http://www.naccho.org/.

[308] Ibid.

to improved health, the vast body of literature spawned by the IOM report assumes it to be true. Thus does one biased federal report pave the way for an extraordinary expansion of federal power, to the detriment of the constitutional structure.

Chapter 6

Federally Funded Research: Shaping Curricula

We all want progress. But progress means getting to the place where you want to be. And if you have taken a wrong turning, then to go forward does not get you any nearer. If you are on the wrong road, progress means doing an about-turn and walking back to the right road; and in that case the man who turns back soonest is the most progressive man.

—C. S. Lewis, *Mere Christianity*

In debates about local control over education, the use of federally funded education research to influence educational policy-setting at the state and local level gets little attention. Yet over the last fifty years, the National Science Foundation (NSF) has been the main federal agency responsible for education research funding, including grants for the development of national math and science standards, curriculum, assessments, and teacher-education programs. The amount of funding the NSF has received from Congress to conduct this research is substantial — $19.8 billion from 1992 to 2016[309] — and its policy-shaping influence has eviscerated state and local control of education.

[309] "NSF Requests and Appropriations History," Budget Internet Information System, https://dellweb.bfa.nsf.gov/.

Deconstructing the Administrative State

During the highly controversial adoption of the Common Core Standards for mathematics and English, claims made by the U.S. Department of Education (USED) and state education officials that the standards were "rigorous" and "research-and evidence-based" puzzled opponents of the standards. In light of independent reports[310] from mathematicians and English language arts experts criticizing the standards' slowed-down academic progression and inclusion of progressive instructional methods, they questioned the research base upon which these officials could make such claims.

[310] For further discussion on the deficiencies of the Common Core Standards, see: Sandra Stotsky and Ze'ev Wurman, *Common Core Standards Still Don't Make the Grade* (Pioneer Institute white paper no. 65, July 2010), http://pioneerinstitute.org/; Mark Bauerlein and Sandra Stotsky, *How Common Core's ELA Standards Place College Readiness at Risk* (Pioneer Institute white paper no. 89, September 2012), http://pioneerinstitute.org/; Prof. Sandra Stotsky, "Common Core Standards' Devastating Impact on Literary Study and Analytical Thinking," Heritage Foundation issue brief, December 11, 2012), http://www.heritage.org/; R. James Milgram and Sandra Stotsky, *Lowering the Bar: How Common Core Math Fails to Prepare High School Students for STEM* (Pioneer Institute white paper no. 103, September 2013), http://pioneerinstitute.org/; Ze'ev Wurman, *Why Students Need Strong Standards (and Not Common Core)* (Washington, D.C.: American Principles Project, 2014), https://americanprinciplesproject.org/; Prof. Anthony Esolen, "How Common Core Devalues Great Literature," *Crisis Magazine*, February 6, 2014; Prof. Marina Ratner, "Making Math Education Even Worse," *Wall Street Journal*, August 5, 2014); Barry Garelick, "Drilling 'Rote Understanding,'" Truth in American Education, July 5, 2017, https://truthinamericaneducation.com; Erin Tuttle and James Wilson, *Common Core Does Not Equal Excellent* (Washington, D.C.: American Principles Project Foundation, 2016), https://americanprinciplesproject.org.

Federally Funded Research: Shaping Curricula

As this chapter will show, the same stranglehold progressive education has over schools of education and the educational establishment dominates federal education research programs and has negatively affected the research base upon which educational decisions are made. Even though such research produces one failed educational program after another, the NSF's education research funding is provided almost exclusively for research programs that advance progressive methods.

As discussed earlier, the NSF was founded with lofty goals of promoting science and advancing national health, prosperity, welfare, and defense. But as with many federal agencies, the NSF has fallen prey to "mission creep," assuming the authority to fund and develop projects that fall outside those intended by its authorizing legislation.

In the area of education research, the "creep" at the NSF has been expansive. For purposes of maintaining a competitive scientific workforce, the authorizing legislation established programs to fund science, technology, engineering, and math (STEM) education, but those were limited to providing university students with fellowships and grants to expand the pipeline of future scientists. Today, that authority has been extended to include NSF programs concerning all aspects of education at every grade level, including research on learning initiatives for children as young as three. For example, the NSF awarded more than $1 million for a grant to early-childhood educators to monitor children ages three through five playing outdoors to determine, among other things, whether they acquired environmentally responsible behaviors.[311] The relevance of this

---

[311] See Dawn Fuller, "UC's Arlitt Center Awarded $1.6 Million NSF Grant to Advance Preschool Learning in Outdoor PlayScapes,"

grant, and many like it, to the intended mission of the NSF is tenuous at best.[312]

University of Cincinnati website, February 9, 2016, http://www.
uc.edu/news/NR.aspx?id=22845.

[312] In 2011, the NSF awarded a $330,124 grant to the University of Cincinnati Arlitt Child and Family Research and Education Center to study an outdoor preschool program called PlayScapes to monitor: (1) children's behavior and movement patterns in the PlayScapes, (2) children's scientific thinking that may occur during play, and (3) how the PlayScapes may fuel children's interest in science. Any parent or teacher could easily explain the benefit of outdoor play for preschool children to these researchers for free. However, there was another angle the researchers were looking to ascertain: whether the program would "condition the children to develop environmental science literacy, which in turn is likely to strengthen a child's ecological identity and lead to environmentally responsible behaviors (ERBs)." The researchers published their findings in a report titled "Can Playscapes Promote Early Childhood Inquiry towards Environmentally Responsible Behaviors?" The report concluded that although the study lacked a proper control group, "our data provide initial support for our hypothesis that natural environments promote explorations and inquiry, fostering ERBs." This questionable finding was enough evidence for the NSF to award another grant for $1,116,905 to expand the PlayScapes program to three other preschool programs, including two Head Start programs in the Cincinnati area. See: R. Alan Wight, Heidi Kloos, Catherine V. Maltbie, and Victoria W. Carr. "Can Playscapes Promote Early Childhood Inquiry towards Environmentally Responsible Behaviors? An Exploratory Study," *Environmental Education Research* 22, no. 4 (March, 2015) doi: 10.1080/13504622.2015.1015495.

How We Got Here

Although the National Science Foundation Act of 1950 authorized and directed the NSF "to develop and encourage the pursuit of a national policy for the promotion of basic research and education in the sciences,"[313] it is unlikely that Congress intended, or ever imagined, that the NSF's role would expand to the funding of math- and science-education programs for students and their teachers in grades pre-K through 12. In fact, the original act doesn't mention K–12 education, only authorizing an education program concerned with "scholarships and graduate fellowships" at the university level.[314]

After the Soviet launching of Sputnik, fears surfaced that the United States lacked the scientific workforce to compete internationally. To increase the number of future scientists, the NSF shifted some of its resources from programs supporting university-level science and engineering students to improving the pool from which these future scientists and engineers would be drawn. It established programs intended to enhance the knowledge and skills of those teaching these future scientists at the secondary level and to improve the curriculum of such instruction in secondary schools.

When Congress passed the NSF Authorization Act of 1973, it amended the original statute to include "science education programs at all levels":

> The Foundation is authorized and directed ... to initiate and support basic scientific research and programs to strengthen scientific research potential and *science*

---

[313] The National Science Foundation Act of 1950, § 3(a)(1).
[314] Ibid., § 3(a)(4) and § 10.

education programs at all levels in the mathematical, physical, medical, biological, engineering, social, and other sciences.[315]

Since that time, the NSF has interpreted the language "at all levels" very broadly. The NSF's interpretation now encompasses pre-K through 12, community colleges, and universities, and even extends to informal settings such as museums, parks, and community centers.

The NSF's Authority, Mission, and Structure

The leadership of the NSF consists of a director, who oversees staff and agency programs, and a twenty-four-member (plus the director, who sits *ex officio*) National Science Board, which establishes the overall policies of the NSF within the framework of national policies set by Congress and the president. In addition, the board serves as an "independent body of advisors to both the President and the Congress," and together with the Director, recommends and encourages the "pursuit of national policies for the promotion of research and education in science and engineering."[316] The director and board members, who serve six-year terms, are appointed by the president and confirmed by the Senate.[317]

The NSF divides its non-administrative activities among seven "directorates": biological sciences; computer and information science and engineering; engineering; geosciences; mathematical

---

[315] PL 92-373 at https://www.gpo.gov/fdsys/pkg/STATUTE-86/pdf/STATUTE-86-Pg528-2.pdf, emphasis added.

[316] See "Background," National Science Board website, https://www.nsf.gov/nsb/about/index.jsp.

[317] See "Who We Are," National Science Foundation website, https://www.nsf.gov/about/who.jsp.

and physical sciences; social, behavioral, and economic sciences; and education and human resources. Each is headed by an assistant director and is further subdivided into divisions.[318]

The NSF doesn't conduct research internally or operate its own laboratories. Rather, it supports the research of scientists, engineers, and educators directly through their home institutions. The NSF's total budget in 2016 was $7.45 billion, which, excluding administrative costs ($349 million),[319] was distributed via grants (74 percent); cooperative agreements (21 percent); and contracts (5 percent). It distributed these funds to more than 2,000 colleges, universities, and academic consortia (78 percent); private industry (14 percent); federally funded research-and-development centers (3 percent); and other (6 percent). In monetary terms, colleges, universities, and academic consortia received $5.5 billion.[320]

How Grant Recipients Are Selected

Every year, the NSF receives about 50,000 proposals from researchers, educational institutions, nonprofits, and others. The assistant director of each directorate selects which proposals will be evaluated for funding, a process that is conducted by NSF-selected "experts." Although the NSF claims that the proposals are reviewed in a "fair, competitive, transparent, and in-depth manner," the identity of the experts who select the proposals for

[318] See the NSF staff organizational chart: http://www.nsf.gov/staff/organizational_chart.pdf.

[319] This amount represents $330 million for administration, $4.3 million for the National Science Board, and $15 million for the Office of the Inspector General.

[320] FY 2017 NSF Budget Summary Brochure, National Science Foundation website, https://www.nsf.gov/.

funding is never disclosed to either the applicants or the public, leaving their qualifications and possible biases unknown to those outside NSF management.[321] This process can lead to research slanted by a funding-induced bias, because the agency may select only reviewers who support its established paradigm, mission, or other funding interest.[322]

Also troubling is the NSF's policy concerning grant reviewers' conflicts of interests. That policy allows the NSF to issue a waiver to allow a reviewer to have a financial interest in the outcome of a proposal. The NSF can also issue a waiver for a reviewer of, for example, grants in which family members, business partners, or employers have a financial interest in the outcome.[323] This policy is particularly troublesome given the NSF's lack of transparency regarding the identity of grant reviewers.

The NSF protects the identity of grant reviewers even from members of Congress. This includes having redacted the names of reviewers from documents produced pursuant to a request by a House of Representatives committee examining NSF grants for fraud and waste.[324] In 1996, an unsuccessful applicant filed a federal-court challenge to this policy.[325] The plaintiff sought

---

[321] "NSF-51: Reviewer Proposal File and Associated Records," National Science Foundation website, https://www.nsf.gov/.

[322] Wojick and Michaels, *Is the Government Buying Science or Support?*, 32–33.

[323] National Science Foundation, *Proposal and Award Policies and Procedures Guide* (Washington, D.C.: National Science Foundation 2017), 55, https://www.nsf.gov/.

[324] Jeffrey Mervis, "Battle between NSF and House Science Committee Escalates: How Did It Get This Bad?" *Science*, October 2, 2014, http://www.sciencemag.org/.

[325] In 1996, a rejected grant applicant sued the NSF in the U.S. District Court for the District of Columbia (*Henke vs. the*

the identities of the reviewers to examine a possible conflict of interest in the selection process. The court, however, upheld the NSF privacy policy under the Privacy Act.

Shaping Education Through the NSF Division of Education and Human Resources

The NSF considers itself "the primary federal agency supporting research ... across all fields of science and engineering and at all levels of science and engineering education."[326] Since 1990 the NSF has centered its education spending in the Directorate for Education and Human Resources (EHR), which supports "bold programs and innovative projects that lead to impact by meeting the needs of students, teachers, researchers, and the public." EHR's mission is stated on its website:

> The mission of EHR is to achieve excellence in U.S. science, technology, engineering and mathematics (STEM) education at all levels and in all settings (both formal and informal) in order to support the development of a diverse and well-prepared workforce of scientists, technicians, engineers, mathematicians and educators and a

---

Commerce Department and National Science Foundation), claiming the policy of keeping reviewers' names confidential masked a possible conflict of interest that resulted in the rejection of his grant. However, the court upheld the NSF privacy policy under the Privacy Act.

[326] NSF Advisory Committee for Education and Human Resources, *Strategic Re-envisioning for the Education and Human Resources Directorate* (Washington, D.C.: National Science Foundation, 2014), 3, https://www.nsf.gov/.

well-informed citizenry that have access to the ideas and tools of science and engineering. The purpose of these activities is to enhance the quality of life of all citizens and the health, prosperity, welfare and security of the nation.[327]

The NSF as an overall science agency has significantly contributed to progress in the hard sciences, including funding 169 Nobel laureates in chemistry (58), physics (65), and medicine (46).[328] The agency claims that its education research projects have been similarly beneficial — "fuel[ing] many important innovations that in turn have stimulated economic growth and improved the quality of life and health for all Americans."[329] But despite these claims of success, the NSF and the U.S. Department of Education have been forced to acknowledge the declining competitiveness of U.S. students on international math and science tests over the past decades (often using such acknowledgment to argue for new federal education programs).

The ineffectiveness of the NSF's education programs can't be attributed to lack of financial support. Since 1980, NSF funding has increased more than tenfold for EHR programs (from $82 million in 1980 to $878 million in 2016).[330] Once a small portion

---

[327] See "About Education and Human Resources (EHR)," National Science Foundation, https://www.nsf.gov/ehr/about.jsp.

[328] See "NSF-Funded Nobel Prize Winners in Science through 2016," National Science Foundation, https://www.nsf.gov/news/news_summ.jsp?cntn_id=100683.

[329] NSF Advisory Committee, *Strategic Re-envisioning*, 3.

[330] "EHR Funding," National Science Foundation, https://dellweb.bfa.nsf.gov/NSFRqstAppropHist/NSFRequestsandAppropriationsHistory.pdf.

NSF spending per program
(2017 proposed budget)

U.S. Arctic Research Commission (USARC)	$1,400,000.00
National Science Board (NSB)	$4,400,000.00
Office of Inspector General (OIG)	$15,200,000.00
Office of Int'l. Science and Eng. (OISE)	$52,100,000.00
Major Res. Equip. & Facility Cnst. (MREFC)	$193,100,000.00
Social, Behavioral, & Econ. Sciences (SBE)	$288,800,000.00
Agency Ops. & Award Mgmt. (AOAM)	$373,000,000.00
Int'l. & Integrative Activities (IIA)	$459,900,000.00
Biological Sciences (BIO)	$790,500,000.00
Education and Human Resources (EHR)	$952,900,000.00
Computer and Info. Science & Eng. (CISE)	$994,800,000.00
Engineering (ENG)	$1,002,700,000.00
Geosciences (GEO)	$1,398,000,000.00
Mathematics and Physical Sciences (MPS)	$1,436,500,000.00

of its research portfolio, educational research is now on equal footing with many of the hard sciences.[331]

In 2016, Congress appropriated $880 million for EHR. Of this amount, $673 million is allocated at the discretion of the NSF director and board. A subcommittee of the board, the Committee on Education and Human Resources, makes recommendations to the full board for consideration and action on the overall strategy for EHR grants.

According to the board's website, this committee "provides guidance and advice on major policy issues related to the NSF Education and Training portfolio, and reviews proposals representing a significant expenditure of agency resources. It also provides advice on major national policy issues in education and human-resource development. The committee makes informal

---

[331] *NSF FY 2017 Budget Request to Congress*, National Science Foundation website, 1, https://www.nsf.gov/.

recommendations, as appropriate, for the board's full consideration and action."[332]

EHR is organized into four separately funded divisions: Graduate Education, Human Resource Development, Undergraduate Education, and Research on Learning in Formal and Informal Settings. According to the NSF website, EHR funds more than 160,000 researchers, teachers, and graduate students through roughly 900 merit-based awards each year. The grant portfolio administered by EHR is so extensive that it includes universities, nonprofits, textbook developers, state departments of education, local school districts, individual schools, and dozens of professional trade associations. Because these grants are often awarded over multiple years, the total number of "active" grants managed by EHR varies. In February of 2017, the NSF grant database reflected 4,513 "active" EHR grants, with total funding at $5.4 billion.[333]

EHR and Progressive Education: The Established Paradigm of Thought in Federal Education Programs

EHR requests for grant proposals almost uniformly include conditions requiring that progressive educational methods form the underlying assumptions of proposals. As with all NSF grants, EHR begins the award process by issuing a solicitation for grant proposals. The solicitation works like a Request for Proposals (RFP), in which the requirements for grant selection are

---

[332] "*Ad Hoc* Committee for the Vannevar Bush Award," National Science Foundation website, https://www.nsf.gov/nsb/committees/archive/ehrcmte.jsp.

[333] "Awardee Information," NSF Award Search: Advanced Search. https://www.nsf.gov/awardsearch/advancedSearch.jsp.

specified; any grant proposal that doesn't meet these conditions is automatically rejected by NSF "experts." Because these solicitations specify the scientific questions deemed by the NSF to be worthy of answering, the proposals themselves impose NSF biases on researchers. As with the global-climate-change research grants discussed earlier, EHR grant solicitations, including those from EHR's Division of Research on Learning (DRL), include assumptions that progressive educational methods will be used.

To review, progressive education advances minimal teacher instruction or guidance in the classroom; the teacher is the "guide on the side," providing the student with activities and hands-on experiences (experiential learning) in which the student "constructs" his own understanding of the material (constructivism). In contrast, traditional education focuses on direct instruction or guided instruction, in which (in math, for example) the teacher formally explains the concept and solutions to the students before they attempt to solve problems. Progressive educational philosophy has been the accepted scientific paradigm of thought around which EHR grants are structured; it shapes the assumptions of the grants and dictates what the results of that research must look like.

EHR awards are generally limited to proposals that require learning through constructivism, inquiry-based learning, problem-based learning, discovery learning, and experiential learning. A search of the NSF grant database[334] comparing awards containing these terms versus those associated with traditional

[334] Active and expired EHR grants from the NSF grant database were searched for the terms using parentheses around the search term. Accessed at https://www.nsf.gov/awardsearch/.

education (direct instruction, guided instruction) confirms a one-sided, biased approach favoring progressive methods. The chart below shows such a comparison, with start dates from the late 1980s through early 2017. While a more exhaustive search of these grants should be conducted to eliminate possible duplicates, the bias reflected in EHR grants toward progressive educational methods is unmistakable.

Progressive Education			Traditional Education		
Search Term	Awards	Total Award Amount	Search Term	Awards	Total Award Amount
Constructivism	227	$138 million	Direct instruction	9	$5.6 million
Inquiry based	447	$261 million	Guided instruction	15	$16.5 million
Problem based	359	$247 million			
Project based	1,853	$1.4 billion			
Experiential learning	3,001	$1.9 billion			
Student centered	305	$224 million			

While the education establishment has formed rhetorical consensus on the superiority of progressive educational methods, there is little scientific evidence to support that consensus. In fact, the current knowledge of human cognitive architecture—the memory structures of the brain (short-term and long-term memory), which are fundamental to how learners think, learn, and solve problems—establishes quite the opposite. This research shows that students learn best through direct instruction, in which they are given information that fully explains the concept and procedures required to be learned.[335]

As reported in *Educational Psychologist*, it's easy to understand why progressive, minimal-guidance methods of education fail to address current research on how the brain processes and stores information: they were developed prior to the current understanding of the structures and relations that constitute human cognitive architecture:

> We now are in a quite different environment because we know much more about the structures, functions, and characteristics of working and long-term memory; the relations between them; and their consequences for learning and problem solving. This new understanding [of the benefits of direct instruction] has been the basis for systematic research and development of instructional theories that reflect our current understanding of cognitive architecture. This work should be central to the design of effective, guided instruction.[336]

[335] P. A. Kirschner, J. Sweller, and R. E. Clark, "Why Minimal Guidance during Instruction Does Not Work: An Analysis of the Failure of Constructivist, Discovery, Problem-Based, Experiential, and Inquiry-Based Teaching," *Educational Psychologist* 41, no. 2 (2006): 75–86, http://cepa.info/3773.
[336] Ibid.

Deconstructing the Administrative State

It's disturbing that EHR—an organization dedicated to supporting "the science of learning"—continues to advocate learning processes that ignore current research on the functions and characteristics of the brain's learning structures, the relationships between these areas, and their consequences for learning and problem-solving.[337] But EHR need not deliver products that work, because it's sheltered from the checks and balances built into the constitutional structure as well as from the forces of a competitive marketplace, in which ineffective products are rightly recognized as obsolete or defective. To keep its preferred programs and policies in use, EHR merely has to keep funding them—and to support federal programs that require states to keep using them. It's a simple, elegant, and highly effective racket.

Progressive Indoctrination Through
EHR's Division of Research on Learning

EHR grants are designed to do more than generate research on education and learning—they provide funding to pilot and implement EHR research programs in U.S. schools. EHR begins the grant process by soliciting proposals for research to develop various educational programs. It then awards grants to educational organizations to pilot such research programs in schools. Finally, it awards grants to implement the program on a large scale. All of this rests on prudential decision-making—in terms of selecting projects and the quality of the resulting products—that takes place largely outside the normal public federal and state processes.

To illustrate the relationship between K–12 education and EHR grants, we'll focus on its Division of Research on Learning in Formal and Informal Settings (DRL). In the larger context

[337] See ibid.

of federal support for education research, the NSF views the DRL as "a catalyst for change" to improve STEM education "at all levels." The NSF claims to accomplish this by challenging researchers in the field "to create the ideas, resources, and human capacity to bring about the needed transformation of STEM education for the 21st century."[338]

One of the DRL's recent solicitations (for 2015 and 2016) allotted $100 million for grants to develop STEM learning, STEM teaching, or STEM assessment models for use by the nation's teachers, schools, districts, and states.[339] Specifically, the DRL solicitation "encourages" grants that can be implemented in current classrooms, schools, and other environments for pre-K–12 students. Proposals must fall into one of five stages: (1) an "exploratory" study, in which researchers investigate "approaches to STEM education problems that establish a basis for the design and development of STEM education innovations or approaches" and create a "theory of action," (2) proposals that build on a theory of action to develop a "proof of concept that one can develop STEM education innovations or approaches," (3) impact studies of previous studies, (4) research to build the capacity of school districts or communities of schools to implement the education innovation or approach on a large scale, and (5) conferences and synthesis proposals to disseminate the findings and recommendations generated by the research.[340]

---

[338] "Research on Learning in Formal and Informal Settings (DRL)," National Science Foundation, https://www.nsf.gov/ehr/drl/about.jsp.

[339] *Discovery Research PreK–12 (DRK–12)* (program solicitation), National Science Foundation, https://www.nsf.gov/pubs/2015/nsf15592/nsf15592.htm.

[340] Ibid.

The research is thus structured to develop STEM educational products and implement them on a large scale throughout the nation's pre-K–12 and teacher-education systems. The intent of these grants is not to simply inform the field of textbook publishers, curriculum directors, school administrators, and so forth about effective science curriculum and testing; rather, it's to ensure the implementation of these federally funded curricula, assessments, and teacher-training programs in the U.S. education system.

The solicitation requires that the proposed models for "STEM learning" respond to the need "for effective implementation of the new *college-and-career-readiness standards* that provide all students with opportunities to learn recommended concepts and practices."[341] This limits researchers to designing products that align to the Common Core State Standards for Mathematics (CCSS-M) and the Next Generation Science Standards (NGSS). Structuring the grant solicitation around a specific set of standards precludes programs aligned to alternative, and perhaps superior, standards.

The DRL STEM assessment grant solicitation also requires the prospective grantee to align his proposal with "college-and-career-readiness standards" to measure students' knowledge of core STEM disciplinary ideas as well as students' "affective constructs, such as engagement, persistence, values and attitudes towards STEM disciplines."[342] Parents might question whether government schools should be delving into such socioemotional realms rather than teaching their children academic content, but as we have seen, progressives believe that is exactly what government schools should be doing. Moreover, the proposals are encouraged to measure students' learning and "other

[341] Ibid., emphasis added.
[342] Ibid.

outcomes" in ways that are "embedded within cyber-enabled learning environments, including virtual environments, on-line classes, simulations, and games."[343] Apparently, the current body of research[344] indicating that digital learning doesn't increase and may even decrease student achievement, especially for disadvantaged students, wasn't sufficient to dissuade the NSF from pursuing this method of "education."

An aspect of this scheme that usually goes unmentioned is the experimentation conducted on students during this research. While the recipients of these grants, primarily faculty at university schools of education and school-district administrators, are certainly aware of this practice, members of Congress may not be. They may not fully understand that by funding EHR and its attendant programs, they are authorizing federal funding for the use of students and teachers as guinea pigs — in many instances, without their consent or knowledge. While the NSF's general policy states that any research involving human subjects must comply with the federal government's "Common Rule" for the protection of human subjects, many NSF education grants are exempt from the rule. The NSF's policy regarding research using "observational or ethnographic methods, cognitive and educational tests, etc." is exempt from consent requirements unless two

---

[343] Ibid.

[344] See Alan C. K. Cheung and Robert E. Slavin, "The Effectiveness of Educational Technology Applications for Enhancing Mathematics Achievement in K–12 Classrooms: A Meta-Analysis," *Educational Research Review* 9 (June 2013): 88–113, http://www.sciencedirect.com/; and James A. Kulik and J. D. Fletcher, "Effectiveness of Intelligent Tutoring Systems: A Meta-Analytic Review," *Review of Educational Research* 86, no. 1 (March 2016): 42–78, http://rer.sagepub.com/content/86/1/42.abstract.

factors are present: "(1) The information would allow subjects to be identified, and (2) Disclosure of the data would reasonably place the subject at risk of harm."[345]

Not only can this research be conducted without institutional review and participants' consent, but many of these grants are for multiple years, which could place students in an experimental curriculum or pedagogy for the entire span of elementary, middle, or high school. This puts children in precarious circumstances if the program turns out to be ineffective or even harmful. Ineffective instruction for such a period could inflict irreversible harm on students' education and negatively affect their prospects for college or future careers.

Would members of Congress want their own children subjected to such a practice? Would anyone? If parents were to object, what options would they have outside of private school or homeschooling if the entire school district is participating in the study? Moreover, NSF-funded research projects, designed to satisfy federally established criteria, are driving fundamental aspects of education policy that should be controlled locally, where the decision-making is closest to parents.

This grant scheme not only uses children as subjects for experiments but probably violates the spirit, if not the letter, of federal statutes prohibiting the federal government from developing or funding curricula, academic standards, or a national assessment (with the exception of the National Assessment of Educational Progress, or NAEP).[346]

---

[345] "Human Subjects," National Science Foundation website, https://www.nsf.gov/.

[346] See 20 USC § 1232(a); Robert S. Eitel and Kent D. Talbert, *The Road to a National Curriculum: The Legal Aspects of the Common Core Standards, Race to the Top, and Conditional Wavers* (Pioneer

Federally Funded Research: Shaping Curricula

Once EHR establishes an instructional program, that program may become immortal—despite lack of any evidence proving its effectiveness. An example of this dynamic is the Connected Mathematics Project. In 1985, the DRL awarded a grant to researchers at Michigan State University to develop an "innovative new curriculum known as *Middle Grades Mathematics Project* (MGMP) materials."[347] The grant funded the development of five curricula units for use by teachers to help transition from "how they typically taught, 'show and practice,' to classrooms that required engagement in mathematical thinking, reasoning, solving, and proving."[348] In other words, it switched teaching from direct instruction (the traditional way of teaching, in which the teacher explains how to solve math problems using the standard algorithm) to a student-centered approach (the progressive, Dewey method, by which students explore a variety of ways to solve computations).

Six years later, the DRL followed up on the MGMP with another grant to Michigan State researchers, this one worth $4.8 million, to develop a "three-year mathematics curriculum for middle school grades" called the Connected Mathematics Program (CMP), based on the MGMP units. Once that grant was completed, the DRL funded additional grants to various institutions to implement the CMP in school districts, including $23 million in grants to train thousands of teachers to teach the CMP.[349]

Institute white paper no. 81, February 2012), http://pioneer-institute.org.

[347] See "MSU Research History: A New Way to Teach Math," Michigan State University website, https://msu.edu/.

[348] See "History of CMP," Connected Mathematics Project, https://connectedmath.msu.edu/about/history-of-cmp/.

[349] $5M to develop, field-test, evaluate, and disseminate CMP to MSU, NSF award no. 9150217; $5M to develop, field-test,

The CMP's curriculum was representative of other math programs funded by the DRL at the time. These programs were intended to shift math instruction away from "doing things the 'right' way to get the 'right' answer"[350] to focus on "inquiry-based, problem-oriented curricula," in which "students become participants in discovery by using fact-based knowledge to think through open-ended problems in a variety of ways."[351]

The use of the CMP in American schools has been extensive. Various editions of the "CMP were used from 1991 to 1997 and from 2000 to 2006 by approximately 390 teachers and 45,000

---

evaluate, and disseminate CMP to MSU, award no. 9619033; $5M for Austin ISD to conduct training for 2,400 K–8 teachers, including CMP, NSF award no. 9619033; $1M for NC to train 378 K–8 teachers in CMP, NSF award no. 9618957; $1M for NC to train 378 K–8 teachers in CMP; $3.5M for NY to train 1,200 teachers, NSF award no. 9731424; $3.5M for NY to train 1,200 teachers, award no. 9730139; $1.25M CD-ROM and CMP in CA, award no. 9619043; $2M to IN for teacher enhancement and curricula implementation, NSF award no. 9619043; $50K for AZ teacher enhancement; $2.85M to MSU to prepare 360 teachers at 10 sites to implement CMP, NSF award no. 9355542; $450K to NY for training 48 teachers, NSF award no. 9553579; $50K to Tufts University to develop two plans: research and education plans geared to providing Connected Mathematics experiences for students from middle school through graduate school; $500K to TSSI for teacher training, NSF award no. 975342; $6M for Showme Center to facilitate and support implementation of CMP, NSF award #9714999. NSF Award Search: Advanced Search. https://www.nsf.gov/awardsearch/advancedSearch.jsp.

[350] National Science Foundation (NSF), *America's Investment in the Future* (Arlington, Va.: National Science Foundation, 2003), 36, https://www.nsf.gov/about/history/nsf0050/index.jsp.

[351] Ibid.

students across the United States. As of September 2004, the program had been implemented in 2,462 school districts, covering all 50 states."[352]

One would hope that such use of the CMP was based on solid research. Yet a report published by the Institute of Education Sciences (IES) found otherwise. Although the NSF and other groups did conduct seventy-nine "studies" of the CMP, the IES report showed those studies to be flawed. None of the seventy-nine met the evidence standards or eligibility screens used by the What Works Clearinghouse,[353] except one that met those standards "with reservations." That one study found "no discernible effects on math achievement."[354]

Despite its failure to improve student math achievement, the CMP is used in almost 30 percent of the nation's middle schools. It's now distributed by Pearson educational publishing company, which describes the program on the company's website as based on a progressive, inquiry-based approach, aligned to the Common Core:

> *Connected Mathematics Project 3*, or CMP3, is an inquiry-based mathematics program for Grades 6–8.... Funded in

[352] *Connected Mathematics Project (CMP)* (Washington, D.C.: What Works Clearinghouse, 2010), 2, https://ies.ed.gov/ncee/wwc/Docs/InterventionReports/wwc_cmp_012610.pdf.

[353] According to the IES website: "The What Works Clearinghouse is an investment of the Institute of Education Sciences (IES) within the U.S. Department of Education that was established in 2002. The work of the WWC is managed by a team of staff at IES and conducted under a set of contracts held by several leading firms with expertise in education, research methodology, and the dissemination of education research." "Who We Are," Institute of Education Sciences website, https://ies.ed.gov/ncee/wwc/WhoWeAre.

[354] *Connected Mathematics Project*, 3.

part by the National Science Foundation, and developed through Michigan State University, CMP3 provides a powerful inquiry model for learning mathematics.

So, the federal government not only funded curricula but funded curricula that pushed a particular — discredited — educational product.[355]

How Federally Commissioned Reports Shape State and Local Education Policy

George DeBoer, a former program director at EHR and leading contributor to the National Science Education Standards (the precursor to the NGSS, which will be discussed later) writes that the development of the NSF science curricula during the 1950s and 1960s was intended to combat the increased use of progressive educational methods.[356] The NSF curricula aimed to replace the content-light, student-centered curricula with one centered on the scientific disciplines and traditional education methods.[357] DeBoer claims that these NSF curricula, written by scientists with subject-matter expertise, were considered "pedagogically unwise" by science educators:

---

[355] "Pearson CMP3 Math Program for Grades 6–8," Pearson website, http://www.pearsonschool.com/.

[356] George DeBoer. "What We Have Learned and Where We Are Headed: Lessons from the Sputnik Era" (paper presented at the Reflecting on Sputnik Symposium: Linking the Past, Present, and Future of Educational Reform, National Academy of Sciences, Washington, D.C., October 1997), http://www.nas.edu/sputnik/deboer1.htm.

[357] Ibid.

This emphasis on disciplinary knowledge, separated from its everyday applications and intended to meet a perceived national need, marked a significant shift in science education in the post-war years.... But by the 1970s most science educators realized that it was pedagogically unwise to focus so heavily on the structure of the disciplines at the expense of the interests and developmental needs of learners.[358]

By the 1970s the NSF education programs had become dominated by progressives, who revamped the science curricula according to their ideology.

Instead of centering on scientific content, the new models were based on the interests of students and society to include "issues of personal and community health, the significance of rapid population growth, and the many factors affecting environmental quality."[359] Where the earlier NSF science curricula were designed to "produce students capable of pursuing a career or degree in the field of science," those of the 1970s through the early 1980s focused on "the broad spectrum of elementary and secondary students, with a special emphasis on the special needs of minorities, women, and the physically handicapped." Sound altruistic and caring? The report continued, "This is especially important for students in the middle and junior high schools. These curriculum materials could focus on the science

---

[358] George E. DeBoer "Scientific Literacy: Another Look at Its Historical and Contemporary Meanings and Its Relationship to Science Education Reform," *Journal of Research in Science Teaching* 37, no. 6 (August 2000): 588.
[359] DeBoer, "What We Have Learned."

and technology basis of essential national problems such as energy, natural resources, and health."[360]

Objections to the new NSF curricula led Congress to reduce federal funding substantially for NSF education programs during the early 1980s. The efforts of progressives at the NSF were derailed, and the NSF found itself on the sidelines of science and math education. But if there is one eternal truth demonstrated by this book, it is that progressives never give up. In 1983 a federal education commission released *A Nation at Risk*, and the NSF, once again, became actively involved in developing math and science programs. According to a 2003 NSF report, *A Nation at Risk* "triggered fresh calls for the setting of national or at least state-level education standards and sent NSF back into the K–12 education arena with a renewed vigor."[361]

A Nation at Risk — Preparing the Ground for Federal Intervention

Most Americans held a positive impression of American schools when President Ronald Reagan took office in 1981, and support for his call to close the newly created U.S. Department of Education (USED) was high. Nonetheless, Reagan's first secretary of education, Terrel H. Bell, worked against efforts to close the USED. Unlike Reagan, Bell believed in an active federal role in education and had testified before a Senate committee in support of President Carter's successful effort to establish the department only a year earlier.[362]

[360] National Science Foundation, *Science and Engineering Education for the 1980s and Beyond* (Washington: White House, 1980), xiv.
[361] NSF, *America's Investment in the Future*, 35.
[362] Terrel H. Bell, *The Thirteenth Man: A Reagan Cabinet Memoir* (New York: Free Press, 1988), 1.

Many people associate Reagan with *A Nation at Risk*, a national report on the status of student achievement that was subsequently used to justify massive centralization of the American education system. Yet, as Bell writes in his 1988 memoir, *The Thirteenth Man*, the Reagan White House had declined his request for a presidentially appointed commission.[363] Reagan wanted to close the USED, and he feared that establishing a national panel would imply a significant federal role in education or even lead to more federal legislation.[364] However, that was exactly what Bell wanted, so he commissioned the report himself.

The resulting report painted a bleak picture of American education. It claimed educational foundations were being "eroded by a rising tide of mediocrity that threatens our very future" and that puts the country's safety and international competitiveness "at risk." It recommended that "government at all levels," including the federal government, must "affirm its responsibility for nurturing the nation's intellectual capital."[365] Bell writes that he was "elated" by the report's "hard-hitting" message and calls for reform.[366] It was just the thing he and other proponents of a strong federal role in education needed to prevent Reagan from closing the USED.

The report cited low test scores of American students on international testing, especially in math and science, to conclude that

[363] Ibid., 116.

[364] Ibid.

[365] National Commission on Excellence in Education, *A Nation at Risk: The Imperative for Educational Reform: A Report to the Nation and the Secretary of Education, United States Department of Education* (Washington, D.C.: National Commission on Excellence in Education, 1983), 17.

[366] Bell, *The Thirteenth Man*, 123.

academic standards had fallen in the United States. To correct the situation, it called on every state to work with established federal education programs to adopt academic standards, to develop assessments to measure students' mastery of those standards, and to create systems to hold schools accountable for meeting the standards. In other words, the report called for states to establish a standards-based system of education.

The report's authors urged governors, legislators, school leaders, teachers, and parents to embrace these federal recommendations as state priorities, and to "incorporate the reforms we propose in their educational policies and fiscal planning."[367] They advocated a top-down approach, with the federal government having "the *primary responsibility* to identify the national interest in education" and state and local officials having "the *primary responsibility* for financing and governing the schools."[368] Essentially, the report called for federal agencies to establish the educational reforms and for the states to implement them. This was the call that the NSF and supporters of a centralized education system had been waiting for to reengage in science- and math-education programs—and they did so with greater authority and influence than in earlier years.

Standards-Based Reforms: Writing New Science Standards

It's important to note that at no point did Congress pass legislation calling for national education standards, nor did it formally charge the NSF with the task of creating them. The only "authority" that agencies such as the NSF and the USED acted on

[367] National Commission on Excellence in Education, A *Nation at Risk*, 32.
[368] Ibid., 32–33.

to incentivize a standards-based education system was a report, commissioned by an unelected secretary of education, describing such a reform as a "national priority." Ironically, Reagan himself made no mention of national standards after the release of *A Nation at Risk*. In fact, he viewed the report's findings as a call to restore local control, not federal intervention:

> I believe that parents, not government, have the primary responsibility for the education of their children. Parental authority is not a right conveyed by the state; rather, parents delegate to their elected school board representatives and State legislators the responsibility for their children's schooling.[369]

The adoption of national standards—or at least the alignment of states' curricula to such standards—had been a long-term goal of the NSF, and *A Nation at Risk* gave it the cover to pursue that goal. It began the process of establishing national math and science standards as well as curricula, assessments, and teacher-education programs aligned to those standards.

The Next Generation Science Standards (NGSS) may be the current national science standards, but they aren't the first. They are simply the latest iteration of previous national standards written in response to the assumed call for national standards issued by *A Nation at Risk*.

The NGSS document credits four "partners" in the "two-step process" used to write the national science standards: the

---

[369] Ronald Reagan, "Remarks on Receiving the Final Report of the National Commission on Excellence in Education," April 26, 1983, American Presidency Project, http://www.presidency.ucsb.edu/ws/?pid=41239.

American Association for the Advancement of Science (AAAS), the National Science Teachers Association (NSTA), the National Academy of Sciences (NAS), and Achieve, Inc.[370] The document also states that the "two-step process" used to write the NGSS consisted of developing (1) a science framework by the National Research Council (NRC; the research arm of the NAS) and (2) based on that framework, the development of a next generation of science standards, led by Achieve. Although the NGSS document claims that the "federal government was not involved in the effort to develop the *Next Generation Science Standards* (NGSS)" and "no federal funds were used" to develop them,[371] it fails to disclose that the framework that the NAS used to craft them was based on previous national science standards funded in part by grants from the NSF and the USED: *Benchmarks for Science Literacy* (1993) and the National Science Education Standards (NSES) (1996).

Benchmarks for Science Literacy (1993)

The NGSS list *Benchmarks for Science Literacy* as a foundational document used to develop the standards.[372] It was written and developed by AAAS in 1993 as part of a three-phase program called Project 2061 — "a long-term initiative of the American

---

[370] Next Generation Science Standards, Executive Summary, introduction (2013), 1, https://www.nextgenscience.org/sites/default/files/Final%20Release%20NGSS%20Front%20Matter%20-%206.17.13%20Update_0.pdf.

[371] "FAQ," Next Generation Science Standards website, https://www.nextgenscience.org/faqs#3.2.

[372] "Standards Background: Research and Reports," Next Generation Science Standards website, https://www.nextgenscience.org/standards-background-research-and-reports.

Association for the Advancement of Science (AAAS) to help all Americans become literate in science, mathematics, and technology."[373] AAAS is an international nonprofit organization dedicated to "advancing science for the benefit of all people" through initiatives in "science policy, international programs, science education, public engagement, and more."[374] EHR has been a substantial funder of AAAS's science-education efforts, providing the AAAS with more than 100 grants worth $101,544,672 since Project 2061 began in the mid-1980s.[375]

With funding from the Carnegie Foundation, the AAAS began Phase I of Project 2061 in 1985 to define "the knowledge, skills, and attitudes all students should acquire as a consequence of their total school experience, from kindergarten through high school." This effort culminated in the publication of *Science for All Americans* in 1989.[376]

The content selected for inclusion in *Science for All Americans* was stated as being based on what would serve as a lasting foundation on which to build more knowledge and consideration of the following:[377]

---

[373] "About Project 2061," American Association for the Advancement of Science website, https://www.aaas.org/program/project2061/about.

[374] "About AAAS," American Association for the Advancement of Science website, https://www.aaas.org/programs/science-and-policy._

[375] See NSF Awards Advanced Search.

[376] American Association for the Advancement of Science, *Science for All Americans* (Washington, D.C.: American Association for the Advancement of Science, 1995), 220. http://webapp1.dlib.indiana.edu/virtual_disk_library/index.cgi/4273355/FID1736/curric/enc2297/2297.htm.

[377] Ibid., xix–xx.

1. *Utility.* Will the proposed content—knowledge or skills—significantly enhance the graduate's long-term employment prospects? Will it be useful in making personal decisions?

2. *Social responsibility.* Is the proposed content likely to help citizens participate intelligently in making social and political decisions on matters involving science and technology?

3. *The intrinsic value of knowledge.* Does the proposed content present aspects of science, mathematics, and technology that are so important in human history or so pervasive in our culture that a general education would be incomplete without them?

4. *Philosophical value.* Does the proposed content contribute to the ability of people to ponder the enduring questions of human meaning such as life and death, perception and reality, the individual good versus the collective welfare, certainty and doubt?

5. *Childhood enrichment.* Will the proposed content enhance childhood (a time of life that is important in its own right and not solely for what it may lead to in later life)?

Science for All Americans embraced a progressive pedagogy. Its chapter on the requirements for supposedly effective teaching and learning practices advocated a constructivist approach and discovery-learning methods.[378]

---

[378] Ibid., 198–209.

Federally Funded Research: Shaping Curricula

Phase II of Project 2061 aimed to transform this report into "blueprints for reform."[379] The NSF took an active role in this phase by providing $21 million in grants to the AAAS and other educational organizations to align curriculum, assessments, and teacher training to *Science for All Americans*. To further the development of curriculum aligned to *Science for All Americans*, the AAAS released *Benchmarks for Science Literacy* in 1993. This quasi-standards document included "statements of what all students should know or be able to do in science, mathematics, and technology by the end of grades 2, 5, 8, and 12," to achieve the "science literacy goals outlined in [*Science for All Americans*]."[380] Since 1993, the NSF has funded thirty-two grants totaling $43 million to various universities, state departments of education, school districts, professional educational trade associations, and other organizations to support the alignment of curriculum models, assessments, and teacher training programs to *Benchmarks for Science Literacy*.[381]

Phase III of Project 2061, which continues today, "overlapped" with the goals of Phase II by collaborating with "scientific societies, educational organizations and institutions, and other groups involved in the reform of science, mathematics, and technology education in a nationwide effort to turn the Phase II blueprints into educational practice."[382]

Project 2061's website claims that the science documents it developed "serve as a foundation for state and national science education frameworks and standards," including the NGSS. It

---

[379] Ibid., 220.

[380] American Association for the Advancement of Science, *Benchmarks for Science Literacy* (New York: Oxford University Press, 1993), xi.

[381] "Awardee Information," NSF Award Search: Advanced Search.

[382] Rutherford and Ahlgreen, *Science for All Americans*, 221.

also states that Project 2061 continues to receive funding from federal agencies—including the NSF and the USED—to develop curriculum and assessment materials:

> Through ... *Benchmarks for Science Literacy* ... and *Science for All Americans*, ... Project 2061 provides a coherent set of K–12 learning goals that serve as a foundation for state and national science education frameworks and standards including the *Next Generation Science Standards*. With funding from the U.S. Department of Education, the National Science Foundation, NASA, and NOAA, Project 2061 develops innovative and engaging curriculum materials that support students' achievement of these science learning goals and tools for evaluating the alignment of curriculum and instruction to standards and the quality of support provided for teachers and students.
>
> ... With support from the National Science Foundation, Project 2061 has developed an online bank of high-quality test items and related assessment resources for use in middle and early high school science, ... and a grant from the U.S. Department of Education is funding the development of assessment instruments for evaluating students' understanding of energy concepts from elementary through high school.[383]

National Science Education Standards (1996)

In 1991 a separate effort, but one connected to Project 2061, was taking place to write national science-education standards.

[383] "About Project 2061," American Association for the Advancement of Science website, https://www.aaas.org/program/project2061/about.

The presidents of several leading science and science-education associations, the U.S. secretary of education, the NSF's assistant director for EHR, and the co-chairmen of the National Education Goals Panel all encouraged the National Research Council (NRC) to play a leading role in developing national standards for science education in content, teaching, and assessment.

The NRC is the principal operating agency of the National Academies of Sciences, Engineering, and Medicine for service in the national interest and for furnishing scientific and technical advice to governmental and other organizations.[384] Today, the National Academies has four parts: the National Academies of Sciences, the National Academy of Engineering, the National Academy of Medicine, and the NRC. The NRC is further divided into research units similar to the directorates at the NSF.

The NRC's mission statement is very similar to the NSF's, and the two agencies collaborate on shared areas of study, such as education, social sciences, engineering and physical sciences. For example, the NRC's Board on Science Education (BOSE), which "investigates how science is learned and taught," has a symbiotic relationship with EHR, with one research organization helping the other to influence national policy. The "core work" of BOSE, for example, is funded by a standing grant from the NSF, which, as we will see below, supported the development of the NGSS.[385]

---

[384] "Articles of Organization of the National Research Council," approved June 1, 2015, National Academies of Sciences, Engineering, Medicine, http://www.nationalacademies.org/nasem/na_070358.html.

[385] "About BOSE," National Academies of Sciences, Engineering, and Medicine website, http://sites.nationalacademies.org/DBASSE/BOSE/DBASSE_066648.

Through the work of BOSE committee members, the NRC published the National Science Education Standards (NSES) in 1996. Funding for this project came from a few private sources and multiple federal agencies, including the NSF and the USED, which is specifically prohibited from funding the development of national standards.[386]

In the introduction to the NSES, Bruce Alberts, then president of the National Academies of Science, made clear that those involved with creating the standards believed they were responding to "a call to action" to follow through on a "national priority":

> This nation has established as a goal that all students should achieve scientific literacy. The *National Science Education Standards* are designed to enable the nation to achieve that goal. They spell out a vision of science education that will make scientific literacy for all a reality in the 21st century. They point toward a destination and provide a roadmap for how to get there.[387]

The NSES document notes that the standards had several important "precursors" that guided their development, including the statements of what all students should know and be able to do

---

[386] National Research Council, *National Science Education Standards* (Washington, D.C.: National Academies Press, 1996), ii. doi:10.17226/4962. Funding for the NCES came from the NSF, the USED, the National Aeronautics and Space Administration, the National Institutes of Health, and a National Academy of Sciences president's discretionary fund provided by the Volvo North American Corporation; the Ettinger Foundation, Inc.; and the Eugene McDermott Foundation.

[387] Ibid., ix.

that were published in *Science for All Americans* and *Benchmarks for Science Literacy*.[388] But perhaps cognizant of federal prohibitions on creating curricula, the NSES authors were careful to emphasize that the standards did not constitute curriculum:

> The importance of inquiry does not imply that all teachers should pursue a single approach to teaching science. Just as inquiry has many different facets, so teachers need to use many different strategies to develop the understandings and abilities described in the *Standards*.
>
> Nor should the *Standards* be seen as requiring a specific curriculum. A curriculum is the way content is organized and presented in the classroom. The content embodied in the *Standards* can be organized and presented with many different emphases and perspectives in many different curricula.[389]

Despite this disclaimer, the authors also stated that the standards "emphasize a new way of teaching and learning about science ... emphasizing inquiry as a way of achieving knowledge and understanding about the world."[390] In addition to these changes, which can be understood only as curricular, the standards were intended to make "changes in what students are taught, in how their performance is assessed, in how teachers are educated and keep pace, and in the relationship between schools and the rest of the community — including the nation's scientists and engineers."[391]

[388] Ibid., 15.
[389] National Research Council, *National Science Education Standards*, 2–3.
[390] Ibid., ix.
[391] Ibid.

Deconstructing the Administrative State

A noteworthy feature of national-standards development during this period was the commissioning and funding of national committees and boards by federal agencies (such as the NRC) to promote the development of national standards. The NSF has awarded millions to commissions and boards, including BOSE at the NRC.

Many in Congress complain that the USED acts as a *de facto* national school board, and in many ways it does. But these multiplying commissions and boards composed of unelected "experts" constitute a much wider circle of national education policy-makers that is beyond the USED. Unlike the USED, they act independently, without congressional oversight or accountability to the people. As evidenced in the creation of the NSES and *Benchmarks for Science Education*, ad hoc national committees are empowered to set national education policies, which constitutionally fall under the purview of the states and localities. By funding these commissions, the federal government pays others to formulate national education policies that the federal government, by law, may not set. This workaround to the Constitution and federal law allows the NSF and the USED to influence public opinion and guide federal and state policy while escaping accountability if, as is often the case, the policy is proven ineffective.

Mediocrity Breeds Mediocrity—
Next Generation Science Standards

A decade later, yet another call to action to improve science education was issued. In 2007, the Carnegie Foundation and the Institute for Advanced Study organized the Commission on Mathematics and Science Education. Through this commission, leaders from a wide range of fields joined forces to study science and mathematics education and make recommendations.[392] One of the commission members was Bruce Alberts, who had led the development of the NSES.

The resulting report was called *The Opportunity Equation*. Like its predecessor *A Nation at Risk*, this report concluded that math and science education in the United States was still—despite (or perhaps because of) perpetual federal intervention—in a state of crisis and, without substantial improvements, the economy and the international standing of the country were at risk. Among the report's recommendations were these:

> To meet the dual demands of equity and excellence in mathematics and science education, the United States will need to pursue a coordinated agenda that includes re-crafting the standards and upgrading the assessments that guide what happens in our classrooms, deploying the talents of our educators more effectively, and aligning our schools and school systems with the task of bringing the diversity of American students to high levels of math and science learning.[393]

Not surprisingly, a key finding of *The Opportunity Equation* report was that new standards would be necessary to transform science education. The old NSES, it claimed, "covered too much content at too superficial a level, and they did little to expand a student's understanding of STEM concepts and their relevance in the outside world." Moreover, the report concluded that science

---

[392] Carnegie Corporation of New York and the Institute for Advanced Study, *The Opportunity Equation: Transforming Mathematics and Science Education for Citizenship and the Global Economy* (New York: Carnegie Corporation), iv, https://www.carnegie.org/.

[393] Ibid., 2.

instruction "was outdated because it underestimated the ability of students to think in sophisticated ways."[394]

The NRC, once again acting on the advice of national "experts," directed BOSE to leap into action (there was no acknowledgement that BOSE's previous leaps had obviously fallen flat). Following the same protocol used to develop the NCES, the NRC directed BOSE to develop a document called *A Framework for K–12 Science Education: Practices, Crosscutting Concepts, and Core Ideas*. As stated earlier, the *Framework* was intended to serve as the basis for new national science standards.[395]

Ironically, the same personnel, standards, and research base that contributed to what *The Opportunity Report* described as a desperate state of science education were selected to drive new standards intended to correct it. As the presidents of the NAS and the National Academy of Engineering wrote in the final draft, the *Framework*:

> builds on the strong foundation of previous studies that sought to identify and describe the major ideas for K–12 science education. These include *Science for All Americans* and *Benchmarks for Science Literacy*.[396]

The committee of "experts" selected by BOSE to perform this task was composed almost exclusively of members who favored a progressive approach to science education. Instead of

[394] "Math and Science Standards," Carnegie Corporation of New York website, https://www.carnegie.org/interactives/opportunity-equation/#!/.

[395] National Research Council, *A Framework for K–12 Science Education: Practices, Crosscutting Concepts, and Core Ideas* (Washington, D.C.: National Academies Press, 2012), x. doi: 10.17226/131.

[396] Ibid.

structuring the framework around the disciplines of science (biology, chemistry, physics, and so forth), four core ideas served as the basis for the standards (life sciences, physical sciences, earth and space sciences, and applied sciences). Development of content and learning expectations for each of the four core ideas in the framework was directed by a "lead design team." Despite the pool of top scientists who could have led this work, only one of the four individuals selected to head the design teams held a Ph.D. in any field of science.[397] Instead, their degrees were in education, and their experience was mostly in curriculum design. Moreover, they had all previously worked on either NSF or NRC education research programs, and two of the four served on the NSES working groups.

Achieve, Inc., the organization responsible for overseeing the development of the Common Core national standards in English language arts (ELA) and mathematics, received a Carnegie Corporation grant to translate the NRC *Framework* into standards. Not surprisingly, the four design-team leaders who developed the *Framework* also served as lead writers of the "new" NGSS, which were released in 2013. Carnegie's website states that the NGSS include "fundamental changes to the way science and math are taught and outline ambitious expectations for what elementary, middle, and high school students should learn each year to be fully prepared for college and careers."[398] Yet there is nothing new about the standards; they mirror the same failed approaches to learning science as did *Science for All Americans*, *Benchmarks for Science Literacy*, and the NSES.

---

[397] Ibid., 365, appendix D, http://www.nap.edu/read/13165/chapter/1#v.

[398] "Math and Science Standards."

Deconstructing the Administrative State

In keeping with the progressive methodology advanced by the previous sets of science standards, the NGSS stress "hands-on exploration and teaching methods that mirror the way scientists conduct research and use the practices, core ideas, and concepts that are common to all of science and engineering." Carnegie further elaborates on the NGSS:

> Instead of taking notes and memorizing facts, students ask questions and design experiments to find the answers. Above all, students learn why science and math matter, how they work, and how they might apply in the outside world. Advocates believe that the guidelines, which states and districts adopt voluntarily, will help students learn how to think critically and creatively—a change that will revolutionize STEM education.[399]

Despite the well-documented federal effort to develop the NGSS's foundational documents, and the NSF grant's funding the "core work" of BOSE, the NGSS website claims there was no federal involvement:

> The federal government was not involved in the effort to develop the *Next Generation Science Standards* (NGSS). It was state-led, and states are deciding whether or not to adopt the NGSS. The work undertaken by both the National Research Council (NRC) and Achieve has been supported by the Carnegie Corporation of New York. No federal funds were used to develop the standards.[400]

[399] Ibid.
[400] "FAQs," Next Generation Science Standards website, https://www.nextgenscience.org/faqs.

Federally Funded Research: Shaping Curricula

Although the eighteen states (plus the District of Columbia) that have adopted the NGSS claim the creation of the standards was a "state-led" process, the NGSS are trademarked and controlled by Achieve. Claims that the NGSS (and Common Core) were state-led are false. The NGSS, especially, rest on decades of fatally flawed, federally funded, progressive policy reports. Like Common Core, the science standards were crafted not by the states but by private entities. Like Common Core, they were marketed to the states as a high-quality product.

This discussion demonstrates how the federal government has manipulated "research" and has created and funded a plethora of boards and commissions to drive the debate about educational content and pedagogy. Even though the federal government supplies only about 10 percent of funding for public education, it exercises a wildly disproportionate influence over what happens in local classrooms. Even when state and local officials appear to be in control, their choices are circumscribed by the progressives' capture of American education, a phenomenon enabled by decades of federal manipulation. And students who spend twelve or more years marinating in the progressive caldron are less likely to emerge with a healthy understanding of and appreciation for the brilliant constitutional structure created by our Founders.

Chapter 7

Federally Funded Parallel Governments

Regionalists aren't equalizing government subsidies; they're employing coercion at every turn, telling the public where and where not to live, where and where not to drive, and raiding voters' wallets whenever possible. Give regionalists half a chance, and they'll annex your town without your consent. Liberty is not a regionalist strong suit.

—Stanley Kurtz, *Spreading the Wealth*, 2012

One way in which the federal government advances the progressive agenda of rule by "experts" is by subduing state and local government through the creation of "quasi-governmental agencies," which we call "ghost governments." These entities operate largely independent of state legislatures, have federally specified policy portfolios, and are structured for political dominance over legislatures and local government. Over time, the extension of federal grants and cooperative agreements to these organizations has increased their influence in state and local policy-setting, thereby creating what is essentially a "federal agent with a local face" through which federal programs can be falsely advanced as state-led.

The effect of this scheme is a parallel governing structure that overrides the will of the people and the authority of state and local elected officials. Policies preferred by the people for their local communities are jettisoned in favor of federally inspired reforms. The façade of local control becomes just that—a shell that hides a mechanism controlled from Washington, D.C.

As described in the case studies below, the federal government uses these ghost-government structures not to help local citizens achieve what they want—which, in this case, may be more efficient, cost-effective transportation in the communities of their choosing—but rather to advance the progressive vision of what a "sustainable" community should look like. It seeks to remake the average American into someone who lives in high-density surroundings, walks or uses public transportation for mobility, and reorders his life in accordance with some bureaucrat's notion of environmental sustainability. Individual liberty simply isn't a value. A citizen's freedom to live his life as he pleases, and to join his fellow citizens in implementing their community priorities, must give way to the experts' decisions. Federally controlled ghost governments allow these "experts" to bypass the benighted rubes and exercise control to implement their version of what is good.

GHOST GOVERNMENT: METROPOLITAN PLANNING ORGANIZATIONS

Under a federal statute reauthorized in December 2015 as the Fixing America's Surface Transportation (FAST) Act,[401] urban

---

[401] Currently, all MPOs are governed by federal legislation called the Moving Ahead for Progress in the 21st Century (MAP-21) Act, as updated by the December 2015 passage of the FAST Act. See Public Law 114-94, 129 Stat. 1312 (2015).

areas with a population of 50,000 or more are required to have a designated metropolitan planning organization (MPO) with "the responsibility of conducting a continuing, cooperative and comprehensive transportation planning process."[402] The MPO planning process is a prerequisite to the area's receiving federal funds for airport, transit, and highway improvements. The FAST Act includes federal funding to cover 80 percent of MPO operating expenses, which generally includes staff salaries, and thus bends the attention of these staffers to Washington, D.C., and away from area residents.

The Bigger Picture: Statewide Transportation Planning

To participate in federal highway programs, a state must have, "by the laws of the State," authorized its highway department "to make final decisions for the State in all matters relating to, and to enter into, on behalf of the State, all contracts and agreements for projects and to take such other actions on behalf of the State as may be necessary to comply with the Federal laws and the regulations" relating to transportation.[403] The state must cede authority for determining what will be an "urban area" for purposes of state transportation projects.[404] The federal highway scheme

---

[402] Federal regulations require urbanized areas with a population in excess of 50,000 to have an MPO. Furthermore, the Department of Transportation designates "as a transportation management area (TMA) each urbanized area with a population of over 200,000 individuals, as defined by the Bureau of the Census" plus "any additional urbanized area as a TMA on the request of the Governor and the MPO designated for that area." 23 CFR §450.310(c).

[403] 23 CFR §1.3.

[404] 23 CFR §1.7.

also requires the state department of transportation to maintain the projects after they are built or to enter into a maintenance agreement with a county or subdivision if it lacks authority for maintenance.[405]

As a further condition of federal funding, the state department of transportation must carry out a continuing, cooperative, and comprehensive performance-based statewide multimodal transportation planning process. This planning process includes the development of a Long-Range Statewide Transportation Plan (LRSTP) for nonmetropolitan areas (those with populations between 2,500 and 49,999), including long-term transportation projects designed to meet national goals required under the FAST Act. Thus, the state's LRSTP is designed not in accordance with the priorities of the state, but to performance measures and targets that advance national goals established under federal law.

The FAST Act also requires the state transportation department to develop short-term Transportation Improvement Programs (TIPs) for nonmetropolitan areas based on the plans established in the LRSTP. Each area's TIP includes a list of transportation projects to be completed within four years and must be included in the overall Statewide Transportation Improvement Plan (STIP) submitted to the Federal Highway Administration (FHWA) and the Federal Transit Administraion (FTA) for approval. With narrow exceptions, only projects included in the STIP can be funded with FHWA/FTA money.[406]

---

[405] 23 CFR §1.27, citing 23 USC §116.

[406] 23 CFR §450.220(a). See also §450.220(b) and §450.330 (project-selection procedures); 23 CFR §450.220(d) (category projects that cannot be funded without a federally approved state transportation plan).

Just as the statewide planning process is required by the FAST Act to produce a long-term and short-term transportation plan for nonmetropolitan areas, a parallel planning process conducted by the MPO is required for urbanized areas with populations of 50,000 or more.[407] The MPO must develop a long-range plan for the urban area within its boundaries called a Metropolitan Transportation Plan (MTP) and a short-term transportation improvement program based on the MTP. Although the TIPs developed by the MPO must "be approved by the MPO and the Governor,"[408] the MTP on which it is based requires only the approval of the MPO. Once the MPO and the governor approve a TIP, it must be included with the nonmetropolitan TIPs in the overall STIP submitted to the FHWA and the FTA for approval "without change, directly or by reference."[409]

In other words, the MPO is responsible for long- and short-term transportation planning for larger, metropolitan areas within its boundaries, and the state transportation department is responsible for smaller, nonmetropolitan areas. The TIPs (short-term plans) developed by both the state and the MPO must be submitted in the STIP (statewide plan) to the FHWA and the FTA for approval.

While the FAST Act requires the MPO to develop the plans in cooperation with the relevant States and the public transportation operators, [410] the MPO is designated by law to carry out transportation planning and thus has control over the process.[411]

---

[407] 23 CFR §450.310(a).
[408] 23 CFR §450.326.
[409] 23 CFR §450.328(b).
[410] 23 CFR §450.330(a). See also 450.220 (project selection).
[411] 23 CFR §450.104.

Moreover, the DOT takes the position that the Act grants MPOs the power to act with the authority of federal law.[412]

Federal law establishes detailed requirements for how the state and the MPOs are to develop these transportation plans, including specifying who must be consulted in the planning process,[413] the type of plan presentation that must be made, and requirements for public comment.[414]

In addition to meeting national goals, federal law requires that these plans facilitate the safe and efficient management, operation, and development of surface transportation systems that will serve the mobility needs of people and freight (including accessible pedestrian walkways, bicycle transportation facilities, and intermodal facilities that support intercity transportation, including intercity bus facilities and commuter vanpool providers) and that foster economic growth while minimizing transportation-related fuel consumption and air pollution in all areas of the state.[415]

Through regulation, the DOT requires several factors to be considered in the transportation-planning process, including the following:

- [Support] the economic vitality of the United States ... especially by enabling global competitiveness, productivity, and efficiency.
- Protect and enhance the environment, promote energy conservation, improve the quality of life, and promote

---

[412] "Metropolitan Transportation Planning: Executive Seminar," U.S. Department of Transportation website, https://www.planning.dot. gov/Documents/MetroPlanning/metroTrans.htm#anatomy.

[413] 23 CFR §450.210 (interested parties, public involvement, and consultation).

[414] 23 CFR §450.208 (coordination of planning-process activities).

[415] 23 CFR 450.200.

consistency between transportation improvements and State and local planned growth and economic development patterns.[416]

MPOs also have responsibility for the federally required Air Quality Conformity Analysis, whereby the MPO must determine that transportation plans will not violate the EPA's National Ambient Air Quality Standards required under the Clean Air Act.

The control of MPOs, and thus the reach of the federal government, extends to any transportation project covered by nonfederal funding if the project adds capacity (widening existing lanes, adding new lanes, constructing bicycle or pedestrian paths, and so forth) to roadway segments that are designated as "regionally significant." Such transportation projects, which include "at a minimum," roads with a functional classification of "minor arterial" or higher and collector roads that intersect with regionally significant projects, must be included in the STIP and, thus, subject to MPO approval.[417]

Boundaries

Federal law charges the governor and the MPO with determining by agreement the boundaries of the metropolitan planning area governed by the MPO, subject to certain federal requirements, including the urbanized area (as defined by the Bureau of the Census) plus contiguous areas expected to become urbanized within twenty years.[418] It defines, too, the outer possible limits

---

[416] 23 CFR §450.206 (scope of the statewide transportation planning process).
[417] 23 CFR § 450.326(f).
[418] 23 CFR § 450.312(a).

of the boundaries.[419] The boundaries may encompass more than one urbanized area,[420] thus giving the MPO cross-jurisdictional authority. For example, the area governed by the Indianapolis MPO encompasses multiple cities and towns outside Indianapolis that the Census Bureau determined to be urbanized. This impinges on political accountability to the people who live in the covered areas, because their city and county councils are no longer in complete control over transportation policy in those cities or counties.

Governance and Administration

Federal law sets parameters on MPO membership and provides a framework for a state's selection of members, even to the point of setting conditions on a governor's selection of members.[421] For MPOs serving an area with a population over 200,000, federal law becomes more prescriptive, requiring that membership include certain local elected officials, officials from certain public agencies, and representatives from transit-provider agencies. It also permits the transit-provider representative to serve as a representative of the local community.

[419] 23 CFR § 450.312.
[420] 23 CFR § 450.312(c).
[421] 23 CFR § 450.310(d)(1). The FAST Act requires that the representation of MPOs with a population over 200,000 people "shall consist of (i) Local elected officials, (ii) Officials of public agencies that administer or operate major modes of transportation in the metropolitan area, including representation by providers of public transportation; and (iii) Appropriate State officials."

Funding

Federal law provides several sources of funding for MPOs. One source is Highway Trust Fund money, which comes from the national gasoline sales tax. The formula used by the secretary of transportation to distribute this money to the states requires that a significant portion of the funds be dedicated for use by the MPOs.[422] The state must pass through these set-aside funds to the various MPOs in accordance with a formula "developed by [the] State and approved by the Secretary" and in accordance with factors dictated by federal law.[423]

The states' total apportionment of federal funding under the Federal-Aid Highway Program (authorized under the FAST Act) was $39 billion in 2016. This funding included grants for the Metropolitan Planning Program[424] and provides 80 percent of

[422] 23 CFR § 450.308(a), referencing 23 USC § 104(d), and 49 USC §§ 5305(d), & 5307).

[423] 23 USC §104(d)(2).

[424] "The purpose of [the Metropolitan Planning Grant program] is to implement the provisions of 23 USC 135, 23 USC 150, and 49 USC 5304, as amended, which require each State to carry out a continuing, cooperative, and comprehensive performance-based statewide multimodal transportation planning process, including the development of a long-range statewide transportation plan and STIP that facilitates the safe and efficient management, operation, and development of surface transportation systems that will serve the mobility needs of people and freight (including accessible pedestrian walkways, bicycle transportation facilities, and intermodal facilities that support intercity transportation, including intercity bus facilities and commuter van pool providers) and that fosters economic growth and development within and between States and urbanized areas, and takes into consideration resiliency needs while minimizing transportation-related fuel consumption and air pollution in all areas of the State, including those areas subject to the metropolitan

each MPO's operating costs; the remaining 20 percent comes from a local match. (Fiscal year 2016 total allocation for the program was $329 million.)[425]

This complex and well-funded scheme — of which very few Americans are aware — eviscerates federalism. It end-runs the role of the state legislature. It enlists the governor as an agent of a federal program. It reconfigures the power structure between the sovereign state and its political subsidiaries. It builds in structures that pretend to reflect public input, or the will of the people, when in fact they do no such thing.

GHOST GOVERNMENT: MPOs AND THE PARTNERSHIP FOR SUSTAINABLE COMMUNITIES

In 2009 the DOT, HUD, and the EPA formed the Partnership for Sustainable Communities (PSC) to coordinate federal housing, transportation, and environmental investments to bring about what the federal government considers to be "sustainable" communities. The Obama administration recognized that these agencies most directly affected the physical form of local communities and were thus best suited to "lead the way in reshaping the role of the Federal government in helping communities obtain the capacity to embrace a more sustainable future."[426]

---

transportation planning requirements of 23 USC 134 and 49 USC 5303." 23 CFR § 450.200.

[425] "Apportionment of Federal-Aid Highway Program Funds for Fiscal Year (FY) 2016," FHWA Notice N. 4510.802, Federal Highway Administration website, January 8, 2016, https://www.fhwa.dot.gov/legsregs/directives/notices/n4510802/n4510802_t1.cfm.

[426] U.S. Department of Housing and Urban Development, Docket no. FR-5396-N-03, Notice of Funding Availability (NOFA)

Each agency would have a specific orchestrated role in fulfilling this vision. HUD would integrate regional planning for sustainable development and invest in sustainable-housing and community-development efforts. The DOT would fund transportation infrastructure that directly supports sustainable development and livable communities. The EPA would provide technical assistance to communities and state governments to help implement sustainable-community strategies, and develop environmental sustainability metrics and practices.[427]

These federal agencies aligned their policies, programs, funding requirements, and performance measures to six "livability principles" designed "to help communities nationwide improve access to affordable housing, increase transportation options, and lower transportation costs while protecting the environment."[428] The livability principles are as follows:

1. *Provide More Transportation Choices.* Develop safe, reliable and affordable transportation choices to decrease household transportation costs, reduce energy consumption and dependence on foreign oil, improve air quality, reduce greenhouse gas emissions, and promote public health.

2. *Promote Equitable, Affordable Housing.* Expand location- and energy-efficient housing choices for people

---

for HUD's Fiscal Year 2010 Sustainable Communities Regional Planning Grant Program 6 (2010).

[427] Notice of Funding Availability (NOFA), 75 Fed. Reg. 36245, 36247 (June 24, 2010).

[428] "About Us," Partnership for Sustainable Communities (PSC) website, https://www.sustainablecommunities.gov/mission/about-us.

of all ages, incomes, races, and ethnicities to increase mobility and lower the combined cost of housing and transportation.

3. *Enhance Economic Competitiveness.* Improve economic competitiveness through reliable and timely access to employment centers, educational opportunities, services and other basic needs by workers, as well as expanded business access to markets.

4. *Support Existing Communities.* Target Federal funding toward existing communities — through strategies like transit-oriented development, mixed-use development, and land recycling — to increase community revitalization and the efficiency of public works investments and safeguard rural landscapes.

5. *Coordinate Policies and Leverage Investment.* Align Federal policies and funding to remove barriers to collaboration, leverage funding, and increase the accountability and effectiveness of all levels of government to plan for future growth, including making smart energy choices such as locally generated renewable energy.

6. *Value Communities and Neighborhoods.* Enhance the unique characteristics of all communities by investing in healthy, safe, and walkable neighborhoods — rural, urban, or suburban.[429]

---

[429] "Livability Principles," website of the Partnership for Sustainable Communities, updated October 31, 2013, https://www.sustainablecommunities.gov/.

Federal Agencies' Grant Coordination
to Effect Changes in Local Communities

The Partnership for Sustainable Communities marks a fundamental shift in the way the federal government structures transportation, housing, and environmental funding programs. The
agencies no longer operate in "silos" with reforms tied to the
individual department, but jointly, with a unified set of reforms
intended to create supposedly more livable, sustainable, and equitable communities. According to the agreement, each agency
committed "to coordinate activities, integrate funding requirements, and adopt a common set of performance metrics for use
by grantees."[430] When grants (which totaled $4.6 billion from
2009 to 2014)[431] from three agencies require the adoption of the
"livability principles," state and local grantees are more likely
to accept the terms than if required by a single agency. This is
what is meant by leveraging federal grants: what one agency's
grants may not be able to effect, the clout of all three—HUD,
the DOT, and the EPA—certainly does.

For example, within the Partnership for Sustainable Communities grant portfolio, those from the EPA totaled $14.8 million.
Alone, this amount would have been insufficient to coerce states
into adopting sustainable policies and programs. However, when
coupled with more than $4 billion in grants from the DOT and
$510 million from HUD, grantees, especially state-level agencies
that depend on federal grant money, are more willing to oblige.

[430] NOFA, 75 Fed. Reg. at 36245, 36247.
[431] See *Partnership for Sustainable Communities: Five Years of Learning from Communities and Coordinating Federal Investments Fifth
Anniversary Report* (hereafter Fifth-Anniversary Report) (Washington, D.C.: Partnership for Sustainable Communities, 2014),
5, https://www.sustainablecommunities.gov/.

By the end of 2014, this approach proved very successful, with more than 1,000 communities in all 50 states, Washington, D.C., and Puerto Rico receiving $4.6 billion in grants and technical assistance through the partnership.[432]

Creating Sustainable Communities through MPOs

Expanding mass transportation and creating transit-oriented developments (TODs) are the two main components through which the PSC sets about to establish sustainable communities. TODs are the "ideal" sustainable community, where land use and transportation planning are integrated. More specifically, a TOD is a compact neighborhood with high-density, mixed-use developments, located within a half mile of a transit stop. A "compact" neighborhood is one in which residents can reach work, school, entertainment, and shopping within a twenty-minute walk. "High-density" development refers to dwellings with a high ratio of dwellings per acre, with a minimum of eight dwellings per acre and no set maximum. "Mixed-use" developments include structures with street-level retail and residential units above.

TODs are also described as "livable communities," where auto travel is unnecessary. As then–Secretary of Transportation Ray LaHood explained it, a "livable community" is "a community where if people don't want an automobile, they don't have to have one; a community where you can walk to work, your doctor's appointment, pharmacy or grocery store. Or you could take light rail, a bus, or ride a bike." Rural and suburban neighborhoods where a car is necessary are not considered "livable" under this definition. TODs were also part of the Obama administration's strategy to combat climate change: reducing

[432] Fifth-Anniversary Report, 5.

the use of automobiles would reduce air pollutants, and reducing urban sprawl would have the added benefit of protecting the natural landscape.

The Obama administration also suggested that TODs improve individuals' health, relying heavily on federally funded research from the NRC's Institute of Medicine to make the claim. The theory is that getting people to walk to transit increases the amount of walking they do, which, in turn, will reduce cardiovascular disease, stem diabetes, and so forth.

The PSC in Practice: The DOT's
Capital Improvement Grants

To advance the PSC's mission, the DOT offers mass-transit grants through the FTA's Capital Investment Grants (CIG) program, which awards competitive grants to state and local government agencies to plan and construct mass-transit systems. As Secretary LaHood revealed in a press release in 2009, CIGs were intended "to achieve a broader goal than simply improving mobility." By including the "livability principles" in the grant requirements, CIGs intended to impose federal policy—sustainable land-use planning and development—on local communities. The CIG requirements are clear on this point, stating that a higher score will be awarded to applicants who can demonstrate that:

1. Local jurisdictions have adopted or drafted revisions to comprehensive and/or small area plans in most or all of the station areas ... which are strongly supportive of a major transit investment [*e.g.*, increased development in the transit corridor and station areas].

2. Local jurisdictions have adopted zoning changes that strongly support a major transit investment in most or

all transit station areas [e.g., increased development density, reduced parking and traffic mitigation].

3. Agencies have adopted effective regulatory and financial incentives to promote transit-oriented development [e.g., development community engaged in station area planning and transit-supportive development and outreach to government agencies to support land use planning].[433]

The scoring rubric used by the FTA to rate grant-application projects is structured so that the "livability principles" are more important than improving transportation. Before 2010, the DOT required cost-effectiveness to be considered above all other factors when awarding CIG grants. In 2010, it changed the rule to require consideration of the broader range of benefits transit can provide, including economic development, a healthier environment, and increased access to opportunities.[434] The FTA scoring rubric now evaluates funding applications based on six factors that are given equal weight: mobility improvements, environmental benefits, congestion relief, cost-effectiveness, land use, and economic development.

However, if the project's capital costs are less than $100 million and the existing weekday transit trips in the proposed

---

[433] U.S Department of Transportation, Federal Transit Administration, *Final Interim Policy Guidance: Federal Transit Authority Capital Investment Grant Program* (Washington, D.C.: Federal Transit Administration, 2016), chap. 2, 22–24, https://www.transit.dot.gov/sites/fta.dot.gov/files/docs/FAST_Updated_Interim_Policy_Guidance_June%20_2016.pdf.

[434] Notice of Proposed Rulemaking (NPRM), 77 Fed. Reg. 3848-3850 (January 25, 2012).

project route are more than 6,000, the application is eligible for a warrant to receive an automatic score of "medium" for mobility improvements, congestion relief, and cost-effectiveness.[435] Thus, any grantee that receives such a warrant need not demonstrate that its proposed project will improve existing and future transportation patterns or is the most cost-effective choice — the most important characteristics of a successful transit project.

Under a warrant, the grantee is left to focus on what's important to forming sustainable communities — aligning the land-use, economic-development, and environmental benefits of the project to the "livability principles." The grantee's score for land use is determined by the station areas' potential for TODs: dense population, high parking costs, and policies to locate legally binding affordable housing in the area.[436] Economic development is measured by "the extent to which a proposed project is likely to induce additional, transit-supportive development in the future," such as interest from developers to build in the area and the transit-friendly zoning policies discussed earlier.[437] Environmental benefit is "based upon the dollar value of the anticipated direct and indirect benefits to human health, safety, energy, and the air quality environment scaled by the annualized capital and operating cost of the project."[438]

In other words, the DOT transit grants are no longer about helping states improve their transportation systems; rather, they are part of a larger federal attempt to socially reengineer communities. Of course, because MPOs have authority over statewide

[435] FTA, *Final Interim Policy Guidance*, chap. 2, 28.
[436] Ibid., 12 et seq.
[437] Ibid., 20.
[438] Ibid., 18.

transportation planning, they play a role in advancing the PSC's vision by aligning transit projects to the PSC criteria.

The PSC in Practice: HUD's
Sustainable Communities Initiative

Mass transit tends to be successful, at least in the sense that people use it, in large urban locales, where many people live in a small geographic area and have access to employment, retail, and services close to their homes. Because these conditions don't exist in many areas, such as large suburban areas with plentiful land, the FTA requires that the optimal conditions be *created* to secure the grant. As part of the Partnership for Sustainable Communities, HUD offered $150 million in grants for a Sustainable Communities Initiative (SCI) "to improve regional and local planning efforts that integrate housing and transportation decisions, and increase the capacity to improve land use and zoning to support market investments that support sustainable communities."[439] Of that total, $100 million was made available for the Sustainable Communities Regional Planning Grant Program, and $40 million was directed to the Community Challenge Planning Grant Program. For the purposes of this chapter, our focus will be on the latter:

> Community Challenge Planning Grants foster reform and reduce barriers to achieve affordable, economically vital, and sustainable communities. Such efforts may include amending or replacing local master plans, zoning codes, and building codes, either on a jurisdiction-wide

[439] "Sustainable Communities Initiative," HUD.gov, https://portal. hud.gov/hudportal/HUD?src=/hudprograms/sci.

basis or in a specific neighborhood, district, corridor, or sector to promote mixed-use development, affordable housing, the reuse of older buildings and structures for new purposes, and similar activities with the goal of promoting sustainability at the local or neighborhood level.[440]

As the recipient of many Community Challenge Planning Grants, MPOs prime their cities to be eligible for PSC grants by including TOD-friendly zoning provisions in the master zoning plans. Unbeknownst to the affected residents, the bureaucrats in the area MPO and the local transit authority are working in tandem with the FTA and HUD to reshape their communities.

The intent of the PSC was to use these grants to increase the capacities of state, regional, and local planning officials to push livability, sustainability, and social equity into land-use plans and zoning.

Note that with the Community Challenge Planning Grants, federal funding is targeted to influence land-use and zoning patterns at the *neighborhood* level: MPOs enter into grant agreements with HUD to reshape a community down to the most local level—often without the consent of any elected body. This grant scheme has impaired the ability of local residents to direct the development of their own neighborhoods.

Circumventing the Democratic Process

The Smart Growth Network was formed to support the PSC in states and localities. The network includes forty organizations representing a variety of interests: national trade associations

[440] Ibid.

(including the Association of Metropolitan Planning Organizations), state-level agencies, national institutions, and nonprofit groups. Through federal grants and cooperative agreements, the PSC provides these organizations with financial and technical assistance to advocate for including the "livability principles" in state and local policies.

These national organizations have given the PSC's reforms the patina of being state-led. By working through local and state chapters, nonprofits, and state agencies, they can mask the fact that the policies and reforms they support were not born locally, but imposed from Washington. If a state legislature refuses to implement the desired reforms of the PSC, the network of organizations is activated to "champion" the implementation of the reform via local government. For example, when legislation to fund a light-rail transit system failed to pass the Indiana state legislature, the local affiliates of the Smart Growth Network and other transit lobbyists were engaged to lobby for mass-transit projects implemented through the local transit agency and financed with federal grants. When imposing federal policies, there's more than one way to skin a cat.

To understand how the PSC network functions to subvert local control, consider the example of the FTA-funded report, published in 2014, entitled *Planning for Transit-Supportive Development: A Practitioner's Guide*. The New Jersey Institute of Technology produced the report to help metropolitan planning organizations, transit authorities, and state and local planners overcome local resistance to federal sustainable-community initiatives. The report acknowledges that the local community "ultimately" controls land-use patterns and outlines a process by which local buy-in can be obtained through a coalition of "champions":

To succeed, transit needs to be accepted and accommo-
dated by the local communities that regulate development
and ultimately control land use. But those communities
must be involved early on and throughout the transit
planning process. [Note that the report specifies that the
local community means the body that regulates land use,
not the citizens of the local community.][441]

In a subsequent chapter, the report further states:

Select champions from the public, private, and not-for-
profit sectors. The private sector often brings funds and
credibility, the public sector offers political savvy and
support, and the not-for-profit sector is able to mobilize
large numbers of people and communicate to a broad
network.[442]

The report concedes that the role of state transit agencies in
coordinating regional land use and transit is a "major challenge"
because transit plans are prepared on a regional level, yet land-
use planning and zoning are implemented on a local level.[443] A
barrier to successful transit, according to the report, is the "dis-
connects" between the federal government, state governments,
regional planning organizations such as MPOs, transit agencies,

---

[441] Federal Transit Administration, U.S. Department of Transportation, *Planning for Transit-Supportive Development: A Practitioner's Guide* (Washington, D.C.: Federal Transit Administration,
2014), sect. 1, 8, https://www.transit.dot.gov/sites/fta.dot.gov/
files/FTA_Report_No._0053.pdf.

[442] FTA, *Planning for Transit-Supportive Development*, sect. 2, 7,
https://www.transit.dot.gov/sites/fta.dot.gov/files/FTA_Report_
No._0054.pdf.

[443] FTA, *Planning for Transit-Supportive Development*, sect. 1, 2.

railroad owners, redevelopment authorities, municipal governments, private developers, business organizations, neighborhood organizations, and lending institutions. Successful transit development "requires an alignment of all of the entities' goals, a shared common vision, an understanding of the implications of their decisions, and an advocate to keep the project a continual priority."[444] It's apparently inconceivable to the report's authors that the "shared common vision" would be anything other than the one embraced by federal bureaucrats.

The real goal is to tap transit-supportive individuals from the above-mentioned groups to convince the locality that the federal and local visions for the community are the same. The report provides a modern-day roadmap to accomplish the goal of progressives, such as Woodrow Wilson, who sought "to make town, city, county, state, and federal governments ... interdependent and co-operative combining independence with mutual helpfulness."[445] It suggests that MPOs and other regional planners recruit members of the local community to facilitate the process:

> *Identify transit-related development leaders from all of the principal organizations.* MPOs, transit agencies, redevelopment agencies, environmental groups, and chambers of commerce — These leaders will be the key points of contact regarding transit-supportive development issues within their organizations and will routinely coordinate with the other point people....

[444] Ibid., 1, 3.
[445] Woodrow Wilson, "The Study of Administration," cited in Pestritto and Atto, *American Progressivism*, 209.

Make sure there is a business case supporting investment in the transit-supportive developments. Most major initiatives benefit from business community support. When elected officials are called on to make investment and approval decisions regarding transit-supportive development, the business community provides justification and support. . . .

Form a not-for-profit transit and transit-supportive development advocacy organization. These groups are dependable and educated supporters of new transit and transit supportive development concepts, and can generate political, financial, and technical support.[446]

Massive "pro-transit" campaigns are designed to dominate the narrative on transit and prevent citizen-led opposition groups —often those living in the transit area with the most to lose— from influencing the process. This creates the appearance that everyone is on the same page with transit supporters. Those opposed to the transit plans find that their influence is limited to applying pressure directly to elected representatives. But that is often a quixotic venture. Once the decision-making process shifts from the legislative process to an agreement between a transit agency and the FTA, there is little any one person or "unconnected" group can do to combat the extensive network built up by transit supporters.

Not only is it fundamentally wrong for the federal government to leverage grants to force specific land-use plans at the neighborhood level; it's also unconscionable for unelected bureaucrats in state transit agencies or MPOs to be allowed to

---

[446] FTA, *Planning for Transit-Supportive Development*, sect. 2, 7.

accept the grant terms on behalf of people they don't directly represent. Perhaps increased public transit and the development of sustainable communities are the priorities for some cities, but the grant process is structured to block consideration of competing ideas.

It's true that in the case of the Community Challenge Planning Grants to alter zoning ordinances, a city or county council or another elected body must vote on whether the final plans are adopted. Yet, when the sought-after federal grant dictates the criteria used in the plan's formation—and when rejecting the criteria means losing the money—it's unlikely that the voting body will be offered any other choice.

MPOs in Practice: IndyGo Case Study

In 2013 the Indiana General Assembly rejected a proposal to fund construction of a massive $1 billion light-rail system in Indianapolis. Legislators found the proposal problematic because Indianapolis, like the state as a whole, isn't conducive to transit use; land is abundant and flat, parking plentiful, and commute times short. Moreover, the largest public-transportation provider in the state, the Indianapolis Public Transportation Corporation (IndyGo), lacked ridership and was forced continually to seek subsidies for operations. For example, rider fares currently cover only 14 percent of IndyGo's operating costs, necessitating heavy tax subsidies to round out the remainder.

Following the New Jersey Institute's "playbook" to a T, transit lobbyists, led by the Indianapolis Chamber of Commerce (Indy Chamber), garnered support to pass a watered-down bill that allowed eligible counties to hold a referendum to raise the local income tax for financing a mass-transportation system (with the caveat that the system could not be light-rail).

Despite a lack of state funding and irrespective of whether the voters subsequently approved the referendum, the Indianapolis Metropolitan Planning Organization (IMPO) in conjunction with IndyGo launched the Marion County Transit Plan (Indy Connect), a billion-dollar transit system including a 70 percent increase in local bus service (shorter wait times between buses, service earlier in the morning and later at night, more efficient transfers, and real-time arrival information) and the creation of three bus rapid-transit (BRT) lines.[447]

IndyGo needed two things to be able to finance Indy Connect: (1) voter approval of the referendum creating a new transit tax to fund the improvements to the existing bus service, and (2) the securing of a series of federal grants through the CIG program to subsidize 50 percent of the $390 million needed to construct the three BRT lines.

IndyGo applied for a CIG grant to finance the construction of the first of three BRT lines, called the Red Line — 13.5 miles long, connecting neighborhoods north and south of the downtown core. This grant would cover 80 percent ($75 million) of the Red Line's total construction costs ($98 million).

The neighborhoods lining the north segment of the planned Red Line route are more residential than commercial. Other than a few intersections along the north route, the majority of the area comprises single-family detached homes. In anticipation of the Red Line grant, the IMPO — working under the guidance of a Sustainable Community Planning grant — rewrote the master plan for the city of Indianapolis to include a new zoning

---

[447] "The Marion County Transit Plan," Indy Connect website, http://www.indyconnect.org/the-central-indiana-transit-plan/the-marion-county-transit-plan/.

ordinance allowing for transit-oriented developments within a quarter-mile radius of the proposed Red Line transit stations.

Residents living along the proposed Red Line route have objected to having their neighborhoods turned into TODs and have petitioned the City-County Council of Indianapolis-Marion County to shut down the Red Line's CIG grant. Yet there is little their council members can do; the grant application didn't require the approval of the city or county council or any signatory under its control, nor did it need approval of the state legislature or the governor — it's strictly an agreement between IndyGo and the Federal Transportation Authority. The concept of representative government simply doesn't apply.

To ensure support for the Red Line and passage of the referendum, the IMPO and IndyGo tapped local "champions" to build support for the transit project among city leaders. Led by the Indy Chamber, a group of nonprofits, business groups, and others came together under the umbrella of a newly formed nonprofit called Transit Drives Indy.[448]

With the financial support of the Indy Chamber (which formed a political action committee to fund pro-referendum activities), Transit Drives Indy launched a million-dollar PR campaign to gain support for the referendum, including a series of information sessions for voters on transit's benefits (no cons were presented); radio and print advertisements; expensive mailers, including flashy pro-transit messages; and paid workers to show up at transit rallies and work the polls on election day.

Citizens opposed to the transit plan found themselves unable to compete under these terms, and the referendum passed

---

[448] See "Thank You to Our Coalition Partners," Transit Drives Indy website, http://www.transitdrivesindy.com/about-us.

with 51 percent of voters supporting it. While transit supporters claimed the vote signaled the city's support for the new transit plan, IndyGo had to mislead the public about the plan's details. In meeting after meeting, representatives from IndyGo and Transit Drives Indy promised voters that the federal funding for the Red Line grant was a "done deal." This was a critical aspect of IndyGo's pitch to voters; without the federal funding it couldn't deliver the transit plan promised to voters. When pressed by transit opponents on whether the federal funding for the Red Line had been received, IndyGo withheld a crucial part of the story: Congress had yet to appropriate the funding, and it was possible the funding might not materialize.

As the facts slowly started to seep out about the uncertainty of federal funding, public opinion toward the referendum began to turn negative — voters didn't want their tax dollars going to construct the Red Line. Shortly before the election, the Chamber and IndyGo released statements promising voters that a vote for the referendum was not a vote for the Red Line; they were separate issues. Reporting to the *Indianapolis Star*, officials from both groups declared that the Red Line would be completely financed with funding from the federal grant and assured the public that if the referendum were to pass, new funding would be used to improve "basic" bus services:

> The vast majority of the $56 million generated by the tax would fix traditional problems vexing basic bus service, such as long waits, short hours of operation and unreliability, rather than running the Red Line rapid transit route.[449]

[449] John Tuohy, "Selling the $56 Million Transit Tax Hike," *Indianapolis Star*, May 16, 2016, http://www.indystar.com/.

Deconstructing the Administrative State

A few months after the election — and with the referendum safely passed — IndyGo changed its story. In a report to the City-County Council, IndyGo admitted that the federal grant wasn't the "done deal" it had promised voters and submitted a new budget in case the funding didn't come through. Without the federal grants money, construction of the Red Line would consume most of the transit tax funding until 2021, and improvements to the existing bus system — what voters thought they approved — would not be made. Such disrespect for the citizen is the foreseeable consequence of placing political authority with unelected experts.

It was a pleasant surprise for transit opponents when President Donald Trump's proposed budget included elimination of CIG funding. Unfortunately, Republicans in Congress acceded to the Left and included 50 percent of the expected Red Line grant in the omnibus spending bill passed in April 2017. Despite the cut in funding required to build the Red Line, IMPO and IndyGo are still moving forward with Indy Connect. As we have learned, progressives never give up.

The Indy Chamber's preference for government-subsidized mass-transit projects over options from the private sector is puzzling to conservatives who believe that business interests are better served in a free-market system. The U.S. Chamber of Commerce and its many state and local chapters, however, often endorse such big-government, progressive programs, claiming they will spur the economy and create more jobs. As will be discussed in chapter 12, the average citizen and small business rarely realize these benefits the same way larger corporations do. The Indy Chamber's support for mass-transit projects, such as the Red Line, is no different — only business, not government programs that raise taxes, can create wealth.

The vice president of the Indy Chamber, Mark Fisher (who conveniently serves on the IndyGo board of directors) stated that "for businesses, reliable transportation means a more productive workforce." The existing transit system, he claimed, had put the city at a "competitive disadvantage" because it wasn't "connecting workers to jobs."[450] Specifically, the Chamber argued that transit-dependent workers were locked out of jobs in high-demand areas not easily accessed by public transit. In other words, low-income workers in the city's core were unwilling to ride the bus for an hour each way to a job that paid only $12 an hour. The Chamber's solution to this situation is to have taxpayers subsidize a better transportation system to make the commute faster for these workers. Of course, the free market would call for a different approach — offer a higher wage. If employers offered more, workers might be able to afford their own transportation or at least be more willing to endure the long bus ride. Obviously, the option of taxpayer-subsidized public transportation works out better for the employers, while the laws of supply and demand favor the employee.

The Affirmatively Furthering
Fair Housing Rule: Bullet Dodged?

The PSC and MPOs are only two examples of how the federal government seeks to undermine state and local government by establishing and implementing regional policy. Another such initiative is HUD's Affirmatively Furthering Fair Housing Rule (AFFH), created by the Obama administration. Like the PSC,

---

[450] "As Marion County Transit Supporters Gear Up for Referendum, Indy Chamber Launches 'Transit Drives Indy' Campaign," Indy Chamber website, June 29, 2016, http://indychamber.com/.

the AFFH (released late in Obama's second term) is designed to leverage the power of multiple agencies to "persuade" cities, suburbs, and neighborhoods to adopt federally preferred policies that break down community boundaries. In this case, the USED, the DOT, and HUD plan to coordinate their work to achieve near-complete economic integration of American society, with no imbalances related to income level, race, and so forth.

Journalist Stanley Kurtz has written the definitive series on the AFFH and how its implementation would limit individual freedom in service of "equity."[451] As Kurtz has explained, under the AFFH any local jurisdiction applying for a HUD Community Development Block Grant must submit an "Assessment of Fair Housing" that analyzes housing occupancy by categories such as race, ethnicity, nationality, and income class. To ensure that there will be imbalances, the AFFH requires the assessment to encompass not just the jurisdiction applying for the grant, but the surrounding region as well (for example, an upscale suburb must include housing data from the nearby city). Imbalances identified, the applicant must determine what factors account for them and then submit a plan to remedy them.

---

[451] See Stanley Kurtz, "Massive Government Overreach: Obama's AFFH Rule Is Out," *National Review*, July 8, 2015, http://www.nationalreview.com; Stanley Kurtz, "Attention America's Suburbs: You Have Just Been Annexed," *National Review*, July 20, 2015, http://www.nationalreview.com; Stanley Kurtz, "Don't Take HUD Money: Feds Will Swallow You Whole," *National Review*, January 11, 2016, http://www.nationalreview.com; Stanley Kurtz, "Democrats Target Wealthy Suburbs: GOP Silent on AFFH," *National Review*, August 29, 2016, http://www.nationalreview.com.

One possible HUD-approved remedy would be to nullify local zoning ordinances and construct high-density, low-income housing. Kurtz explains:

> By obligating all localities receiving HUD funding to compare their demographics to the region as a whole, AFFH effectively nullifies municipal boundaries. Even with no allegation or evidence of intentional discrimination, the mere existence of a demographic imbalance in the region as a whole must be remedied by a given suburb. Suburbs will literally be forced to import population from elsewhere, at their own expense and in violation of their own laws. In effect, suburbs will have been annexed by a city-dominated region, non-residents.[452]

The requirement that local jurisdictions import population to remedy the artificial imbalances means the transportation and education systems will have to be "regionalized" as well. This is where the USED and the DOT come in—to implement policies designed to break down naturally developed lines of demarcation between suburbs and neighborhoods, on the one hand, and cities on the other.

In fact, the secretaries of the three federal agencies issued a "Dear Colleagues" letter[453] "calling on local education, transportation, and housing leaders to work together on issues at the intersection of our respective missions in helping guarantee full

---

[452] Kurtz, "Attention America's Suburbs."

[453] HUD Secretary Julián Castro, Education Secretary John B. King Jr., and Transportation Secretary Anthony R. Foxx to "Colleagues," See https://www2.ed.gov/documents/press-releases/06032016-dear-colleagues-letter.pdf.

access of opportunity across the country." Such collaboration would include planning sites for new schools in consultation with housing and transportation officials, or redrawing or eliminating attendance boundaries, to ensure "that high-performing schools serve diverse populations, including high-need students." It would also require local transportation officials to provide "ease of access to critical housing, school, and transportation resources for students, teachers, parents, and the broader [read: regional] community." Obviously, as with the PSC, mass transit would be critical.

All these possible remedies would go into the plan that the grant applicant must submit to HUD for approval. And to ensure the remedies are as broad as possible, the AFFH requires a "community participation" process in developing the plan that would involve activists from throughout the region, not just from the jurisdiction applying for the grant. So, radical "community organizers" based in the nearby city would have a say in how a suburb structures its neighborhoods, schools, and transportation.

What if the local citizenry objects to these policies that are designed to obliterate their communities? It wouldn't matter — to get the HUD money, the plan would have to be implemented. But it's also likely that the affected citizens wouldn't know any of this was happening until it was too late.

Now that President Trump has replaced Julián Castro with Ben Carson at HUD, there is hope that the AFFH will be rolled back. Carson had previously criticized Obama's attempts to "legislate racial equality."[454] But Carson hasn't withdrawn the rule,

[454] Joseph Lawler, "Carson at HUD Spells Trouble for Obama Diversity Rule," *Washington Examiner*, November 25, 2016, http://www.washingtonexaminer.com.

vowing instead to "reinterpret" it in an as-yet-unrevealed manner.[455] Unless HUD now completely overhauls the AFFH, or better yet, withdraws it, local jurisdictions will have to exercise extreme caution in applying for federal housing grants. Grabbing the money without considering the consequences can mean turning over their housing, education, and transportation systems to regional authorities controlled by the distant bureaucrats of Washington.

As this discussion shows, the federal government has built structures that can be activated without congressional authorization or other accountability to the people. The Trump administration might eliminate the PSC or the AFFH, but the next president could restore those initiatives and others. When it comes to constructing the edifice to impose federal power, the hard work has already been done.

Chapter 13 describes possible remedies for such schemes. Any remedies will have to address programs that (1) meddle with the relationships among various branches of state government or between state government and its subsidiaries (cities, counties, towns), (2) manipulate grant requirements of multiple federal agencies for the purposes of leveraging funding to implement policies and programs that Congress didn't originally fund, and (3) require establishment of particular boards and commissions in or by state and local government. As long as agencies of the administrative state are left free to engage in collaborative and creative schemes to subordinate state and local autonomy to the

---

[455] Joseph Lawler and Al Weaver, "Ben Carson: HUD Will 'Reinterpret' Obama Housing Discrimination Rule," *Washington Examiner*, July 20, 2017, http://www.washingtonexaminer.com.

federal will, the ideals of liberty and representative government will remain in peril.

Case Study: Credit Mobilier Redux (by Jason Arp)

To show how perverse public-private partnerships can be, we have included the following piece by Jason Arp, a member of the Fort Wayne, Indiana, City Council.

In the 1860s America was at war with itself. Washington was in search of a unifying accomplishment, something to reiterate the manifest destiny of continental expansion. To accomplish this, Congress created the Union Pacific Railroad to construct a transcontinental railroad. The Union Pacific issued shares at par through Credit Mobilier, which, unbeknownst to the public, was owned by Union Pacific stockholders. It then sold the shares at a loss to investors, including several members of Congress. Credit Mobilier was the sole provider of services to Union Pacific, which, in turn, billed the United States government on a "cost plus overhead" arrangement. In the end, the Union Pacific Railroad, a privately owned company, owned a transcontinental railroad that the taxpayer paid $100 million to construct for $50 million.

New Markets and Regional Cities

Flash forward nearly 140 years to the final days of the Clinton administration. Vice President Al Gore had been marketing the Community Renewal Tax Relief Act of 2000 for much of the year, touting the change in the way public-housing investment would be done, through public-private partnerships driven through Treasury Department incentives to banks. The Bush administration was the first to administer the new tool to redirect tax money to local governments for the projects of their choosing.

Federally Funded Parallel Governments

New Markets tax credits are awarded to Community Development Entities within city or county governments. Two and a half billion dollars was distributed in the first two years (2001–2002). In total, the treasury has distributed $50.5 billion as of fiscal year 2016 to the New Markets program, ostensibly for the purpose of providing low-income housing in underserved urban areas.

New Markets tax credits are a boon to local "press release economics," a term coined by Tad DeHaven, former OMB deputy director under Indiana Governor Mitch Daniels. These credits are combined with other tax-credit financing (such as Historic Tax Credits), local tax increment financing (TIF), local grants, and state matching funds grants (Regional Cities). As illustrated below, these schemes not only give politicians bragging rights for attracting investment and development, but also shower private investors with millions of dollars of taxpayer money — risk-free.

The Florida Model

Here is how this scam works as applied to a particular problem. In the early twenty-first century, small and mid-sized cities across America were supposedly losing their young talented people to big cities such as San Francisco and New York. Richard Florida, Ph.D., addressed the problem in *The Rise of the Creative Class*, which prescribed hefty doses of public funding on "quality of place" initiatives to "attract and retain talent." These slogans became the marching orders and the rationale to make the most of the New Markets tax credits.

In the town where I serve on the city council, we have had several of these "quality of place" projects. I will describe the most egregious. The table below illustrates the proposed financing for The Landing, in millions of dollars.

Senior mortgage (U.S. Treasury CDFI)	4.00
New Markets Tax Credits "Equity"	6.70
Regional Cities	7.00
Historic tax credit "equity"	4.00
HUD/City HANDS loan	2.50
City endowment loan	2.50
City tax increment financing loan	2.50
Downtown development trust	1.25
Streetscape grant	2.50
Developer equity	3.25
Total financing	34.70

When this project is completed, it will have used $10 million of local money, $7 million of state money, and $14 million of federal money to build apartments at $280,000 apiece (where the average home price is $100,000), which will rent for 65 percent more than the average rent in the city. It will include thousands of square feet of commercial property to be offered at subsidized rates. The present value of the cash flows (the rents less expenses) of the development is $11 million (using a 6 percent discount rate), fully one-third of the stated construction costs and dollars "invested." The best part: the developer gets all of its $3.25 million "equity" returned at deal closing as a "development fee." The more than $20 million in overpayment will go to inflated costs of design construction and legal fees. Three to one: a ratio that would make the Credit Mobilier crooks blush.

Chapter 8

Grants in Aid to States and Localities

A habit of not thinking a thing wrong, gives it a superficial appearance of being right, and raises at first a formidable outcry in defense of custom. But the tumult soon subsides. Time makes more converts than reason.

— Thomas Paine, *Common Sense*, 1776

Mario Loyola, an attorney and senior fellow at the Texas Public Policy Foundation, contends that taxing the states' residents and then conditioning the receipt of such funds on the states' acceptance of federal dictates is "confiscatory, coercive, and profoundly corrosive to the federal structure of our Constitution" and "threatens to blow away what few constitutional limits remain on federal power."[456] Loyola argues that "the entire practice of federal grants to state governments ought to be abolished." He cited the Supreme Court's warning in *U.S. v. Butler* (1936) that "the federal taxing and spending power" has a great potential to

---

[456] Mario Loyola, "Why States Have to Push for Federal Funds," *National Review*, February 22, 2012, http://www.nationalreview. com/.

"become the instrument for total subversion of the governmental powers reserved to the individual states."[457]

Loyola and Richard A. Epstein, a professor of law at New York University, write in the *Atlantic* that the excessive number of federal mandates attached to federal grants has "turn[ed] states into mere field offices of the federal government, often against their will, in turn creating a host of structural problems" and obscuring the "vital divide" between federal and state government. They offer the example of the Medicaid program:

> On the surface, it looks like a federal matching-grant for state health care programs targeted at the needy. In fact it is the opposite: a way to rope states into match-funding a federal program. Federal Medicaid funds come with so many strings attached that states have little room to deviate from federal dictates—except by expanding their programs to fiscally unsustainable levels, which Medicaid actually encourages the states to do.[458]

The expansion of federal grants-in-aid to states and localities over the last fifty years underscores the acceptance of this practice. In 1960, for example, federal grants to states and localities totaled $7 billion, accounting for 7.6 percent of federal outlays, 1.3 percent of GDP,[459] and 12 percent of state and local

---

[457] Ibid.

[458] Richard A. Epstein and Mario Loyola, "The United States of America," *Atlantic*, July 31, 2014, https://www.theatlantic.com/politics/archive/2014/07/the-federal-takeover-of-state-governments/375270/.

[459] Robert J. Dilger, *Federal Grants to State and Local Governments: A Historical Perspective on Contemporary Issues* (CRS Report No.

spending.[460] By 2015, this amount had increased to a staggering $624.4 billion, representing 16.9 percent of federal outlays, 3.5 percent of total GDP,[461] and 30 percent of state expenditures.[462] These intergovernmental grants finance various functions of state and local government. According to a Congressional Research Service report, in fiscal year 2018 health care is anticipated to account for more than half of total outlays for federal grants to state and local governments (an estimated $432.5 billion in fiscal year 2018, or 61.5 percent of the total), followed by income security ($107.1 billion, or 15.2 percent), transportation ($61.5 billion, or 8.7 percent), education, training, employment, and social services ($59.5 billion, or 8.5 percent), community and regional development ($16.5 billion, or 2.4 percent), and all other ($26.3 billion, or 3.7 percent).[463]

Moreover, many federal programs, such as Medicaid, require the state to match a percentage of federal grant dollars with state dollars, which increases a state's spending and reduces resources available for state priorities.

R40638) (Washington, D.C.: Congressional Research Service, 2017), 7, https://fas.org/sgp/crs/misc/R40638.pdf.

[460] Elliott Dubin and Trevor Ahouse, "Trends in State and Local Finances: 1960 to 2015," *Journal of Multistate Taxation and Incentives* 26, no. 8 (November–December 2016), Exhibit 12, http://www.mtc.gov/getattachment/Trends-in-State-and-Local-Finances-1960-to-2015-(JMT-Nov-Dec-2016).pdf.aspx.

[461] Dilger, *Federal Grants*, 7.

[462] Dubin and Ahouse, "Trends in State and Local Finances," Exhibit 12.

[463] Dilger, *Federal Grants*, 5.

Using Federal Grants to
Undermine State Legislatures

The influence of federal grants varies depending on how the grant is distributed. The federal government uses three types of schemes: block grants, categorical formula grants, and project-based competitive grants. Block grants comprise a small portion of federal grants-in-aid, with categorical formula grants and project grants comprising the vast amount of federal grants to states and localities.[464]

Block grants are typically large, fixed-amount grants to state and local governments, allocated through a statutory formula based on area population or other demographic features, such as poverty level.[465] For example, 70 percent of the amount distributed to urban areas and cities under the Community Development Block Grants (CDBG) is allocated to cities and urban counties meeting required minimum population thresholds, collectively known as "entitlement communities." The remaining 30 percent of funds appropriated for CDBG formula distribution is allocated among the 50 states and Puerto Rico for distribution to small or "non-entitlement communities."[466] Every state and every area meeting the requirements of an "entitlement" or "non-entitlement" community will automatically receive its share of the amount allocated by Congress to that program.

Conservatives often favor block grants because the funds have fewer spending restrictions and grantees generally retain the

---

[464] Megan Randall, Sarah Gault, and Tracy Gordon, "Federal Aid to Local Governments," Urban Institute, September 2016, 2, http://www.urban.org/sites/default/files/2016.09.07_state_of_cities_fact_sheet.pdf.

[465] GAO/HEHS-95-74 Block Grants 3.

[466] 42 USC §5306(a)(3) and §5306(d)(1).

primary administrative authority. President Trump, for example, has called for Medicaid to be consolidated into a block grant to give states more spending discretion. Block grants, however, still come with strings attached. Congress can include set-asides, which require a portion of the funds to be spent for a federally prescribed activity; ceiling limits, which set the maximum amount a state may spend on a specific purpose; and state matching requirements, which mandate state program contributions.[467] State flexibility can be further limited by the additional layers of regulations imposed by the federal agencies administering the program. For example, the CDBG program has more than 156 pages of statutes and regulations.[468]

Like block grants, categorical formula grants are allocated using a statutory formula, but with much more prescriptive state spending requirements. For example, Title I of the Elementary and Secondary Education Act (ESEA), recently reauthorized as the Every Student Succeeds Act (ESSA), allocates funds through four statutory formulas that are based primarily on census poverty estimates and the cost of education in each state. The funds must be used to assist local educational agencies (LEAs — bureaucratese for "school districts") and to schools with high numbers or high percentages of children from low-income families to help ensure that all children meet "challenging" state academic standards.[469] While the stated purpose of Title I funds may not seem

[467] GAO/HEHS-95-74 Block Grants 29.

[468] See *Title 24: Housing and Urban Development*, HUD Exchange website, https://www.hudexchange.info/resources/documents/24-CFR-Part%20-570-CDBGs.pdf.

[469] See "Improving Basic Programs Operated by Local Educational Agencies (Title I, Part A)," "Purpose," https://www2.ed.gov/programs/titleiparta/index.html.

particularly prescriptive, the authorizing legislation includes 162 pages of statutory requirements and endless regulations issued by the USED to which the state must also align its education policies.

Project grants (also known as competitive grants), the most restrictive type of federal grant, are awarded on a competitive basis. The competition "winners" are determined by criteria that are generally established by the federal agency administering the grant. For example, from 2010 through 2011 the Obama administration held three rounds of Race to the Top (RttT) grant competitions through which it awarded $4.35 billion to states that agreed to implement an extensive list of education reforms. Included among these were adopting the Common Core standards, linking student test scores to teacher evaluations, building longitudinal data systems to collect information on students and teachers, and investing in and expanding state-run early-childhood education programs.

With respect to policy adoption, RttT wasn't an *if-then* competition in which a state promised to adopt policies if it received money — bad as that would be. Rather, states put themselves in a stronger position and gained more points in the competition against other states by demonstrating their unconditional commitment to the federal policies — no matter the results of the competition.[470] The administration thus accomplished its objectives by merely luring states to pursue the money. Most states applied for the first round of RttT grants, which were awarded to only two states — Tennessee ($500 million) and Delaware ($100

[470] U.S. Department of Education, *Race to the Top Program Executive Summary*, November 2009, 4, https://www2.ed.gov/programs/racetothetop/executive-summary.pdUf.

million). In total, 19 states were eventually awarded RttT grants, with the largest allocated to Florida and New York ($700 million each) and the smallest to Kentucky ($17 million).

The administration needed such a mechanism because its policies were unpopular with most Americans and would not have survived the checks and balances embedded in American government. The student and family databases, for example, are contrary to American notions of privacy and exist to provide more information, and thus power, to the administrative state and to increase the transfer of taxpayer money to politically favored private enterprises. The Common Core standards are of poor quality and lock children into a slow academic progression, making it difficult for teachers to teach above the standards and rather forcing them to teach the same centralized mediocrity that is tested by the same centralized tests.[471]

States adopted these and other problematic policies to score points on the competition, not because the people wanted them. And the competition itself consisted largely of a conversation between the state education bureaucracies and the federal executive branch; in most states, there was no input from the legislature.[472]

Grants made to state agencies diminish the authority of the governor and state legislature. They make the state agency beholden to the federal agency. They also necessitate a larger state bureaucracy to administer the grant, and this in turn creates a constituency that bends toward the federal agencies and away from the state legislatures and the governor and, thus, the people.

---

[471] Emmett McGroarty and Jane Robbins, *Controlling Education from the Top: Why Common Core Is Bad for America* (Pioneer Institute white paper no. 87, May 2012), http://pioneerinstitute.org/.
[472] Ibid., 4–8.

Using Federal Grants to Undermine
State Authority Over Local Government

The 2015 Catalog of Federal Domestic Assistance identifies 824 programs with local governments or communities as beneficiaries, sometimes as the direct grantee and sometimes as the ultimate recipient of money granted to the states to subgrant.[473] In some cases, such a grant is channeled through the state executive, which acts as a pass-through of the funds to local government. More often, these grants are channeled through a state agency, which negotiates the terms of the grants and disburses the funds, often without the requirement of the governor's or legislature's approval. Under Title I, for example, the state department of education submits the grant application to the USED and disburses the funding to local school districts based on the number of low-income students in those districts. While the grant requires the application to be submitted to the governor, it doesn't require his approval.

The federal government also offers grants directly to local government, bypassing the state government completely. These grants might include no financial or administrative involvement from the state. Some federal-local grants even bypass the local unit of government and are made directly to special-purpose districts, municipal authorities, and private organizations; good examples are the Federal Transit Authority Capitol Improvement Grants (CIGs) awarded to transit authorities, and HUD's sustainable-communities grants offered to MPOs, examined in chapter 7.

---

[473] Randall, Gaunt, and Gordon, "Federal Aid to Local Governments," 2.

Grants in Aid to States and Localities

The Race to the Top-District program (RttT-D),[474] launched in 2012, was an almost $500 million grant program allowing LEAs (school districts) to compete directly for federal money without going through the state government. But of course, the only way for a school district to get the money was to commit to implement federal policies. These included adopting specific teacher, principal, and superintendent evaluation systems; measuring students against "college- and career-ready" standards, which means Common Core; and connecting preschoolers' data to K–12 and higher-education data.[475] An "Absolute Priority" for receiving a grant was to commit to "personalized learning,"[476] which ultimately will mean adopting a more technocratic approach to education so that students' brains can be mapped by sophisticated software and algorithms.[477] If the federal government could not persuade state officials to adopt these policies, it would simply bypass the state and appeal to cash-strapped school districts themselves.

Through round one of RttT-D, the USED awarded $383 million to sixteen grantees representing fifty-five schools.[478] It made

---

[474] See "Race to the Top—District Competition," U.S. Department of Education website, July 30, 2013, 1, https://www.ed.gov/category/keyword/race-top-district-competition.

[475] U.S. Department of Education, *Race to the Top—District Executive Summary*, August 2012, https://www2.ed.gov/programs/racetothetop-district/2012-executive-summary.pdf.

[476] Ibid.

[477] Emmett McGroarty and Jane Robbins, "Not a Conspiracy Theory: Educrats Discover Alarming New Ways to Data Mine Our Children," *Conservative Review*, August 12, 2016, http://www.educationviews.org/conspiracy-theory-educrats-discover-alarming-ways-data-children/.

[478] "Department of Education Invites Districts to Apply for $120 Million in Race to the Top Funds to Support Classroom-Level

five additional grants worth a total of $120 million in round two.[479] When poured directly into local schools, half a billion dollars can buy a lot of support for federal policies. This practice undermines a state's authority to govern its subdivisions or otherwise to provide, in the state constitution or other state law, the conditions under which subdivisions operate.

The use of federal-local grants dates back to the nineteenth century, when federal aid was provided to local governments for internal improvements related to functions expressly or at least arguably allocated to the federal government (construction of roads, railroads, canals, and so forth, for the promotion of commerce; postal services; and immigration and customs facilities).[480] The years between the New Deal and the Great Society saw an increase in the use of federal-local grants for purposes outside the scope of federal authority, such as grants for public housing and eradication of blight and decay, poverty, and congestion.[481] Progressives of those eras contended that such federal interference was necessary because the states had been either unwilling or unable to address the persistent social ills that had befallen cities during the early twentieth century.[482]

Reform Efforts," U.S. Department of Education website, July 30, 2015, https://www.ed.gov/.

[479] See "Awards—Race to the Top District (RTT-D)," U.S. Department of Education website, last modified September 25, 2015, https://www.ed.gov/.

[480] Advisory Commission on Intergovernmental Relations, *State Involvement in Federal-Local Grant Programs: A Case Study of the "Buying In" Approach* (Washington, D.C.: U.S. Government Printing Office, 1970), 10n1.

[481] Ibid., 11.

[482] Ibid.

Grants in Aid to States and Localities

Many progressives of the time dwelled on the contention that the states had become an obstacle to federal reforms. Among these critics was Professor Charles E. Merriam, a prominent voice of the progressive movement and an adviser to President Franklin Roosevelt. Merriam wrote:

> In many instances the state is a fifth wheel as far as city government is concerned. The state will neither grant autonomy to the cities, nor will it assume the burden of administrative supervision over them. The state will neither rule, nor permit anyone else to rule over the metropolitan regions.[483]

A report generated in 1969 by the now defunct American Commission on Intergovernmental Relations (ACIR)[484] detailed what it was about the structure of state governments that Merriam and other progressives believed was flawed and prevented the state from enacting the types of reforms they believed necessary. It cited, among other factors, check-and-balance provisions

---

[483] Charles E. Merriam, "The Federal Government Recognizes the Cities," *National Municipal Review* 23 (1934): 108.

[484] The American Commission on Intergovernmental Relations was an independent agency authorized by Congress from 1953 to 1996 "to strengthen the American federal system and improve the ability of federal, state, and local governments to work together cooperatively, efficiently, and effectively." It consisted of six members of Congress appointed by the House and Senate leadership; four governors; three state legislators; four mayors and three county officials appointed by the president from nominations by the respective national associations of state and local governments; and three private citizens and three representatives of the federal executive branch appointed directly by the president.

in state constitutions that impaired the governors' authority to act unilaterally, such as legislative veto powers, shared budget-making responsibilities, and gubernatorial term limits. Moreover, legislative authority to place property-tax-rate caps and limits on the amount of debt the localities can borrow had "shackled" the localities in raising and borrowing funding to solve their problems on their own. It argued that, absent changes, the states couldn't be effective partners to the federal government in solving the nation's problems.[485]

The chief criticism of the states' governance structure boiled down to the powers granted to state legislatures, because they denied the governor and local leaders the authority to unilaterally enact federal reforms. Under this view, state legislatures aren't seen as a safeguard for individual rights and freedoms against an all-powerful executive, but rather as an impediment to the executive's ability to push federal policies through the political process.

While President Lyndon Johnson believed that states could not be trusted to initiate necessary improvements, he found the federal government unable to manage the growing number of federal-local grant programs without their administrative and financial assistance:

> While the states complain of being bypassed when the federal government deals directly with local governments, they often forget that this occurs because of lack of action on their part. Only a few states contribute to the construction of housing, sewage treatment, or water systems. Yet for some time federal aid has been provided for

[485] Advisory Commission on Intergovernmental Relations, *State Involvement*, 12.

such projects. Furthermore, congressional authorization for federal-local programs has been increasing because of the failure of the states. We will welcome your "buying in" to these federal-local programs, for it would simplify administrative problems both for us and for local governments if we worked through the state instead of dealing directly with numerous local officials.[486]

If states would just do what the feds want, Johnson argued, life would be simpler for all parties.

To alleviate the administrative burden to federal agencies, the ACIR recommended that federal-local grants be consolidated and channeled through the state (or state agencies) on the condition that the states agreed to "buy into" such programs and provide financial and administrative assistance:

> Federal funds for a particular program in a particular State should be routed through the State if and when two basic conditions are met: establishment of adequate administrative machinery, and provision of State financial aid to cover a substantial portion of the non-Federal share of project costs. If the State chooses not to meet these conditions, then a direct Federal-local relationship should obtain regarding the operation of the program in that State.[487]

Relative to direct federal-local grants, under such an arrangement the state would gain "increased state supervision of local program development and closer review of completed applications

---

[486] Ibid., 22.
[487] Ibid., iii.

in order to ensure that they conform to the standards and conditions attached to the state aid."[488] Like current federal grant schemes, this shifted financial and administrative burdens to the states yet maintained federal control over local policies.

The "buy in" arrangement undermines state sovereignty by directing state funding and resources toward the federal government's policy preferences, by again creating a constituency of state bureaucrats, and by blurring responsibilities for the programs and thereby the accountability due to citizens. In a sense, the federal government is telling the states that unless they are willing to lose all policy control via direct federal-local funding, they have to pony up money and be satisfied with the crumbs of control that the feds toss their way.

Another recommendation made by the ACIR at this time to ease the administrative headache of federal-local grant programs was to consolidate multiple grant applications into a single application, or a "consolidated state plan." The supposed intent of grant consolidation was to encourage states and localities to interrelate various federal grant programs and to facilitate effective program administration by the federal government.[489] Today, many federal programs, such as Medicaid, state highway grants, and education grants under ESSA, are submitted through a consolidated state plan. Under ESSA, for example, multiple education grant programs are applied for via a single grant application, which, in general, requires each individual grant program to meet the goals of the overall state plan.

[488] Ibid., 5.

[489] Advisory Commission on Intergovernmental Relations, *Fiscal Balance in the American Federal System*, vol. 1 (Washington, D.C.: Government Printing Office, 1967), xxii.

In many ways, the "buy in" approach and use of consolidated plans have given rise to the current structure of federal-state relationships, which empowers the federal government over the states and, as Epstein and Loyola point out, has turned the states into "mere field offices for the federal government."

A NATION OF LAWS?
FEDERAL GUIDANCE DOCUMENTS

The Obama administration infamously used guidance documents —an indefinite term that encompasses pronouncements based on interpretations of statutes, regulations, and executive orders— to drive its policy agenda. Its aggressive use of such devices illuminates the immense, largely unchecked power of the bureaucracy to intimidate states and citizens. Many, and perhaps most, statutes, regulations, and grant documents have some gray area that needs interpretation, and there the federal bureaucracy steps in.[490]

Some of the Obama administration's most notorious guidance documents related to education. In October 2010, the USED's Department for Civil Rights (OCR) responded to what it called a "pandemic" of bullying in schools by issuing a "Dear Colleague" letter[491] threatening civil-rights penalties if schools failed to address alleged bullying in the way the OCR preferred. The OCR used this letter to create a new standard for "harassment" under

---

[490] For a discussion of the significance of such guidance documents, albeit from a perspective different from that of these authors, see Mantel, "Procedural Safeguards."

[491] Assistant Secretary for Civil Rights Russlyn Ali to "Colleague," Office for Civil Rights, U.S. Department of Education website, October 26, 2010, https://www2.ed.gov/about/offices/list/ocr/letters/colleague-201010.pdf.

federal law; to alter Supreme Court authority on the issue; to reinterpret existing statutes so as to expand liability; and to restrict students' First Amendment rights to free speech and free exercise of religion.[492]

Several years later, Obama's OCR, along with the Department of Justice, issued another guidance letter threatening schools that refused to open up restrooms, locker rooms, sleeping quarters (on overnight trips), and possibly sports teams to both sexes.[493] Once again, the administration unilaterally expanded federal statutory law, this time to cover discrimination based on "gender identity" as well as sex.[494] (The Trump administration has rescinded this guidance, but at this writing its policy toward complaints based on gender identity is unclear.)[495]

Because both of these guidance documents rested on such shaky legal foundations, it's likely they wouldn't have been enforced if challenged in court. Indeed, the gender-identity guidance was preliminarily enjoined by a federal court in a lawsuit filed by multiple states.[496] But states and schools are loath to

[492] Emmett McGroarty and Jane Robbins, "Bullying and Civil Rights," *Public Discourse*, January 12, 2012, http://www.thepublicdiscourse.com/2012/01/4526/.

[493] See "U.S. Departments of Education and Justice Release Joint Guidance to Help Schools Ensure the Civil Rights of Transgender Students," U.S. Department of Education website, May 13, 2016, https://www.ed.gov/.

[494] Jane Robbins, "New Transgender Letter from Trump Administration Should Have Parents on Alert," *National Pulse*, June 26, 2017, https://thenationalpulse.com/commentary/new-transgender-letter-from-trump-admin-should-have-parents-on-alert/.

[495] Ibid.

[496] Josh Gerstein, "Judge Reaffirms Nationwide Ban on Obama Transgender School Bathroom Policy," *Politico*, October 19,

initiate litigation because of the enormous cost in time and resources. Too often, federal bureaucrats need merely to hint at expensive legal action or loss of federal funding, and state officials assent to whatever the guidance requires. The states are always on the short end of a massive power imbalance, and federal bureaucrats take every advantage of their superior position. Requirements for the submission of state plans to the federal government serve to increase that power imbalance, as state bureaucrats strive to craft an acceptable plan. The love of (federal) money may not be the root of all evil in the deterioration of state autonomy, but it's close.

CASE STUDY: THE NSF's USE OF GRANTS TO CHANGE STATE EDUCATION POLICY

Chapter 6 discussed the NSF's office of Education and Human Resources (EHR) State Systemic Initiatives (SSI) program. This program provided grants to twenty-four states and twenty-two major urban school districts to make "fundamental, comprehensive, and coordinated changes in science, mathematics, and technology education through attendant changes in policy, resource allocation, governance, management, content and conduct."[497]

2016, http://www.politico.com/story/2016/10/obama-transgender-school-bathrooms-texas-judge-ruling-229973.

[497] Michael McKeown, David Klein, and Chris Patterson, "National Science Foundation Systemic Initiatives: How a Small Amount of Federal Money Promotes Ill-Designed Mathematics and Science Programs in K–12 and Undermines Local Control of Education, Michael McKeown Mathematically Correct," in *What's at Stake in the K-12 Standards Wars: A Primer for Educational Policy-makers*, ed. Sandra Stotsky (New York: Peter Lang

In signing the grant agreements, states and school districts committed themselves to the NSF reform agenda: implementation of standards-based curricula; teacher training on that curricula; assessments of student performance based on the standards; and reforming state and local policies, governance structures, and allocations of federal, state, and local resources to support the transformation to a standards-based education system. In a 1997 press announcement, the NSF admitted that the purpose of the grants was to "spur local officials and the public to undertake a comprehensive and sustained reform of their entire approach to education—from curriculum to class scheduling to teacher professional development—by first overhauling math and science teaching."[498]

Until the late 1980s, the NSF's math and science programs were made available to schools without strings attached. But the SSI program changed that. In reviewing the program biologist and former NSF Fellow Michael McKeown noted that the SSI exceeded the authority of the federal government:

> The problem is that this NSF program implicitly if not explicitly mandates the use of certain sets of standards instead of others (including those developed by the states themselves), as well as certain curricular, instructional, and classroom management practices instead of others.[499]

Publishing, 2000), 288, http://www.csun.edu/~vcmth00m/chap13.pdf.

[498] "Urban School Superintendents Form Coalition to Share Innovations and Tackle Obstacles" (news release 97-030), National Science Foundation website, April 24, 1997, https://www.nsf.gov/.

[499] McKeown, Klein, and Patterson, "National Science Foundation Systemic Initiatives," 292.

Grants in Aid to States and Localities

To alleviate any confusion about what, in its view, constituted effective, standards-based education, the NSF mandated
a progressive approach to instruction:
- Mathematics and science are learned by doing rather
  than by passive methods of learning such as watching a
  teacher work at the chalkboard. Inquiry-based learning
  and hands-on learning more effectively engage students
  than lectures.
- The use and manipulation of scientific and mathematical ideas benefits from a variety of contributing perspectives and is, therefore, enhanced by cooperative problem
  solving.
- Technology can make learning easier, more comprehensive, and more lasting.
- This view of learning is reflected in the professional
  standards of the National Council of Teachers of Mathematics, the American Association for the Advancement of Science, and the National Research Council
  of the National Academy of Sciences.[500]

Grant recipients also had to align local, state, and federal
funding to SSI efforts. For instance, to meet the conditions of
the NSF grants, Cleveland, Ohio, devoted half its available bond
referendum funding for instructional materials aligned to the
standards-based reforms required under the SSI. The Fresno,
California, school system allocated $31 million in USED Title I
funds to implement the SSI grant—even though SSI grants of
this type approximated only $3 million.[501] By 1999, states had

[500] Ibid., 295.
[501] Ibid., 291–292.

matched $250 million in NSF-SSI grants with $311 million in state and local funding.[502]

McKeown notes that in its annual report, the Texas SSI program had claimed to exert influence over "the largest and most important sources of money for education in the state 'in ways that reflect our mission.'"[503] The report claimed that SSI grants influenced the expenditure of approximately $2 billion dollars annually of federal and state monies. And in its 1999 budget request to Congress, EHR noted that the SSI program had driven "policy and legislative changes for facilitating and sustaining systemic reform and gains in student performance in impacted school districts."[504]

According to McKeown, while the NSF grants had forced major reforms, the presumed academic improvement did not materialize. He cited the program in Texas as an example:

> In short, no valid and reliable data have been generated to date in Texas to support SSI's claims for academic success. The absence of quantitative data for SSI programs in Texas replicates the situation in other states. A five-year analysis of SSIs sponsored by NSF itself could not find enough test score data to support claims that NSF-endorsed mathematics and science programs raise academic achievement or reduce the achievement gap between student populations.[505]

---

[502] Education and Human Resources FY 1999 Budget Request, https://www.nsf.gov/about/budget/fy1999/ehr4web.htm.

[503] McKeown, Klein, and Patterson, "National Science Foundation Systemic Initiatives," 311.

[504] Education and Human Resources FY 1999 Budget Request.

[505] McKeown, Klein, and Patterson, "National Science Foundation Systemic Initiatives," 323.

But the NSF was undaunted by the failure of its program to improve student achievement. It drove the use of textbooks (including the Connected Mathematics Project textbook series discussed in chapter 6) and instructional materials aligned to the National Council of Teachers of Mathematics standards. Although the SSI grant program is now defunct, its policies and priorities live on; a standards-based education aligned to progressive pedagogy is the status quo. That is the intent of leveraging federal grants to make "systemic" change: to implement institutional changes that remain in effect long after federal funding dries up.

Chapter 9

The Plight of State Legislators

*The State Legislatures will jealously and closely watch the opera-
tions of this Government, and be able to resist with more effect
every assumption of power, than any other power on earth can
do; and the greatest opponents to a Federal Government admit the
State Legislatures to be sure guardians of the people's liberty.*[506]

—James Madison, *Annals of Congress* June 8, 1789

The process for governance set forth in the Constitution grants
each branch of government a separate role: the legislature writes
the law, the executive implements the law, and the judiciary
interprets the law. The ever-expanding power of the administrative state, however, has blurred the separation of powers. The
administrative state issues regulations having the force of law,
enforces these regulations, and judges any infractions to these
rules. The melding of the three roles into the administrative state
has damaged not only the separation of powers at the federal
level, but also the division of federal and state authority.

State legislatures were intended to be the bulwark of the federalist structure, but the influence of the administrative state on

[506] 1 Annals of Cong. 457, June 8, 1789 (Joseph Gales, ed. 1790).

the lawmaking process at the state and federal levels, combined with the lack of resources at the state level, has limited the ability of state legislatures to fulfill their constitutionally ordained role.

WEAKENED AUTHORITY OF STATE LEGISLATORS RESULTING FROM IMBALANCE OF RESOURCES

State legislatures are very busy places during the legislative session. On average, 1,800 bills will be introduced during the session, and 300 of them will pass.[507] Because most state legislatures weren't designed to process so many bills during a single session (which in some states is as short as 30 days), their capacity to legislate effectively can be diminished.

The National Conference of State Legislatures (NCSL) determines the capacity level of state legislatures based on three factors: the size of the legislature's staff, the amount legislators are compensated, and the amount of time they spend on the job.[508] With few exceptions, the NCSL found that more populous states have a greater capacity to legislate due to more staff, full-time compensation rates, and longer legislative sessions. Legislators in high-capacity states such as California, New York, and Pennsylvania generally have a large, year-round staff available to them (an average of 1,340 staff members per legislature), are

---

[507] See "How Efficient Is Your State Legislature? Nearly All Are More Effective Than Congress," FiscalNote, March 10, 2016, https://fiscalnote.com/2016/03/10/how-efficient-is-your-state-legislature-nearly-all-are-more-effective-than-congress/.

[508] See "Full- and Part-Time Legislatures," National Conference of State Legislatures website, June 14, 2017, http://www.ncsl.org/research/about-state-legislatures/full-and-part-time-legislatures.aspx.

compensated at a higher rate (an average salary of $81,079), and devote the most time to their legislative duties (82 percent).

Legislators in medium-capacity states such as Indiana, Wisconsin, and Tennessee have a smaller staff (an average of 479), are compensated at a lower rate ($43,429), and devote less time to their legislative duties (70 percent).

Legislators in low-capacity states such as New Hampshire, Georgia, and Kansas have a smaller staff that is mostly part-time (169), are compensated the least ($19,197), and devote the least amount of time to legislative duties (54 percent).

The capacity of state legislators to process the numerous bills laid before them is also determined by the amount of time they spend in session. While most state legislatures meet every year, a few (Texas, Montana, North Dakota, and Nevada) meet only every other year, which tends to make the number of bills introduced very high and the capacity for analysis low. The length of time spent in regular session also varies: most legislatures meet between 30 to 160 days in regular session, while some (Idaho, Illinois, Michigan, New Jersey, New York, North Carolina, Ohio, Pennsylvania, Rhode Island, Vermont, and Wisconsin) meet year-round.

The compressed time schedule during session makes legislating a hurried and, in some cases, almost frantic process. Even if a legislator has the time to read every bill he is expected to vote on, he probably won't have time to cross-reference it to other bills, interacting provisions, or underlying affected statutes. Federal agencies, lobbyists, and special-interest groups take advantage of this chaos and push through bills that, if fully understood, might not pass.

A problem that is exacerbated by the imbalance of resources is simply the lack of information available to state legislators.

Deconstructing the Administrative State

As the scope of government programs and policies grows, so too does the scope of knowledge necessary to cast an informed vote. No single legislator can personally analyze every bill and gather the relevant facts and information necessary to make an informed decision. Because they lack personal staff to assist them, many legislators rely on others, particularly lobbyists, to help them.

In the Indiana General Assembly, for example, four state representatives share a single legislative aide. Obviously, one-fourth of a legislative aide doesn't go far in terms of sorting through thousands of pages of bills each session and conducting the necessary research and due diligence. To aid legislators, most state legislatures offer fiscal and legal analysis and bill drafting through a nonpartisan legislative service agency, and party leadership often has a caucus budget for research, legal, and public-relations staff. While these resources are helpful to state legislators, they are simply not enough.

The number of staffers available to members of Congress, on the other hand, dwarfs that of state legislatures. In 2015, congressional staff numbered 19,625, including committee staff, personal staff, leadership staff, and officers of the house staff. There are also joint committee staff, support agency staff, and miscellaneous staff (such as Capitol Police). The largest cohort was for members of Congress's personal staff—6,030 in the House and 3,917 in the Senate.[509]

The unequal amount of resources between state and federal lawmakers empowers the federal government over the states.

---

[509] Table 5-1: Congressional Staff, 1979–2015, Brookings Institution website, https://www.brookings.edu/wp-content/uploads/2017/01/vitalstats_ch5_tbl1.pdf.

Well-funded and attractively presented initiatives from the federal government and its affiliated special-interest organizations are laid before state legislators, who have neither the time nor the research resources to examine them objectively and perhaps debunk the propaganda. When federal policies are backed by the power of Congress, federal agencies, and a variety of organizations with influence in their communities, even legislators who want to defend state sovereignty are outgunned.

These disparities make the fight to defend the constitutional structure an unfair battle from the start. If the capacity of the state legislature is already stretched thin by a lack of resources and time, how can the legislature be expected to check the power and influence of the behemoth federal government?

The next sections will detail how the administrative state undermines the decision-making process of state legislators in two ways: (1) the administrative state uses its power to place considerable political pressure on lawmakers to adopt federal priorities, and (2) it uses its regulatory power to implement its preferred policies and programs outside the normal legislative process (via rule-making, grants, and so forth), which cuts state legislators out of the decision-making process.

HOW FEDERAL AGENCIES APPLY POLITICAL PRESSURE TO INFLUENCE STATE LAWS

As explained in other chapters of this book, federal policies tend to originate at the agency level—for example, standards-based education reform with the USED, mass-transit grants with the DOT, and public-health expansion with the U.S. Public Health Service. Once a federal agency decides to push a policy, it applies political pressure to advance legislation.

Deconstructing the Administrative State

Step one is to legitimize the reform as a social imperative. This is accomplished by commissioning biased research conducted to justify rather than to evaluate the proposed policy. Despite the perhaps questionable science underpinning the research, it's used to build consensus among "experts" in the field, state-level agencies, lobbyists, national associations, and nonprofits. These groups, some of which will benefit financially if the reform becomes policy, serve as a conduit for federal agencies to lobby lawmakers at the federal and state levels in support of legislation to implement the reform.

Once such legislation is passed by Congress or state legislatures, history suggests it's only a matter of time before the reform fails. The agency will then start the process over again, replacing the failed reform with one very similar and predictably more

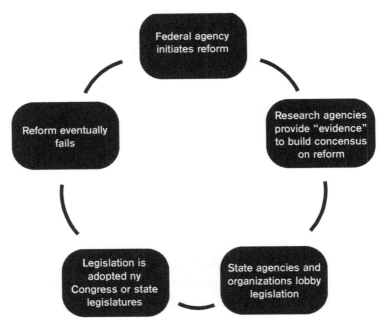

expansive and expensive, and the states under political and financial pressure will likely adopt it. Many legislators, of course, are amenable to doing the federal government's bidding and work in cooperation with lobbyists and agents of federal and state departments to adopt federal requirements into state law. When federal funding represents 30 percent of the state's budget, obliging the federal government is the politically expedient thing to do; constituents can be swayed by the additional spending capacity these federal programs bring to the state. The financial relationship with the federal government provides state legislators, who may be constrained by balanced-budget amendments and limited state revenues, the means to finance attractively packaged programs. Although the states could levy taxes to finance these programs, why should they? The feds will do it for them and save them the political fallout.

State legislators who realize that the purported short-term benefits of federal funding are offset by long-term financial burdens and loss of state sovereignty face an uphill battle convincing the public, and even some conservative legislators, to shun the federal programs. In most cases, uncertainty over whether the state will lose funding for failure to adopt specific laws or policies is enough to quell any efforts at pushing back — even when federal law is plainly in the states' favor. No Child Left Behind, for example, expressly prohibited the secretary of education from mandating a particular set of standards, yet the fear of losing Title I money or other federal benefits (a fear stoked, duplicitously, by USED bureaucrats)[510] dissuaded many legislators from voting to repeal Common Core.

---

[510] See Caitlin Emma, "The Price of Common Core Repeal," *Politico*, August 28, 2014, http://www.politico.com/.

Deconstructing the Administrative State

The Common Core issue illustrates another problem. Even though student achievement has declined nationally since the standards were adopted, the USED, the U.S. Chamber of Commerce, the National Association of State School Boards, the National Association of School Administrators, teachers' unions, and even state departments of education and local school administrators continue to oppose legislation to repeal the standards. They do so not because Common Core increases student academic achievement (it clearly doesn't) but because they follow a progressive agenda (or, in the case of the Chamber of Commerce, a workforce-development agenda) into which Common Core fits nicely. But overwhelmed state legislators are generally unaware of this agenda; instead, they see these entities as objective "experts" on which they will rely because they lack the resources to challenge the consensus argument.

State legislators who continue to be influenced by these lobbyists and nonprofits appear to know little about the history of federal education programs. From *A Nation at Risk* in 1986, through Goals 2000 and No Child Left Behind, to today's Common Core and the recently passed ESSA, these same groups have consistently advocated for failed programs that increase federal control of education. Each time, they claimed these programs would result in higher standards, better student assessments, increased graduation rates, and "college- and career-readiness," yet the experiment always ended with the bars lowered, student achievement further behind, and students less prepared for a fulfilling life. But despite this uninterrupted record of failure, the federal government and its affiliated nonprofits and lobbyists continue to exercise outsized influence in state policy-making.

Over and over, the federal government, through its attendant agencies, repeats this cyclical process with lawmakers to advance big-government reforms that don't work. In many ways, this process is the culmination of early progressives' idea of experimental public-policy-setting, where unelected bureaucrats — unmoored from the Constitution and political accountability — continually experiment with policies in the hope of one day achieving social efficiency. This is tyranny by experts — and state legislators are either unwilling or unable to stop it.

How Federal Agencies Direct State Policies through Regulation

A particularly effective way for the federal government to shape state law is to enact sweeping legislation that extends its tentacles into the states. The policy of a broad federal law will eventually be adopted at the state level, as state law generally conforms to federal law. For example, in the three years after the Affordable Care Act passed in 2010, 546 new state laws were enacted in response; 510 were passed to comply with the act, and only 36 were passed to challenge or provide an alternative to the act.[511] Federal agencies responsible for administering the federal program then issue myriad regulations to which state law must also conform, putting state law into the hands of unelected federal bureaucrats. If the state doesn't conform to the new federal regulations, the federal agency will often threaten the loss of funding.

---

[511] "Health Reform: 2011–2013 State Legislative Tracking Database," National Conference of State Legislatures website, last updated January 2014, http://www.ncsl.org/research/health/health-reform-database-2011-2013-state-legislation.aspx.

Deconstructing the Administrative State

Congress also empowers federal agencies to undermine the role of state legislatures when, as described in chapter 8, it requires a state to submit a "state plan" to federal agencies in its application to participate in a federal program. In general, federal laws under which a state plan (more accurately called a "federal plan") must be submitted don't require the consent of the state legislature. Instead, the state plan is submitted with the signature of the official of the state agency responsible for administering the program. For example, ESSA requires the signature of only the state superintendent of education, not the governor or any legislative officials. Thus, legislatures are usually cut out of the decision-making process used to develop the state plans and are unaware of the various assurances and promises made by the state agency on the state's behalf. In fact, as in the case of Common Core, the legislatures may be unaware even that the federal program exists and that their states are participating. Their only involvement is generally after the fact — to make sure state laws conform to the state plan.

Thus does the federal government convert the state legislatures and executive agencies into little more than agents to implement federal policies. And while the state executive agencies may at least be aware of the federal programs and mandates, the legislatures are frequently left in the dark until it's too late — until the programs are already embedded and protected by the federal government and a phalanx of well-funded special-interest groups. This is not the way the Founders intended state policy-making to work.

Chapter 10

The Pursuit of Happiness

A Short Note on Life, Liberty, and Property

*You are a man, and so am I. God created both, and made us
separate beings. . . . In leaving you, I took nothing but what
belonged to me, and in no way lessened your means for obtaining
an honest living. Your faculties remained yours, and mine became
useful to their rightful owner.*[512]

—Frederick Douglass, letter to Thomas Auld,
who had held Douglass in slavery, September 3, 1848

The administrative state can enjoy the authority and resources
necessary to manage society only if it grabs power from states, and
ultimately from citizens. The modern-day administrative state particularly benefits from using new technologies in the management
of people. The science of administration demands nothing less.

Progressives unravel the bundle of individual rights with a
narrow characterization of the right to property. That view doesn't
hold the right to property as intimately connected to, and flowing
from, the individual. Rather, as Walter Rauschenbusch argued,

[512] Transcript accessed at Letters of Note, ed. Shaun Usher, http://
www.lettersofnote.com/.

property must be "made to serve the public good, either by the service its uses render to the public welfare, or by the income it brings to the public treasury." Property must "be made more directly available for the service of all"; in a word, it must be depersonalized. As early progressives termed it, we must "resocialize property."[513] Of course, the by-product of that is an individual who has no security and who remains at the mercy of the State (and its experts).

Properly viewed, the right to property, in both its philosophical and legal meanings, serves as a bulwark against the bureaucratic tendency to develop ever more ways to amass power. It is an inextricable part of the classic liberal formulation, used by John Locke and others, of "life, liberty, and property" as the overarching description of individual rights.[514] In its full philosophical meaning, property encompasses all things proper to man by nature, including "Lives, Liberties and Estates."[515] To that end, in his essay "Property," James Madison noted that man has property not only in his "land, or merchandize, or money" but also in "his opinions and the free communication of them." Madison continued:

> He has a property of peculiar value in his religious opinions, and in the profession and practice dictated by them.
>
> He has a property very dear to him in the safety and liberty of his person.

---

[513] Walter Rauschenbusch, "The Socializing of Property," in *Christianizing the Social Order* (New York: Macmillan, 1912), 419–429, reprinted in Pestritto and Atto, *American Progressivism*, 117–124.

[514] John Locke, *Second Treatise*, chap. IX, sect. 123. See also chap. VII, sects. 87–89.

[515] Ibid., chap. IX, sect. 123.

He has an equal property in the free use of his faculties and free choice of the objects on which to employ them.

In a word, as a man is said to have a right to his property, he may be equally said to have a property in his rights.[516]

Madison warned, "Where an excess of power prevails, property of no sort is duly respected. No man is safe in his opinions, his person, his faculties or his possessions. Where there is an excess of liberty, the effect is the same, tho' from an opposite cause." The purpose of government, he contended, is "to protect property of every sort; as well that which lies in the various rights of individuals, as that which the term particularly expresses."[517]

Properly considered, the rights to life, liberty, and property establish a fluid continuum of rights. An individual's right to life, of course, inheres with his existence. His right to liberty expresses his rights to action: for example, to develop and employ his faculties, to earn a living, to express himself in verbal and written form, to develop associations with others, and to practice his faith. His liberty rights include, too, his right to exploit and protect his real and personal property. His right to property encompasses the right to possess the product of his liberties. It includes his real property, personal property, and intellectual property. It also includes the associations he has formed with others and with the Creator.[518]

---

[516] James Madison, "Property," Lexrex website, http://www.lexrex. com/enlightened/AmericanIdeal/honor_to_founders/not_just_ material.htm.

[517] Ibid.

[518] For a general discussion of these issues, see Peter Laslett, introduction to John Locke, *Two Treatises of Government* (Cambridge:

Deconstructing the Administrative State

Progressives tend to narrow the meaning of "property" and to disconnect it from the individual, to make it an object separate from the individual and subject to exploitation by government. That dynamic plays out, rather blatantly, in the traditionalist versus progressive interpretations of the Second Amendment: traditionalists hold the right "to keep and bear arms" as encompassing both personal property and liberty rights, while progressives argue that it's an impersonal matter intertwined with state sovereignty and militia authorities rather than with personal liberty.[519] The Supreme Court eminent-domain case *Kelo v. City of New London* shows a more nuanced application of the conflicting views of property.

The Court in *Kelo* held that government may use its eminent-domain powers to take property from a private party (*Kelo* involved fifteen homes owned by various private parties) and give it to another private party for purposes of economic development.[520] Earlier case law had established that government may take property from a private owner only for public ownership, such as for a park or highway, or for transfer to a private party if the purpose is a future "use by the public"—a use that can be exploited by people generally—such as for a common carrier railroad or a public utility.

Cambridge University Press, 1988), 101ff.

[519] See, *e.g.*, District of Columbia v. Heller, 554 U.S. 570 (2008): "There seems to us no doubt, on the basis of both text and history, that the Second Amendment conferred an individual right to keep and bear arms" (at 595). In a dissent joined by three other justices, Justice Stevens argued that the Second Amendment "was a response to concerns ... that the power of Congress to disarm the state militias and create a national standing army posed an intolerable threat to the sovereignty of the several States." Ibid., 637 (Stevens, J., dissenting).

[520] Kelo v. City of New London, 545 U.S. 469 (2005).

Over the previous century, the Court had expansively interpreted—that is, weakened—the Fifth Amendment requirement that government "takings" be for a "public use." The Court in *Kelo* observed that it had "long ago rejected any literal requirement that condemned property be put into use for the general public."[521] It continued, "Indeed, while many state courts in the mid-19th century endorsed 'use by the public' as the proper definition of [the Fifth Amendment requirement that a taking be for] public use, that narrow view steadily eroded over time."[522] Resting on that logic, the *Kelo* Court held that the literal interpretation was "impractical given the diverse and always evolving needs of society" and that, therefore, it would affirm its line of cases interpreting "public use" to mean "public purpose," not use by the public.[523]

In dissent, Justice O'Connor wrote that the Court had abandoned the "long-held, basic limitation on government power" that a "law that takes property from A and gives it to B . . . is against all reason and justice."[524] She continued:

Under the banner of economic development, all private property is now vulnerable to being taken and transferred to another private owner, so long as it might be upgraded—*i.e.*, given to an owner who will use it in a way that the legislature deems more beneficial to the

---

[521] Ibid., 479, quoting Hawaii Housing Authority v. Midkiff, 467 U.S. 229, 244 (1984). The Fifth Amendment states, in pertinent part, "nor shall private property be taken for public use without just compensation."

[522] Ibid.

[523] Ibid., 480.

[524] Ibid., 494 (O'Connor, J., dissenting), quoting Calder v. Bull, 3 U.S. 386 (1798).

public—in the process. To reason, as the Court does, that the incidental public benefits resulting from the subsequent ordinary use of private property render economic development takings "for public use" is to wash out any distinction between private and public use of property—and thereby effectively to delete the words "for public use" from the Takings Clause of the Fifth Amendment.[525]

The Fifth Amendment's two conditions—that the taking be for a "public use" and that "just compensation" be paid—provide "safeguards against excessive, unpredictable, or unfair use of the government's eminent-domain power—particularly against those owners who, for whatever reasons, may be unable to protect themselves in the political process against the majority's will."[526] But the Court took a very narrow view of the nature of the property being protected, merely noting that it does "not minimize the hardship the condemnations may entail, notwithstanding the payment of just compensation."[527] The seized property is but a thing for which the owner will be paid—not something rising to the level of intimate liberty rights.

In a separate dissent, Justice Thomas argued that the Constitution demands greater protection. He began, "Long ago, William Blackstone wrote that 'the law of the land ... postpone[s] even public necessity to the sacred and inviolable rights of private property.'"[528] Having expanded the meaning of "public use"

---

[525] Ibid., 494.
[526] Ibid., 496.
[527] Ibid., 489.
[528] Ibid., 505 (Thomas, J., dissenting), quoting *Commentaries on the Laws of England* 1 (1765): 134–135.

to mean "public purpose," the Court expanded "public purpose" to mean a "more productive" use and then deferred to government to decide what satisfies that term. This led to anomalous results. As Justice Thomas observed:

> The Court has elsewhere recognized "the overriding respect for the sanctity of the home that has been embedded in our traditions since the origins of the Republic" when the issue is only whether the government may search a home. Yet today the Court tells us that we are not to "second-guess the City's considered judgments" when the issue is, instead, whether the government may take the infinitely more intrusive step of tearing down petitioners' homes.[529]

Justice Thomas concluded by drawing out the personal nature of rights in property:

> The consequences of today's decision are not difficult to predict, and promise to be harmful. So-called "urban renewal" programs provide some compensation for the properties they take, but no compensation is possible for the subjective value of these lands to the individuals displaced and the indignity inflicted by uprooting them from their homes. Allowing the government to take property solely for public purposes is bad enough, but extending the concept of public purpose to encompass any economically beneficial goal guarantees that these losses will fall disproportionately on poor communities. Those communities are not only systematically less likely

---

[529] Ibid., 518, internal citations omitted.

to put their lands to the highest and best social use, but are also the least politically powerful. If ever there were justification for intrusive judicial review of constitutional provisions that protect "discrete and insular minorities," surely that principle would apply with great force to the powerless groups and individuals the Public Use Clause protects. The deferential standard this Court has adopted for the Public Use Clause is therefore deeply perverse. It encourages "those citizens with disproportionate influence and power in the political process, including large corporations and development firms," to victimize the weak.[530]

As the dissents noted, the evisceration of the Fifth Amendment's private-property protections puts the ownership of private property in peril to subjective, even arbitrary, evaluations of economic benefit. The history of the land at issue in *Kelo* makes that point: More than ten years after the property owners' lands were taken and their homes bulldozed, the land still lay empty.[531]

The full sense of "property" provides a bulwark against government's natural tendency to expand its powers. It demands that government give wide latitude to individuals and their rights to form their identity, or property. Without a proper respect for an individual's property, in the fullest sense of the word, government forges ahead in its natural tendency to absorb more power. For example, it embarks on ever new schemes to collect and analyze data—unrelated to national security—on citizens. It reinterprets laws and regulations, in ways that are wholly unfaithful to the

---

[530] Ibid., 521–522, internal citations omitted.
[531] Ilya Somin, *The Grasping Hand: Kelo v. City of New London and the Limits of Eminent Domain* (Chicago: University of Chicago Press, 2016), 4.

statutory language, to authorize itself to collect and share more and more information about citizens.[532] It delves into students' "self-awareness, self-management, social awareness, relationship skills, and responsible decision-making."[533] In the cramped progressive view of property, none of this is an infringement.

The conflict over the philosophical meaning of "property" plays out in another area—the federal government's capturing vast tracts of land so that they can never be owned by the people. The traditionalist American concept of real property is that, except for narrow, limited federal needs, lands would be made available to the states so that they could be conveyed to citizens. As explained in the next chapter, the progressive concept is the opposite: that the administrative state will claim as much property as possible—managing natural resources, states, and people alike. Increasingly, government has adopted the progressive view and "protected" more and more land from state and private ownership. The progressive march against the constitutional structure is nothing more than a narrowing of the individual's realm, involving less access to land, less power over government, and less security in one's property and in one's liberty.

---

[532] See Emmett McGroarty, Joy Pullmann, and Jane Robbins, *Cogs in the Machine: Big Data, Common Core, and National Testing* (Boston: Pioneer Institute, 2014), http://pioneerinstitute.org/download/cogs-in-the-machine-big-data-common-core-and-national-testing/; Emmett McGroarty and Jane Robbins, "How the Feds Are Tracking Your Kid," *New York Post*, December 27, 2011, http://nypost.com/.

[533] Jane Robbins, "The Latest Big Education Fad, Social-Emotional Learning, Is As Bad as It Sounds," Townhall, August 8, 2016, https://townhall.com/.

Chapter 11

Federal Control of State Lands

*Land is the only thing in the world that amounts to anything, for
'tis the only thing in this world that lasts.*

—Gerald O'Hara, to his daughter Scarlett,
in Margaret Mitchell, *Gone With the Wind*

It is self-evident that the project of managing society requires a
large degree of control over natural resources. To that end, the
progressive Walter Rauschenbusch wrote in *The Socializing of
Property* (1912), "Our States and the federal government should
keep all the land they still have and henceforth lease it instead
of selling."[534] "Public health and public wealth alike demand its
social ownership."[535]

A brief overview of the history of federal and state sovereignty over lands is necessary to understand why control over
lands is so important to state autonomy, and why the federal
government's relatively new policy of gobbling up as much state

---

[534] Walter Rauschenbusch, "The Socializing of Property," in *Christianizing the Social Order* (New York: Macmillan, 1912), 419–429,
reprinted in Pestritto and Atto, *American Progressivism*, 117–
124, 120.
[535] Ibid., 119.

territory as possible usurps constitutional principles of federalism. While eastern states enjoy control over the lands within their borders, many western states have seen the federal government usurp their rightful control over millions of acres of state lands. This federal land grab not only deprives state legislatures of substantial authority but also makes the federal government, and its policy, a dominant factor in public policy within the states. The federal government controls large swaths of economic opportunity, if not the existing economy. It employs or contracts with a cadre of citizens who would otherwise be employed by the state or private business. Thus, economic opportunity itself lies in the grip of the federal government.

At the end of the Revolutionary War, the original thirteen states (plus Vermont, Kentucky, and Tennessee, which were the next three to enter the Union) received whatever unoccupied Crown holdings were present within their borders.[536] This was in keeping with the states' determination to maintain their status as sovereign jurisdictions, with separate constitutions, governments, statutes, courts, taxes, and so forth.[537]

Seven of the original states claimed land extending beyond their western borders,[538] but all recognized that new states would eventually be carved out of the western lands. Disputes about

---

[536] John W. Howard et al., "Legal Analysis of the Legislative Consulting Services Team Prepared for the Utah Commission for the Stewardship of Public Lands" (December 9, 2015) (hereafter Legal Analysis), 11, *citing* Thomas Donaldson, *The Public Domain: Its History, with Statistics,* H.R. Ex. Doc., No. 47, pt. 4, at 30–55 (3rd Sess., 1880)(3rd ed., 1884), http://le.utah.gov/interim/2015/pdf/00005590.pdf.

[537] Legal Analysis, 16.

[538] Ibid., 21.

how these lands would be handled began during the war and continued throughout the Articles of Confederation period, into the time of the Constitutional Convention. Ultimately, the states that claimed western lands ceded them to the national government pursuant to the terms of the Northwest Ordinance, which provided for a temporary government in those western lands until they were sufficiently populated to be admitted to the Union "on an equal footing with the ... original States."[539]

Throughout the years-long negotiations over this issue, the understanding among all parties was that Congress would accept the ceded territories not to build a bank of federal lands, but rather on a temporary basis to dispose of them for the benefit of the new states. This understanding, of course, aligned with the universal agreement that states would retain sovereignty over all matters not explicitly granted to the federal government by the Constitution.

The new Constitution contained a new-states-admission clause[540] in Article IV, Section 3 to govern the admission process. Without much debate, the drafters included the "Property Clause" to give Congress the power to dispose of western lands:

> The Congress shall have Power to dispose of and make all needful Rules and Regulations respecting the Territory or other Property belonging to the United States;

---

[539] Ibid., 32.

[540] "New States may be admitted by the Congress into this Union; but no new State shall be formed or erected within the Jurisdiction of any other State; nor any State be formed by the Junction of two or more States, or Parts of States, without the Consent of the Legislatures of the States concerned as well as of the Congress."

and nothing in this Constitution shall be so construed as to Prejudice any Claims of the United States, or of any particular State.[541]

In 1789, shortly after the Constitution's ratification, Congress reenacted the Northwest Ordinance to initiate the creation of new states from the western lands ceded by the original states.[542] This act "confirmed the process for admission of new States and the 'primary disposal of the soil'" over which Congress now exercised control.[543] But the emphasis on "disposal" of these lands illustrated the understanding that federal dominion was to be temporary.

From 1790 until 1802, the states that claimed western lands ceded them to the United States pursuant to agreements providing that the territory would be "faithfully disposed of" for the use and benefit of the United States and each state.[544] Indeed, "the overarching motive of all policy with respect to the disposition of public land was in the advance of civilization and the expansion of the nation and its commerce through the use of land not only as a resource but as an inducement for the promotion of settlement."[545] The goal was not to "protect" the lands but to put them to work under the control of the new states.

To accomplish this, Congress pursued various avenues for placing the land in the hands of people who would develop it, including aggressive sales and even giving the property away to

---

[541] U.S. Constitution, Art. IV, § 3.
[542] Legal Analysis, 43.
[543] Ibid.
[544] Ibid., 44 (discussing NC and GA cessions).
[545] Ibid., 49.

settlers through the Homestead Act.[546] "This Act resulted in settlement across the nation and the development of homes, towns, communities and commerce to the general benefit of the nation."[547] Not until after the Sixteenth Amendment was ratified in 1913 to impose a federal income tax did the federal government stop selling public lands as a source of funding.[548]

As the western states joined the Union, each did so pursuant to enabling legislation governing the respective responsibilities of the federal and new state's governments.[549] The clear implication of, if not an express statement in, the enabling acts was that Congress would dispose of the lands previously held by the federal government for the benefit of the new states.

But during the twentieth century and into the twenty-first, the federal government has reoriented its lands policy away from development to "protection"—which requires continuing or even increasing federal control to the detriment of state sovereignty. In 1976, through the Federal Land Policy and Management Act (FLPMA), Congress declared it the policy of the United States, not that most federal lands be disposed of for the benefit of the states, as had been the case for almost two centuries, but that "public lands be retained in Federal ownership"[550] absent certain conditions.

The plethora of mechanisms for implementing this reversal of policy includes designating national parks, national monuments,

[546] Ibid., 50.
[547] Ibid.
[548] Ibid.
[549] See, *e.g.*, Utah Enabling Act, chap. 138, 28 Stat. 107 (1894).
[550] Federal Land Policy and Management Act, Public Law No. 94-579, 90 Stat. 2743,
43 USC § 1701(a)(1) (1976).

national recreation areas, national historical sites, national historical trails, national forests, national wilderness areas, national conservation areas, national wildlife refuges, national recreation trails, and national scenic byways. No one objects to reasonable protected-area designations such as national parks, but the federal government's lust for control has, in the view of many citizens, exceeded the bounds of reason.

The federal government has removed millions of acres from control of western states such that some states now exercise sovereignty over only a small percentage of their land. In Utah, for example, the federal government controls more than 66 percent of the state's land (more than 36 million of the state's 54.3 million acres).[551] In Nevada, the percentage of federally controlled land is an astounding 85 percent.[552] The federal government now owns and controls more than 50 percent of lands west of the "fault line" created by the 104th meridian (roughly, the line tracking the eastern borders of Montana and Wyoming and continuing south), compared with only 5 percent of lands east of those states.[553]

Although most federal land grabs are accomplished by Congress, the federal Antiquities Act[554] allows the president to issue

[551] Roger E. Banner et al., *Rangeland Resources of Utah* (2009), 9–23, https://extension.usu.edu/. See also Carol Hardy Vincent, Laura A. Hanson, and Carla N. Argueta, *Federal Land Ownership: Overview and Data* (Washington, D.C.: Congressional Research Service, 2017), https://fas.org/sgp/crs/misc/R42346.pdf.

[552] David Johnson and Pratheek Rebala, "Here's Where the Federal Government Owns the Most Land," *Time*, January 5, 2016, http://time.com/4167983/federal-government-land-oregon/.

[553] See American Lands Council, http://www.americanlandscouncil.org.

[554] Antiquities Act of 1906, Public Law No. 59-209 (codified at 54 USC § 320301ff.).

executive orders designating potentially vast areas as national monuments and therefore removed from state control. Not surprisingly, President Obama surpassed all his predecessors by seizing 553 million acres for federal "protection."[555] His last use of the Antiquities Act—designating 1.35 million acres in Utah and 300,000 acres in Nevada as national monuments—outraged citizens of those states. Then-Rep. Jason Chaffetz (R-UT) decried the Utah designation as "a slap in the face to the people of Utah, attempting to silence the voices of those who will bear the heavy burden it imposes."[556]

There is no more effective means of usurping state autonomy than depriving the state of control over its own lands. The economic consequences of such action are enormous. As Ken Ivory of the advocacy organization the American Lands Council (and elected state representative in Utah) puts it:

[Federal lands policy] is killing Western communities, draining money right out of our kids' education, closing off recreation and grazing access, burning up western forests, and locking up trillions of dollars in abundant natural resources in western communities.[557]

[555] Coral Davenport, "Obama Designates Two New National Monuments, Protecting 1.65 Million Acres," *New York Times*, December 28, 2016, http://www.nytimes.com/2016/12/28/us/ politics/obama-national-monument-bears-ears-utah-gold-butte. html.

[556] "Jason Chaffetz, U.S. Congressman, Chaffetz Outraged by Obama Decision to Impose Unwanted Midnight Monument in Utah," press release, December 28, 2016, https://www.nytimes. com/2016/12/28/us/politics/obama-national-monument-bears-ears-utah-gold-butte.html.

[557] See American Lands Council.

Deconstructing the Administrative State

Particularly galling to many in the western states is the denial of access to the enormous natural wealth lying beneath the surface of these federally controlled lands. In 2013, the Institute for Energy Research estimated that the total worth to the economy of fossil fuels on federal lands, excluding Alaskan coal, is $150.5 trillion.[558] The locked-up western lands also contain rich deposits of other minerals. According to the National Mining Association, lack of access to these deposits forces the United States to be "import-dependent for 19 key mineral resources and more than 50 percent import-dependent for an additional 24 mineral commodities used in everyday manufacturing and defense applications"—even though U.S. mineral reserves, much of them on federal lands, are estimated to be worth $6.2 trillion.[559]

Federal law does grant states a share of federal mineral receipts,[560] and local governments small payments from the Payment in Lieu of Taxes[561] and Secure Rural Schools and Self-Determination Act.[562] These payments are intended to compensate for removing the land from state and local economic development. But western-state government officials argue that the payments do not begin to make up for the lost revenues and that the states

[558] Institute for Energy Research, "Federal Assets above and below Ground," January 17, 2013, http://instituteforenergyresearch. org/.
[559] National Mining Association, "Leading the World in Resources, Trailing the Competition in Access," September 11, 2016, http:// nma.org/.
[560] See "Leasing and Selling Federal Lands and Resources: Receipts and Their Disposition," EveryCRSReport.com, April 4, 2011, https://www.everycrsreport.com/.
[561] Public Law No. 94-565 (1976).
[562] Public Law No. 106-393 (2000).

can oversee these lands much more efficiently than can D.C. bureaucrats.

Not only does such action negatively affect the state's economy by removing potentially productive land from circulation—with the attendant decrease in state tax revenues—but it marginalizes the elected state legislature as a minor policy-maker in control of minor territory. The major policy-maker in such circumstances, of course, becomes the distant, unaccountable bureaucrats of the federal government. When this happens, the federalist system empowering sovereign states is turned on its head.

Some western states are beginning to fight back against this massive territorial overreach. Over the past several years Arizona, Colorado, Idaho, Montana, Nevada, New Mexico, Utah, and Wyoming have begun exploring actions ultimately to reassert state control over some lands seized by the federal government.[563] As stated by the American Lands Council, the goal is to recover "the lands that were intended to be multiple-use federal lands, NOT National Parks, military bases, Indian reservations or congressionally designated wilderness areas."[564] The boldest of these legislative actions is Utah's 2012 Transfer of Public Lands Act (TPLA),[565] which demanded that the federal government

---

[563] For a discussion of the various state initiatives, see Donald J. Kochan, "Public Lands and the Federal Government's Compact-Based 'Duty to Dispose': A Case Study of Utah's H.B. 148—The Transfer of Public Lands Act," *Brigham Young University Law Review* 2013, no. 5 (2014): 1133, 1139–1141n23–29, http://digitalcommons.law.byu.edu/lawreview/vol2013/iss5/3.

[564] See "Get the Facts," American Lands Council website, http://www.americanlandscouncil.org/get_the_facts, emphasis in the original.

[565] Utah Code Ann. § 63L-6-101ff. (West 2012).

extinguish its title to twenty to thirty million acres of land in Utah by the end of 2014. The federal government has so far clung to its ill-gotten gains. To date the state has not sued to enforce the statute, but it has several strong arguments should it decide to do so.

From a federalism perspective, Utah can show that federal law, through the FLPMA, violates the Equal Sovereignty Principle by treating the state as unequal in sovereignty compared with eastern states that have control over the vast majority of their lands.[566] A related argument is that the FLPMA violates the Equal Footing Doctrine (requiring that new states be admitted on an "equal footing" with the original states).[567] A third strong argument is a contract-based theory that the federal government is in breach of promises it made, either explicitly or implicitly, in Utah's Enabling Act when Utah became a state in 1894 — promises creating a duty to dispose of federal public lands within the state.

Though the issue hasn't been joined in court, the federal government would presumably defend its position by arguing a broad interpretation of the constitutional Property Clause, giving Congress "Power to dispose of and make all needful Rules and Regulations respecting the Territory or other Property belonging to the United States."[568] But the many weaknesses of that argument,[569] both legal and historical, create hope that a court might enforce the bargain Utah thought it had made in 1894.

[566] Legal Analysis, 2, 54–72.
[567] Ibid., 2–3.
[568] U.S. Constitution, Art. IV, § 3.
[569] See Kochan, "Public Lands," 1167–1169.

Federal Control of State Lands

Inspired by Utah's example, other western states may fight back against the obliteration of their autonomy by a grasping federal government. If the states are to enjoy the most fundamental principle of sovereignty, the battle is long overdue.

Chapter 12

Winners and Losers

If, in the opinion of the people, the distribution or modification of the constitutional powers be in any particular wrong, let it be corrected by an amendment in the way which the Constitution designates. But let there be no change by usurpation; for though this, in one instance, may be the instrument of good, it is the customary weapon by which free governments are destroyed.

—George Washington, Farewell Address, 1796

Bending Government to Benefit Special-Interest Groups

The progressive preference for large, powerful government with administration by experts conflicts with economic reality: that economic players will always—always—learn how to game the system. A relatively small federal government of strictly enumerated powers, with most power resting with the states and the people, minimizes the opportunities for mischief against citizens' liberties. But when the federal government is so expansive and powerful that fortunes can be made or lost depending on how it operates, average Americans, whose voices constitutional federalism was designed to protect, find it difficult to compete with the moneyed players. They will be hard-pressed even to have their causes heard by congressional leadership and the necessary committees. In *The Theory of Economic Regulation*, George Stigler explained:

> The state — the machinery and power of the state — is a potential resource or threat to every industry in the society. With its power to prohibit or compel, to take or give money, the state can and does selectively help or hurt a vast number of industries.[570]

Government interventions — whether regulatory schemes or participation in the marketplace as a customer — often have benefits to both sides of an issue, as well as ancillary benefits to compliance practitioners such as attorneys and accountants. Savvy players will work to bend government action in their favor in a variety of ways, including (1) accessing transfers of money in the form of subsidies, grants, and contracts and (2) using regulatory schemes to gain an advantage over competitors.

Transfers of Money

Stigler observes that "an industry with power to obtain governmental favors usually does not use this power to get money: unless the list of beneficiaries can be limited by an acceptable device." The reasoning is that the availability of subsidies — essentially free money — will attract new players into the field and thereby reduce the benefits of the free money by increasing competition. The political situation, though, can lend itself to an industry's seeking other cash transfers.

---

[570] George Stigler, "The Theory of Economic Regulation," *Bell Journal of Economics* 2, no. 1 (Spring 1971): 3.

The federal government has expanded tremendously since Stigler published his observations in 1971. Now it can create or drive a market, as it has in the case of centralized student databases. Beginning in 2002 with the Education Technical Assistance Act, and continuing through the America COMPETES Act (2007) and Race to the Top (2010), the federal government incentivized the establishment of statewide longitudinal data systems to track children from pre-K through entry into the workforce. Such a vast surveillance-and-tracking system created highly lucrative opportunities for vendors and data experts.[571] Likewise, a "stimulus" bill would attract the attention of affected industries (such as construction, or, in the case of President Obama's RttT program, education) to capture money for the benefit of existing players ready to pounce on the federal spending opportunity.

Regulatory Strategies

Regulatory schemes raise the bar for new entrants into the field and give larger enterprises an advantage over their smaller competitors. This can be done through licensing requirements and complex reporting requirements that necessitate devoting resources to licensing and regulatory compliance. As Todd Zywicki noted: "Where the regulation transfers wealth to a given industry or to certain firms within that industry, those parties will favor the regulation, not oppose it."[572] Writing in 1999 about the state of environmental regulation, Zywicki observed that regulation

[571] McGroarty, Pullmann, and Robbins, *Cogs in the Machine*, 11–14.
[572] Todd J. Zywicki, "Environmental Externalities and Political Externalities: The Political Economy of Environmental Regulation and Reform," *Tulane Law Review* (February 1999): 856–857.

can benefit an industry or subsets of it by increasing demand for the industry's product or by making it difficult for competitors to enter the market. It can also give certain segments of the industry an advantage over other segments. For example, a regulation requiring installation of an expensive smoke scrubber on a factory will favor larger companies over smaller ones.[573] The same is true of a regulation requiring substantial compliance reporting, necessitating the retention of attorneys, compliance officers, and so forth.[574]

As an example, Zywicki pointed to the Weyerhaeuser Company's reaction to the controversial spotted-owl issue in the 1990s. Federal regulators, clamping down on the timber industry in the northwest in an effort to save the owl's habitat, had forced Weyerhaeuser to stop logging on 320,000 acres of its land. The company responded by hiring wildlife biologists to search for spotted owls on federally owned lands, and thereby advanced an effort that resulted in over five million acres of that land being placed off-limits to logging. The result: higher lumber prices, marginalized competition from smaller companies, and increased profits for Weyerhaeuser.[575] One commentator noted: "As *The Wall Street Journal* summarized the benefit to Weyerhaeuser of spotted owl protections, 'owl-driven profits enabled the company to earn $86.6 million in the first quarter [of 1992], up 81% from a year earlier.'"[576]

---

[573] Ibid., 864.
[574] Ibid., 811.
[575] Ibid. 873–874.
[576] Todd J. Zywicki, "Environmental Externalities," 873–874, citing Bruce Yandle, *Common Sense and Common Law for the Environment: Creating Wealth in Hummingbird Economies* (Lanham, MD: Rowman and Littlefield, 1997), 74.

IMPERATIVE: SHUT THE PEOPLE OUT

Commentators and pundits are fond of debating whether the American people care about the issues of the day. The refrain is that people are not engaged. We disagree with the pessimists and argue instead that millions of Americans who care deeply about their country find themselves shut out by application of Stigler's theory to the political class. Just as private interests will game the political system to their advantage, so will savvy politicians, including members of Congress. The self-serving strategies they employ have the effect of shunning and thwarting citizen engagement.

Developments over the last twenty years initially bolstered citizen engagement in policy-making. Three key recent developments set the stage. First, in the 1990s, the Internet blossomed as a popular vehicle for the real-time exchange of information and for policy research. Citizens now had instant access to vast collections of law, policy, history, and science. With the rise of social media, the ordinary person's political opinion was given a wider audience, which challenged the narrative out of Washington. In the respect of that equilibrium, the republic was back on the keel of the Founding generation.

Second, the attacks of September 11, 2001, rekindled the American spirit.

Third, as President Obama engineered passage of the Affordable Care Act (ACA), a well-informed citizenry tracked the legislation, informed themselves on the subissues, and flooded town-hall meetings and demonstrations in the states and in Washington.

That show of force—of citizen engagement—threatened the political establishment. In particular, it threatened the political class who had constructed a grand casino in which anyone with money could play, and where those with more money would win bigger. Those with comparatively little or no money—the American people—could visit, but not participate in any meaningful fashion. The door must be shut on them and on their citizen groups, such as the Tea Parties, 9/12 groups, and citizen privacy groups, to keep them from interfering with policymaking. As discussed below, congressional leadership had ready solutions to the problem.

STANCHING THE FLOW OF INFORMATION

When elected to Congress, members must generally make a decision: Will they pursue leadership positions, or will they do the bidding of the people who elected them? If they pursue the former, members must raise campaign money for the party, which breeds influence—and perhaps just as detrimental—crowds out the voices of the people. The evidence demonstrates that, for Republicans, playing this game is incompatible with compiling a conservative voting record. (See "How Big Business Controls Both Parties in Congress," below, for a discussion of why big-money interests reject conservatism.) Their new moderate voting record is difficult to explain to constituents and risks the threat of activists' descending upon Washington. To avoid that, party leadership uses its control of legislative procedure to hide members' support for bad legislation.

Leadership uses three legislative "tricks" to "black out" information. The first is restricted layovers, whereby leadership limits access to legislative drafts until just before the bill is voted on. University of Utah political-science professor James Curry explains that, by keeping the bill's content secret until the last minute, leadership can get objectionable legislation passed with minimal opposition:

> Most significant legislation is complex, addressing numer-
> ous issues and engaging a multitude of political interests.
> The final language reflects carefully fashioned compro-
> mises among a handful of important players in Congress,
> the private sector, and the administration. If opponents
> can raise a controversy or otherwise publicize unpopular
> aspects of a bill, or if rank-and-file lawmakers focus on
> information that may push them toward opposition, these
> delicate compromises could be derailed, jeopardizing pas-
> sage of the bill.[577]

House rules require bills to be posted for three days before a floor vote, presumably to allow members and the public a fair opportunity to weigh in. The Rules Committee, however, may issue a special rule to waive that requirement. Curry's research found that, with respect to important legislation, from the 101st through the 111th Congress (*i.e.*, from January 3, 1989, to January 3, 2011), 50 percent of bills lay over less than the required seventy-two hours, with almost 30 percent lying over less than twenty-four hours.[578]

Working through the Rules Committee, party leadership also inserts "self-execution" rules into legislation before a vote is taken. As Curry explains, these rules allow leadership to include last-minute amendments in a bill being considered on

---

[577] James M. Curry, *Legislating in the Dark: Information and Power in the House of Representatives* (Chicago: University of Chicago Press, 2015), 78.
[578] Ibid., 92.

the House floor — including the substitution of a completely new bill:

> Special rules are written in private by the majority staff of the Rules Committee at the direction of the majority leadership. As such, the specific contents of the rule are not known until the Rules Committee markup. Second, self-executing provisions are typically not written with readability in mind. Rather than a series of amendment-like provisions that would strike and insert text at different points in the bill, self-execution often occurs as a single provision that strikes everything and replaces the entire bill. This type of editing makes it much more difficult for lawmakers to assess what changes have been made and to what effect, since they must analyze all of the new draft to identify the alterations.[579]

From the 101st through the 111th Congress, the use of this information-hiding mechanism increased dramatically. In the 101st Congress, less than 6 percent of all special rules had a self-executing provision, but by the 111th Congress, more than one-third of all special rules had a self-executing provision.[580] Such rules vest party leadership with the authority to rewrite legislation behind closed doors, after the bill has been through the legislative process, and with no time for other legislators or the people to analyze the changes. Members must vote blindly or vote against party leadership.

When a bill is written clearly and concisely, the citizen or legislator has a reasonable opportunity to understand its intent

[579] Ibid., 98.
[580] Ibid., 98–99.

and consequences. However, bills are often written using complex language replete with technical jargon. Complexity can be further increased by creating omnibus bills that are hundreds of pages long and cover a multitude of issues.[581] Even if lawmakers or citizens have time to read such a bill, they cannot understand it without expending an enormous amount of additional time to research its ramifications. This allows objectionable provisions to go unnoticed, leaving members unaccountable for their vote.

Notably, Curry's research found that more than one of these information-restricting procedures tend to be used on bills considered a priority to majority leadership, showing an intentional effort to keep citizens in the dark.

Eight years ago, Republicans accused Democrats of ramming Obamacare through Congress in a nontransparent process. Current Speaker of the House Paul Ryan criticized the Democrats, arguing that real reform of the healthcare system required a "sincere, open discussion." He argued that Congress and the White House had focused their public efforts on "platitudes and press conferences, while the substance and the details have remained behind closed doors."[582] Sounding a common theme among Republican leadership at the time, then-Speaker John Boehner chastised Democrats for misrepresenting the bill and ignoring the concerns of constituents: "Shame on each and every one of you who substitutes your will and your desires above those of your fellow countrymen." He warned that they would do so at their own peril: "This is the People's House. And the

---

[581] Ibid., 102–106.

[582] Paul Ryan, "Government Puts Itself, Not Patients, in Control of Care," *Journal Sentinel*, JS Online, July 19, 2009.

moment a majority forgets it, it starts writing itself a ticket to minority status."[583]

But Republican leadership, now in the majority, has not rejected the tactics used by Democrats; rather, it has embraced and "perfected" the process to avoid the political fallout experienced by Democrats. Despite the odious manner in which Obamacare was pushed through Congress, there was at least some degree of openness. The bill was publicly vetted for over a year, including congressional hearings, committee markups, and contentious town halls. The American people learned of many of the controversial provisions in the bill, and the more they knew, the angrier they became. To all that, the takeaway for Republican leadership was, sadly, that to pass legislation the American people might not like, the flow of information must be controlled.

As the Obamacare-repeal debacle in early 2017 has shown, under Speaker Ryan's leadership Republicans have embraced the same underhanded tactics used to pass Obamacare, including writing bills behind closed doors; dropping long, complicated bills on the floor at the last minute; and expecting members to vote on bills without time even to read, much less analyze, them. But the Republican leadership isn't taking the same risk of provoking voter backlash by holding congressional hearings, public committee markup sessions or, Heaven forbid, a series of town halls. Instead, they have limited the flow of information to keep the people in the dark.

Another example is the December 2015 passage of ESSA, the bill that reauthorized President Johnson's Elementary and Secondary Education Act and amended No Child Left Behind

[583] 156 Congressional Record No. 43, March 21, 2010, bk. II, 5.

(NCLB). The legislation had been due for reauthorization in 2007. But rather than wait for a year and the possibility of a Republican president, and despite clarion calls for "reining in" the federal government and restoring local control over education, Republican leaders colluded with their Democratic colleagues and the lame-duck president to engineer passage of a bill that codified much of President Obama's objectionable education policy.[584] And they did it all behind closed doors — with no transparency about who was drafting the bill, almost no public hearings, no town halls, and only two days between the unveiling of the 1,061-page bill and the vote.[585] Moreover, they sheltered the bill from public debate by labeling it "bipartisan," which, according to Senate Majority Leader Mitch McConnell, kills public interest:

> The only way the American people would know that a great debate was going on was if the measures were not bipartisan. When you hang the "bipartisan" tag on something, the perception is that differences have been worked out, and there's a broad agreement that that's the way forward.[586]

With a Democrat in the White House, this strategy seemed to work. Republican leadership orchestrated passage of legislation

---

[584] Emmett McGroarty, "Obama Administration Reveals GOP Leaders' Betrayal on Common Core in Ed Bill," The Pulse 2016, December 21, 2015, https://thenationalpulse.com/.

[585] Emmett McGroarty, "Republican Leadership Plans to Ram Massive Education Bill through Congress," The Pulse 2016, December 2, 2015, https://thenationalpulse.com/.

[586] Joshua Green, "Strict Obstructionist," *Atlantic* (January/February 2010), https://www.theatlantic.com/.

supported by the political class (whose interests are tied to those of the donor class) and claimed it was the best they could do and still avoid a veto. But now Republican leadership faces a dilemma: pass legislation that genuinely fulfills its campaign promises, or protect the interests of its donors.

As Rep. Ken Buck (R-CO) writes in his book *Drain the Swamp: How Washington Corruption Is Worse Than You Think*, too many members of Congress are serious only about getting reelected. Toward that end, Buck explains, House leadership views keeping wealthy campaign donors happy as the surest way to maintain its majority. It thus pressures members to raise money for the National Republican Congressional Committee (NRCC), a political committee devoted to increasing the Republican majority in the House.

During the 2016 election cycle, the NRCC raised $170 million,[587] with about one-third coming from candidates' and lawmakers' fund-raising accounts. Speaker Ryan's campaign committee was the largest NRCC donor at $5.1 million, followed by Majority Leader Kevin McCarthy's at $2.8 million, and John Boehner's at $2 million. The top industries making corporate donations were securities and investment ($16 million), oil and gas ($6.7 million), and real estate ($6 million).

To wield influence in Congress, Buck explains, members must raise money for the NRCC:

> Most Americans don't realize that influence in Congress comes with a price tag. Members are required to pay for

---

[587] See "National Republican Congressional Cmte," "Top Contributors, 2016 Cycle," OpenSecrets.org, https://www.opensecrets.org/parties/contrib.php?cycle=2016&cmte=NRCC.

committee assignments. Chairmen are required to pay for their chairmanships. The Speaker, Leader, and Whip compete for the leadership position and then must pay millions of dollars for the honor of holding the office. Lobbyists, corporations, and wealthy individuals who need something from Congress raise the money.

For Republicans, all the money raised by these charges goes to the National Republican Congressional Committee (NRCC), supposedly to help get members elected. The reality is that NRCC funds are used to coerce members to vote with the leadership. When members don't vote the "right way," the funding dries up from the donor class, members are pressured to step down from their committee assignments, and the NRCC refuses to help finance their campaigns.[588]

A bill in Congress must first pass out of the committee to which it is assigned. This gives the committee members considerable power in shaping the agenda. And of course, each committee has its own "constituency" of groups and business organizations that want to see their policies advanced.

According to Buck, House committees are tiered into "A," "B," or "C" committees, depending on the ability of their respective special-interest groups to donate to the Republican Party. The House Committee on Appropriations, for example, is designated an "A" committee, because its agenda is of interest to a wide spectrum of wealthy special-interest groups whose fortunes ride on federal-agency budgets and lucrative

[588] Ken Buck, *Drain the Swamp: How Washington Corruption Is Worse Than You Think* (Washington, D.C.: Regnery, 2017), 13.

government contracts. Although there is no official listing of dues, Buck reveals that veteran members must raise $450,000 for the NRCC to serve on "A" committees and $220,000 to serve on "B" committees. For a chair position, the dues increase to $1.2 million for "A" committees and $875,000 for "B" committees.[589]

Rep. Bob Massie from Kentucky has also criticized the process, telling *USA Today* that leadership warns new members that "committees all have prices, and don't pick an expensive one if you can't make the payments."[590] He likens the process to "extortion" and argues that it should be illegal to make one's effectiveness as a taxpayer-compensated member of Congress contingent on one's ability to raise campaign cash:

> Just like you shouldn't be making phone calls asking for money from an office that's paid for with taxpayer dollars (something that is prohibited), they shouldn't be able to withhold or extend committee assignments that are official duties and official titles based on fundraising.[591]

Serving on an "A" committee can be quite helpful to representatives in raising donations for their campaigns. As Buck explains, wealthy corporations and their lobbyists spend millions of dollars every year to influence committees. During the 2016 election cycle, members belonging to Financial Services (oversees the financial-services industry), Energy and Commerce

---

[589] Buck, *Drain the Swamp*, chap. 3.

[590] Deirdre Shesgreen and Christopher Schnaars, "Lawmakers' Dues to Party: 'Extortion' or Team Effort?" *USA Today*, May 25, 2016, https://www.usatoday.com/.

[591] Ibid.

(oversees general interstate and foreign commerce), and Ways and Means (crafts tax policy), all of which are "A" committees, received $85 million,[592] $73.5 million,[593] and $67.6[594] million in donations to their campaigns. Compare this haul to Education and the Workforce, a "B" committee, whose members received only $35.8 million in campaign donations during the same period.[595] The sad lesson? It pays to butter up to special interests.

As *USA Today* reports, the NRCC has benefited significantly due to the fundraising efforts of "A" committee chairmen: Financial Services Committee Chairman Jeb Hensarling ($5.6 million), Ways and Means Committee Chairman Kevin Brady ($1.6 million), and Energy and Commerce Chairman Greg Walden (former NRCC chairman) ($10 million).

[592] "House Financial Services Committee," "Sectors Contributing to Members of this Committee, 2016 Election Cycle," OpenSecrets. org, https://www.opensecrets.org/cong-cmtes/overview?cmte=HFIN&cmtename=House+Financial+Services+Committee&cong=115.

[593] "House Energy and Commerce Committee," "Sectors Contributing to Members of this Committee, 2016 Election Cycle," OpenSecrets.org, https://www.opensecrets.org/cong-cmtes/overview?cmte=HENE&cmtename=House+Energy+and+Commerce+Committee&cong=115.

[594] "House Ways and Means Committee," "Sectors Contributing to Members of this Committee, 2016 Election Cycle," OpenSecrets.org, https://www.opensecrets.org/cong-cmtes/overview?cmte=HWAY&cmtename=House+Ways+and+Means+Committee&cong=115.

[595] "House Education and the Workforce Committee," "Sectors Contributing to Members of this Committee, 2016 Election Cycle," OpenSecrets.org, https://www.opensecrets.org/cong-cmtes/overview?cmte=HEDU&cmtename=House+Education+and+the+Workforce+Committee&cong=115.

Rep. Walden's appointment as chairman of the Committee on Energy and Commerce over competitor Rep. Joe Barton came as no surprise to those who understand the game. Barton had more experience than Walden, having served on the committee since 1987 (including as chairman from 2004 to 2007). Nonetheless, as reported by the *Hill*: "Republicans watching the contest said Walden's work at the National Republican Congressional Committee—where he helped secure the GOP's largest majority since the Great Depression, raised millions of dollars for candidates and limited Republican losses in last month's elections—helped him nail down the chairmanship."[596]

This pay-to-play scheme sidelines conservative representatives and puts more "moderate" representatives in control of committees. In fact, the most powerful committees are currently chaired by members scoring below the average for House Republicans (65 percent) compiled by Heritage Action,[597] the political-advocacy arm of the conservative Heritage Foundation: Rep. Rodney Frelinghuysen of Appropriations (45 percent), Rep. Kevin Brady of Ways and Means (62 percent), and Rep. Walden of Energy and Commerce (46 percent). The exception is Rep. Hensarling of Financial Services (83 percent).

Of the twelve subcommittee chairmen for Appropriations, eight fall below Heritage Action's 65 percent average. Some of these score in the lowest percentile of any Republicans, including Rep. Charlie Dent of the Appropriations Subcommittee on Military Construction, Veterans Affairs, and Related Agencies

[596] Devon Henry and Scott Wong, "Walden to Head Powerful Energy and Commerce Committee," *Hill*, December 1, 2016, http://thehill.com.

[597] See "Scorecard," "Top House Performers," Heritage Action for America, https://heritageactionscorecard.com/.

(29 percent), and Rep. Mario Díaz-Balart of the Appropriations Subcommittee on Transportation, Housing and Urban Development, and Related Agencies (35 percent). As a whole, the thirty members of the Appropriations Committee have compiled a sub-par average score of 58 percent from Heritage Action.

Obviously, having a conservative voting record isn't a prerequisite for party assignments; in fact, leadership apparently considers it worthy of a demerit. The twenty-four Republican members of the powerful Committee on Ways and Means earned an average score of 63 percent from Heritage Action, with some members, such as Reps. Carlos Curbelo, David Reichert, Tom Reed, and Patrick Meehan, scoring as low as 20 to 30 percent. To be fair, some members of Ways and Means scored better than the Heritage Action average, including Reps. Sam Johnson (89 percent), George Holding (89 percent), Kenny Merchant (88 percent), and Diane Black (85 percent). But the number of members with less conservative voting records exceeds those with more conservative records 14 to 11.

A logical consequence is that members would feel pressured to "put party over principle" and support defective policies that risk the stability of the nation in exchange for short-term political favors. Moreover, this structure encourages members to duck tough issues in favor of political expediency. Doing so maintains the status quo, and thereby secures the nation's largesse to donors. The passage of the omnibus spending bill in April 2017 is a case in point. Despite holding both the presidency and majorities in both houses of Congress, Republicans increased non-defense spending instead of cutting it, while making numerous concessions to the Left (including funding for Obamacare subsidies, Planned Parenthood, and sanctuary cities).

The Founders were not naïfs; to the contrary, their understanding of human nature and its effect on political systems was extraordinary. But the influence of progressivism—with its gradual but relentless expansion of federal power to the detriment of the states—has chipped away at the barricades protecting liberty and vastly increased the motivation for special interests to manipulate the system.

How Big Business Dominates Both Parties in Congress

An enduring myth of American politics is that "big business" and big government are antagonists—that big business wants small government.[598] Many Republican and libertarian-leaning citizens recognize that both the taxpayer and businesses benefit when government stays out of the way, and they reasonably assume that business leaders share that interest. This assumption holds true for many small-business owners who struggle to compete in a highly regulated market. But the opposite is true of large multinational corporations, for which doing business with the federal government can be very lucrative, and which can benefit financially from manipulating government policy. When large corporations reject the free-enterprise system in favor of governmental back-scratching as a means of wealth creation, the interests of business and fiscally conservative citizens part ways.

Powerful corporations use their influence in Washington, D.C., to secure an unfair advantage in the marketplace by advancing big-government programs that extract wealth from

[598] Timothy P. Carney, *The Big Ripoff: How Big Business and Big Government Steal Your Money* (Hoboken, N.J.: John Wiley and Sons, 2006), 3.

taxpayers and redistribute it to corporations. Business groups, such as the U.S. Chamber of Commerce, often spin this as improvement to the economy, but the benefits are narrow, and the harm to the citizen is great.

As government increases in size, so too does its ability to regulate industry and redistribute tax revenues in the form of government contracts, subsidies, and low-interest government loans. But through high-priced lobbyists and generous political donations, large corporations influence Congress in ways smaller businesses cannot. The Export-Import Bank (Ex-Im) is one program that illustrates this racket.

Ex-Im supporters claim the program benefits small American businesses by providing low-interest, government-backed loans to foreign countries to purchase their exports. In 2015, however, Boeing Company received more money than any other company from the sale of its products to foreign buyers that used Ex-Im financing—a whopping $5.5 billion.[599] Boeing spent $22 million on lobbying (lobbying reports don't break expenditures down by issue) to ensure that its interests were put first, but that's a small sum relative to the amount at stake. It pays to pay a lobbyist.

Large corporations also lobby for tax loopholes or special exemptions to improve their bottom line. In 2004, for example, various American corporations spent $282.7 million lobbying Congress to pass the American Jobs Creation Act. This law provided American companies a one-time tax-rate reduction from 35 percent to 5.25 percent on income earned by their overseas

[599] Catherine Ho, "Ex-Im Backers Spent Record Amounts Lobbying Government in 2015," *Washington Post*, January 28, 2016, https://www.washingtonpost.com/.

subsidiaries upon returning the money to the United States. A study conducted by the University of Kansas estimated that ninety-three U.S. companies spent $282.7 million on lobbying expenditures and received $62.5 billion in tax savings, or a 220:1 return on investment. The corporations that repatriated the most money operated within the manufacturing sector: Pfizer, Inc. ($37 billion); Merck and Company ($15.9 billion); Hewlett-Packard Company ($14.5 billion); Johnson & Johnson ($10.8 billion); and IBM ($9.5 billion).[600] Their competitors in the same tax class but with solely U.S.-based operations paid the full 35 percent tax rate.

Tax cuts and money flowing into the country are good. But on this matter, dig deeper, and there are problems. Lobbyists had claimed the bill would lead to the creation of 660,000 jobs in 2005 as a consequence of American companies' repatriating $265 to $406 billion in offshore earnings.[601] The Kansas study concluded that these companies redirected the earnings to shareholders (and corporate officers and directors often own large blocks of shares) rather than directly investing them in job creation.[602] Distributions to shareholders are also usually a good outcome. But other corporations and their shareholders also suffer from the high corporate tax rate. They too could have used relief, and such relief would also produce good outcomes. Instead, a well-funded few crowded out the whole for the attention of Congress.

[600] Raquel Meyer Alexander, Susan Scholz, and Stephen Mazza, "Measuring Rates of Return for Lobbying Expenditures: An Empirical Analysis Under the American Jobs Creation Act," *SSRN Electronic Journal* (April 2009): 15.

[601] Ibid., 9.

[602] Ibid., 16.

In *Liberal Fascism*, Jonah Goldberg discusses the collusion between big business and government as a form of "creeping fascism." Contrary to the view of many on the Left who blame the Right for creating such a system, Goldberg sees it differently.[603] He describes the fascist bargain between the industrialist and the state:

> You may stay in business and own your factories. In the spirit of cooperation and unity, we will even guarantee you profits and a lack of serious competition. In exchange, we expect you to agree with — and help implement — our political agenda.[604]

Goldberg observes that the "moral and economic content of the agenda" varies according to who is in power. But he rejects any notion that such fascistic arrangements are "inherently right-wing":

> If you understand the right-wing or conservative position to be that of those who argue for free markets, competition, property rights, and the other political values inscribed in the original intent of the American founding fathers, then big business in Fascist Italy, Nazi Germany, and New Deal America was not right-wing; it was left-wing, *and* it was fascistic. What's more, it still is.[605]

Businesses both big and small have an interest in securing the conditions that bring about the lowest cost and highest price for

---

[603] Jonah Goldberg, *Liberal Fascism: The Secret History of the American Left from Mussolini to the Politics of Meaning* (New York: Broadway Books, 2007), 290.

[604] Ibid.

[605] Ibid.

their goods and services, resulting in the highest profit margin. To be truly "pro-free market" or "pro-capitalist" is to embrace competition, which is nothing more than economic choice for workers and consumers. A free-market government will protect the right of individuals to give their free consent and will therefore stand guard against fraud, deceit, and coercion. Because the basis of capitalism is free exchange, it shuns exchanges that are rigged: those in furtherance of fascism, socialism, and all forms of collectivism. Similarly, it abhors the use of government to give one corporation or one business sector a leg-up on others or on the individual citizen.

Many are puzzled by the idea that any business — big or small — would support progressive big-government policies that raise taxes and create unnecessary, job-crushing regulations. Although it's true that such policies are an obstacle to all businesses, they hit smaller companies harder. Larger corporations have the resources to hire lawyers and accountants to find ways to lower their taxes and navigate a highly regulated environment. Smaller companies, in contrast, tend to operate in the margins, and the extra costs often put them out of business. In effect, big business supports big-government policies because they provide a means of eliminating their competition.

The U.S. Chamber of Commerce, one of the country's largest lobbying organizations, is often viewed as an advocate for "pro–free enterprise" interests. However, the Chamber has a history of pushing for bigger, more centralized government, which indicates a preference for "pro-business" policies instead. Its support of demonstrably harmful government economic policies may come as a shock to the mom-and-pop shops and small businesses the Chamber includes in the three million businesses it claims to represent. Yet few are aware that in 2012, more than half of the

$164 million the Chamber collected in fees and dues came from only 64 companies, suggesting the Chamber might be more likely to advocate for the interests of a select group of large corporations, not the majority of small businesses.[606]

In the name of economic development, improving the workforce, and creating jobs, the Chamber and its state affiliates have lobbied for many of the problematic policies and programs discussed in this book: regional development grants, mass-transit projects, sustainable development, and the Common Core standards.[607] Such efforts come at the expense of the larger community in the form of increased taxes on income and property, depressed wages, and defective academic standards that lock children into a low-quality workforce-training education.

Even more remote from the interests of average Americans is the International Chamber of Commerce (ICC), which lobbies organizations such as the World Bank, the United Nations (where it has observer status), and the G20 to promote "international trade, responsible business conduct and a global approach to regulation to accelerate inclusive and sustainable growth to the benefit of all."[608] The ICC condemned President Trump's decision to withdraw from the Paris Climate Agreement as bad for the global economy.[609] As for the U.S. Chamber, it had a record of opposition to the agreement and had co-sponsored a 2017

---

[606] David Brodwin, "The Chamber's Secrets," *U.S. News and World Report*, October 22, 2015, https://www.usnews.com/.

[607] "Issues," U.S. Chamber of Commerce website, https://www.us-chamber.com/issues.

[608] International Chamber of Commerce, https://iccwbo.org/about-us/.

[609] "ICC Reacts to US Paris Agreement Withdrawal," International Chamber of Commerce, https://iccwbo.org/.

report[610] that concluded it would cost the economy, by 2040, $3 trillion and the loss of 6.5 million industrial jobs; however, the Chamber announced it was "neutral" on the withdrawal — perhaps in part because some of its biggest supporters (ExxonMobil, Dow Chemical, Citigroup, and PepsiCo) supported it.[611] What happened to protecting American businesses, jobs, and taxpayers from higher energy prices?

According to the Heritage Foundation, the Paris Agreement was the "open door for egregious regulation, cronyism, and government spending that would have been as disastrous for the American economy as it is proving to be for those in Europe. [The Paris Agreement] would have raised energy prices, killed jobs and cost the average family of four $20,000 by 2035."[612] Katie Tubb, a policy analyst with Heritage, argues that big business supports the Paris Agreement for the same reasons it supports big government:

> Big business and big government often go hand-in-hand. Big businesses generally can absorb and adapt to the costs of complying with burdensome regulation, of which Paris

[610] Dr. Paul Bernstein, Dr. Sugandha Tuladhar, Dr. David Montgomery, and Bharat Ramkrishnan, "Impacts of Greenhouse Gas Regulations on the Industrial Sector," NERA Economic Consulting website, March 2017, http://www.nera.com/publications/archive/2017/impacts-of-greenhouse-gas-regulations-on-the-industrial-sector.html.

[611] Ari Natter, "Paris Pullout Pits U.S. Chamber against the Likes of Exxon Mobil, Citigroup," World Oil website, June 9, 2017, http://www.worldoil.com/.

[612] Nicholas Loris and Edwin J. Fuelner, "Heritage Applauds Paris Climate Agreement Withdrawal," Heritage Foundation website, June 1, 2017, http://www.heritage.org/environment/commentary/heritage-applauds-paris-climate-agreement-withdrawal.

is a wellspring.... Smaller companies have a much harder time complying, which means less competition for big business. This is especially true if big business can influence the substance of regulations to favor themselves or freeze out competitors. I think in other cases, these large companies are just looking for PR points. [613]

Myron Ebell, director of the Center for Energy and Environment at the Competitive Enterprise Institute, told the *Daily Signal* that companies such as BP and Shell are European companies and that it's impossible to do business there without "towing the political line." But he added that there might be an additional reason. "The only way to get the price of gas back up is to kill coal," he said. "The Paris Agreement kills fossil fuels, but it kills coal first."[614]

In his book *The Big Ripoff: How Big Business and Big Government Steal Your Money*, Timothy Carney refutes "the standard assumption [which] seems to be that government action protects ordinary people by restraining big business, which, in turn, wants to be left alone."[615] He argues that the facts point in an entirely different direction:

"The greatest trick the devil ever pulled," said Kaiser Soze in the film *The Usual Suspects*, "was convincing the world he didn't exist." In a similar way, big business and

[613] Fred Lucas, "The Possible Reasons Big Corporations Are So Eager for Trump to Break His Promise on Paris Climate Deal," *Daily Signal*, May 26, 2017, http://dailysignal.com/2017/05/26/possible-reasons-big-corporations-eager-trump-break-promise-paris-climate-deal/.

[614] Ibid.

[615] Carney, *The Big Ripoff*, 2.

big government prosper from the perception that they are rivals instead of partners (in plunder).[616]

In case after case, Carney lays out how every significant introduction of government regulation, taxation, and spending from the Progressive Era to the present has benefited some big business. Government action often springs not from a need to protect society from corporations, but in response to corporations that want to undermine the free-market system to get a leg-up on competitors or otherwise to secure financial gain.

Progressive Era accounts of government's stepping in to regulate predatory monopolies, such as U.S. Steel, are yarns spun to mask old-fashioned collusion. Quoting historian Gabriel Kolko, Carney explains that the "dominant fact of American political life at the beginning of the [twentieth] century was that big business led the struggle for the federal regulation of the economy."[617] The truth, Carney concludes, is that big steel firms feared that free competition would undermine their predatory monopolies, so they asked government to intervene and the government happily obliged.[618]

Despite the near monopoly that U.S. Steel enjoyed at the time, company owners were surprised to see profits decline. After the failure of a series of "gentlemen's agreements" among remaining competitors to fix prices, steel magnate Andrew Carnegie himself asked government to step in.[619] Quoting Kolko again, Carney writes, "Having failed in the realm of economics, the efforts of the United States Steel group were to be shifted to

[616] Ibid, 5.
[617] Ibid, 41.
[618] Ibid, 39–40.
[619] Ibid.

politics."[620] And the consequent regulations had the effect of setting prices and production standards—all of which impeded U.S. Steel's competition.

This same attitude prevailed among big-business leaders who joined forces with progressives during World War I to form the War Industries Board (WIB). Run by "dollar-a-year-men" from the world of finance and business, they set prices, trade quotas, and profits during the war. These "businessmen-turned-bureaucrats" took full advantage of their positions "to establish and enforce what amounted to cartel arrangements for the various industries."[621]

New Dealers continued the practice of putting businessmen in charge of setting regulations and policies to which their industries would be subject. "They invited one industry after another to write the codes under which they would be regulated (as they had been begging to do in many cases)." In doing so, "it was not only inevitable but *intended* for big business to get bigger and the little guy to get screwed.... In business after business, [he] was crushed or at least severely disadvantaged in the name of 'efficiency' and 'progress.'"[622]

The "dollar-a-year-men" still serve in government, repeatedly moving through the revolving door between public service and the private sector. After spending a few years as legislative staffers or employees of a federal agency, many move on to positions with top lobbying firms or powerful corporations, where they are well paid to use their insider knowledge and connections

---

[620] Ibid.

[621] Goldberg, *Liberal Fascism*, 293, quoting Robert Higgs, "Crisis and Quasi-Corporatist Policy-Making: The U.S. Case in Historical Perspective," *The World and I*, November 1, 1988.

[622] Goldberg, *Liberal Fascism*, 293.

in Congress to make sure their clients' agendas are met. And many former members of Congress are pivotal players in this revolving-door game.

As Rep. Buck explains, after a congressman retires or gets defeated, he rarely goes home. He uses his clout on Capitol Hill to make a handsome salary as a D.C. lobbyist. In its "Revolving Door Report," the Sunlight Foundation found that the percent of former lawmakers turned lobbyists jumped from 3 percent in 1974 to nearly 50 percent in 2014. At that time, 415 former members of Congress were paid to influence former colleagues.[623]

In Washington, three streams of influence are guiding the ship of state. Progressivism needs a bigger government to attain rule by experts. Powerful crony businesses encourage bigger government and the government contracts that go with it. They also look for regulatory advantages over their smaller rivals and entrepreneurs. The political establishment willingly entertains both, to bolster its election coffers and perhaps too its post–service job prospects. And the citizen and reform-minded members of Congress get elbowed off the stage.

---

[623] Dan Friedman, "Former Congressmen Make Huge Salaries as Lobbyists While Still Collecting Congressional Pensions," *NY Daily News*, May 24, 2014, http://www.nydailynews.com/.

Chapter 13

Solutions

But the Americans are, above all, a problem-solving people. . . .
They will not give up. Full of essential goodwill to each other and
to all, confident in their inherent decency and their democratic
skills, they will attack again and again the ills in their society, until
they are overcome or at least substantially redressed. . . . The great
American republican experiment is . . . still the first, best hope for
the human race.

—Paul Johnson, A History of the American People, 1997

The overarching theme of this book is that government is no longer citizen-directed in a meaningful sense. In their century-long march, progressives have made huge advances, *de jure* and *de facto*, in reconfiguring the constitutional structure. Crony businesses welcome bigger government as a source of more revenue and as a tool for squashing competition. For its part, Congress has created a massive federal bureaucracy to the extent that Congress itself can no longer provide a meaningful check or balance, and it has created a system of incentives that bends its ear to large moneyed interests and crowds out the voice of the people. The federal government overall has hollowed out the independence of state governments and perverted them into mere federal field agents. It has enfeebled state governments and excused them from having to make many of the hard decisions of governance. The mass of problems is too great, and time too little, to expect the Supreme Court to reverse all its flawed decisions in a timely way.

Over the past thirty years, various attempts at incremental and single-issue reform have had at most minor impact and have done nothing to deflect progressivism's transformational domestic policy goals or the relentless movement toward a bureaucratic administrative state. Systemic changes are needed.

The American people seem to understand this moment. They also sense that a new approach is necessary. The election of Donald Trump demonstrates above all that the American people are worried about the course of the republic. After all, Trump won 30 states with 306 electoral votes by running an improvisational, iconoclastic campaign not just against most aspects of progressivism but against the Republican establishment as well.

Nonetheless, we are witnessing once again that even electing a president committed to returning power to the people won't guarantee success. In the 1980s, federalism was central to President Reagan's agenda. He declared:

> Our next major undertaking must be a program ... to make government again accountable to the people, to make our system of federalism work again. Our citizens feel they've lost control of even the most basic decisions made about the essential services of government, such as schools, welfare, roads, and even garbage collection. And they're right. A maze of interlocking jurisdictions and levels of government confronts average citizens in trying

to solve even the simplest of problems. They don't know where to turn for answers, who to hold accountable, who to praise, who to blame, who to vote for or against.[624]

Reagan then attempted to deliver on his 1980 campaign pledge for elimination of the Education and Energy Departments. He specified $28 billion a year in federal excise taxes for a transition fund to be built up for states to pay for assuming federal programs and grants. Reagan promised to "shortly send this Congress a message describing this program. I want to emphasize, however, that its full details will have been worked out only after close consultation with congressional, State, and local officials."[625]

Needless to say, Reagan's 1982 proposal sank without a trace and is almost completely forgotten today. The Education and Energy Departments chug along unscathed. And Reagan was no slouch at gaining the nation's attention. Why did he have so little success regarding federalism, an issue he deeply cared about?

The answer is the same as it is now. The administrative state is masterful at enmeshing elected officials in its web. Consequently, there was never any serious effort to address the details Reagan promised "that will have been worked out only after close consultation with congressional, State, and local officials." The "consultation" about the subject of governmental realignment that Reagan sought — which levels of government would lose money and power or (alternatively) assume responsibility for curing major headaches — would take a very long time, then or

---

[624] Ronald Reagan, State of the Union message, January 26, 1982.
[625] Ibid.

now. There is simply little or no institutional backing for restoring the constitutional balance crafted by our Founders.

The bureaucracy won't reform itself or limit its power unless it is forced to, and Congress won't take serious steps in that direction unless it in turn is forced to. What is needed now is a citizen groundswell that reclaims the constitutional structure as the guarantor of self-government and individual rights. Such a movement would create the political atmosphere to enact the necessary solutions.

REMEDIES FOR THE FEDERAL GOVERNMENT TO IMPLEMENT

- Enact the Regulations from the Executive in Need of Scrutiny Act (REINS). This bill would require Congress to pass a joint resolution of approval after a federal agency proposes a major regulatory rule in order for the rule to take effect. It sets forth the congressional approval procedure for major rules and the congressional disapproval procedure for nonmajor rules. This bill will give Congress a powerful tool for providing appropriate oversight of the executive agencies and for retaining accountability for the laws it passes. It would help rein in the administrative state.
- Overturn the *Chevron* Deference doctrine. *Chevron* directs courts to approve an agency's interpretation of an ambiguous statute as long as that interpretation is a "reasonable" or "permissible" reading of the statute. Because this doctrine leads to wildly unfettered power by unaccountable bureaucracies, either the Supreme Court or Congress must act to rein it in.

Solutions

- Return to the states specific, inherently state functions, *e.g.*, education, housing, and community and regional development.
- Prohibit tying congressional committee appointments to fund-raising.
- Enact legislation providing that a state or state subdivision (counties, cities, towns, and so forth) may withdraw at any time from a federal grant, memorandum of understanding, or cooperative agreement, without penalty and without repayment of federal monies already obligated.
- Prohibit federal agencies from making grants directly to a state subdivision.
- Make research institutes accountable to Congress and the president, just as are other government agencies. Make directors of such institutes subject to the same appointment, confirmation, and terms of service rules as cabinet secretaries. Make their boards advisory in nature and subject to service at the pleasure of the president.
- Prohibit the federal government from establishing, requiring the establishment of, financing, or affecting the membership of state and local boards and commissions.
- Require federal agencies to give state legislatures and governors actual notice of any monies being transferred to state agencies or to state subdivisions.
- Change federal land policy so that western states are on equal footing with eastern states.
- End the requirement of sixty votes to end Senate debate on legislation, completing the trend of recent years that has seen abolition of the filibuster for all presidential nominations to the judicial and executive branches. For

more than a century, we have seen a growing federal government, an expansion that far exceeds the constitutional design. The filibuster rule raises the bar for serious reform, making obstruction easy for progressives and too often providing conservative legislators with a ready-made excuse for inaction. It is difficult to imagine a significant deconstruction of the administrative state under a sixty-vote minimum for ending legislative debate.

REMEDIES FOR STATE GOVERNMENTS TO IMPLEMENT

• Enact legislation requiring state agencies to give notice to the legislature of submissions to the federal government for discretionary funding in excess of $1 million.
• Elected state officials must have the ultimate responsibility for all funding coming into the state and for all consequences of that funding.
• Enact legislation proscribing state subdivisions from entering into a contract or grant with the federal government except when the legislature has expressly consented.
• Establish a Commission on Federalism. Utah established such a commission and, pursuant to the authorizing legislation, the legislature carried out a review of federal practices and incursions. The commission issued a groundbreaking report in 2017.
• Pass a resolution calling on the state's congressional delegations to sponsor legislation to protect state sovereignty. Utah has already passed such a resolution.

Conclusion

Of all tyrannies, a tyranny sincerely exercised for the good of its victims may be the most oppressive. It would be better to live under robber barons than under omnipotent moral busybodies. The robber baron's cruelty may sometimes sleep, his cupidity may at some point be satiated; but those who torment us for our own good will torment us without end for they do so with the approval of their own conscience.

—C. S. Lewis, *God in the Dock*

In 2014, Obamacare consultant Dr. Jonathan Gruber made news when two videos surfaced with his analysis of the process that produced the statute. In the first video he made these comments (reiterated in the second):

> Lack of transparency is a huge political advantage. And basically, call it the stupidity of the American voter or whatever, but basically that was really, really critical for the thing to pass.... Look, I wish ... we could make it all transparent, but I'd rather have this law pass than not.[626]

[626] Cheryl K. Chumley, "Obamacare's Jonathan Gruber Caught on Second Tape Calling Voters 'Too Stupid,'" *Washington Times*, November 12, 2013, http://www.washingtontimes.com/.

Deconstructing the Administrative State

These remarks crystallized several aspects of progressive philosophy: that individual citizens are incapable of directing public policy, that experts know better and should be making the important decisions, and that deception may be necessary to overcome citizens' ignorant opposition to policy that is in their own best interests.

Those who seek to control us for our own good are the most dangerous of tyrants.

This work has demonstrated the inevitable decline of individual freedom and self-government that results from abandoning the Founders' view of the individual. If the individual is not a precious human being made in the image of the Creator; if he has no natural rights that men may not rightfully infringe; if he exists in a childlike state such that he is incapable of making good decisions that affect his own life and society as a whole—then the Constitution is an outdated shackle that must be jettisoned so that the aristocracy of experts can assume control for the good of the whole.

Progressives believe the American Experiment has failed, and they are doing their best to make it so. They need bigger government to facilitate rule by experts, they need to wreck the constitutional structure, and they need the American people to lose their strength of character, to become subservient and weak, and as part and parcel, to accept a dumbed-down education for their children.

The federal government meddles with the functioning of state government—funding it and thereby undercutting the authority of the legislature, which alone should be controlling the state purse. It bends the state bureaucracy toward Washington, making it less responsive to the legislature and even the governor. It complicates and obfuscates the functioning of state government, making it a federal agent and making it difficult for citizens to identify what government, what body, is responsible for poor decisions.

For its part, the Supreme Court implores the states to stiffen their spines and act like sovereign bodies, but it ignores the fact that the states can't do so because the federal meddling has impaired the checks and balances within, and functioning of, state government. The Court rightly lectures that our system of dual sovereignties is designed not only to protect the integrity of state government for its own sake, but to also protect the rights of citizens. But it fails to recognize that principle when it has the occasion to protect that structure.

Progressives have two powerful allies in their mission. One is the large, politically connected businesses that view big, centralized government as a source of profit and a tool for subduing the competition. They pay lip service to American principles and values while assiduously manipulating the government to procure and protect financial gain.

The second is Congress. It created the administrative state that has now become so massive that Congress cannot provide any check or balance. And now it has created an incentive system that favors a growing state. Perhaps its greatest political sin, though, is that it has elbowed citizens off the policy stage. As any activist knows, the constant legislative response, even for indisputably important issues, is: "We don't have time for that."

Elites in both parties know how to deal with anti-establishment politicians, whether in the White House or in Congress. With control of the mainstream media, academia, Hollywood, and Big Business, they create a false narrative. They ostracize the noncompliant politician as ignorant, unhinged, or a country bumpkin—one whose blundering ways will wreak havoc. But what they can't handle, what they fear, is the American people.

The American people themselves must rise, or watch the magnificent American Experiment crumble and disappear. But is it realistic to expect the electorate to respond to this call?

We believe so. It is a generation's honor to stand with our greatest champions of liberty: George Washington, the creators of the Declaration of Independence and the Constitution, the Revolutionary armed forces, and all the subsequent men and women who have fought, and who fight, for the cause of liberty.

Consider, too, what our Founders faced: the necessity of armed rebellion against the mightiest fighting force on earth, with the rebellion actively opposed by a not insubstantial number of Loyalists. And consider the relatively recent revolutions in Eastern Europe and the Soviet Union. On the strength of ideas and peaceful demonstrations, freedom-loving citizens overthrew one of the most brutal and oppressive regimes mankind has ever known. Our task pales in comparison.

In their genius, the Framers created and entrusted to us the tools to protect what they bequeathed. We simply need to affirm and insist on adherence to that for which our ancestors risked everything so that we would be free. Just as the Founding generation did, we need to educate ourselves, our children, and our neighbors. We need to rise and demand that the ship of state be put back on course.

The long fight against progressivism is almost over, and it is nearly lost. Our final demise will be rapid, exacerbated as Western civilization collapses around us. We are down to our last check and balance—our last shield against both disorder and tyranny. We have left only the American people themselves. But that is our strongest check, our greatest earthly hope.

Conclusion

Posterity, you will never know how much it cost the present generation to preserve your freedom. I hope that you will make a good use of it. If you do not, I shall repent in heaven that ever I took half the pains to preserve it. (John Adams)

About the Authors

Emmett McGroarty is a senior fellow at the American Principles Project Foundation. He is a graduate of Georgetown University and Fordham School of Law.

Jane Robbins is a senior fellow at the American Principles Project Foundation. She is a graduate of Clemson University and Harvard Law School.

Erin Tuttle is a policy analyst at the American Principles Project Foundation. She is a graduate of Indiana University.

American Principles Project Foundation

The American Principles Project Foundation is a 501(c)(3) organization dedicated to the fundamental principles on which our country was founded—universal principles embracing the notion that we are all created equal, endowed by the Creator with certain unalienable rights, and among these are life, liberty, and the pursuit of happiness.